Disarmament Issues

Treaties, Agreements, Conventions and Statements Prohibiting the Use of Nuclear, Biological and Chemical Weapons, and Banning Nuclear Tests

Disarmament Issues

Treaties, Agreements, Conventions and Statements Prohibiting the Use of Nuclear, Biological and Chemical Weapons, and Banning Nuclear Tests

Volume–1

Edited by

Rahul K. Bhonsle

Col. Ved Prakash

K.R. Gupta

ATLANTIC

PUBLISHERS & DISTRIBUTORS (P) LTD

Published by

ATLANTIC

PUBLISHERS & DISTRIBUTORS (P) LTD

7/22, Ansari Road, Darya Ganj,
New Delhi-110002
Phones : +91-11-40775252, 23273880, 23275880, 23280451
Fax : +91-11-23285873
Web : www.atlanticbooks.com
E-mail : orders@atlanticbooks.com

Branch Office
5, Nallathambi Street, Wallajah Road,
Chennai-600002
Phones : +91-44-64611085, 32413319
E-mail : chennai@atlanticbooks.com

ISBN 978-81-269-1502-6 (Vol. 1)
ISBN 978-81-269-1503-3 (Vol. 2)
ISBN 978-81-269-1504-0 (Set)

Printed in India at Nice Printing Press, A-33/3A, Site-IV, Industrial Area, Sahibabad, Ghaziabad, U.P.

Preface

The issue of disarmament is as old as the invention of arms itself. Disarmament has been often suggested as a way of minimizing destruction during the war. But the fact remains that no invention on earth, including the dynamite, has been ever deliberately destroyed by sensible human beings. Stockpiling of weapons for defensive purposes always had state approval until the end of the World War II. The coming of nuclear weapons with their immensely devastative capabilities has made the pacifists to plead for immediate and complete disarmament. Though the term 'disarmament' may literally mean doing away with all kinds of weapons, in today's context it has become synonymous with 'nuclear disarmament'. The term, however, also includes disarmament of chemical, biological (bacteriological), toxic, cyber, and other recently invented weapons of mass destruction.

Over the last couple of years, there has been a resurgence of interest in the subject of nuclear disarmament. It is known that the desire for a nuclear weapons free world (NWFW) had disappeared from the radar of the international community after 1995, until 2007, though there were reasons for this phenomenon. Once the indefinite and unconditional extension of the NPT had been obtained at the NPT Extension and Review Conference in 1995, the nuclear weapon states (NWS), having ensured against any further proliferation, went back to reinforcing nuclear deterrence as the bedrock of their national security strategies. In the decade following this seminal event, the NWS retreated to their comfort zones, having shut the door against the non nuclear weapon states (NNWS).

Consequently, the issue of universal nuclear disarmament was either paid mere lip service or completely ignored by the policymakers in the NWS. Meanwhile, sudden end of the U.S.-U.S.S.R. confrontation, consequent to the end of the Cold War era in 1991—and as a result, the unravelling of the Soviet Union—meant a reduction in the fear of a nuclear Armageddon. As a natural corollary to all this, NNWS and NGOs that had been at the forefront of the cause of the nuclear disarmament through the years of Cold War, were also lulled into a state of comfort.

Nuclear disarmament issues, by and large, revolve around two major concerns: (i) acquisition of nuclear weapons by 'states of proliferation concern' that perceive an asymmetric advantage in this weapon against a more powerful adversary; and (ii) the possibility of non-state actors acquiring the nuclear capability and unleashing nuclear terrorism on the unwary world. The second concern results from the realization of inadequacy of deterrence against these new threats posed by the non-state actors which are harbouring suicidal tendencies and are of extremist persuation. Classical deterrence, built on sheer numbers, will not work against these irrational actors. After all, success of deterrence in the past has been premised on the rationality of the players.

In order to translate its concept of nuclear disarmament into reality, India has tried to make use of every opportunity in multilateral fora to get the international community to pursue it consensually. Within the U.N. and outside it, through appeals, proposals and action plans, India has constantly and consistently striven to realize an NWFW.

Post-1998, there was a perceptible waning of interest in disarmament. Even if some critics find it curious, this shift in India's passion for disarmament after the 1998 tests, some analysts say is demanded by country's national security parameters in the changed strategic environment post-indefinite extension of the NPT. Even if critics see greater evidence of the predominance of realpolitik with a shift in focus to building of a credible nuclear deterrence, the Indians ask simply: Is not this shift unavoidable in the changed security situation created by nuclearised neighbourhood, particularly an unpredictable China? Yet again, a strong nuclear India is also demanded by its emerging power status.

There is a lack of seriousness on the part of NWS about the objective of universal nuclear abolition—given the past Indian experience and the entangled web of present international relations. Consequently, recent initiatives, including the one by President Obama, are seen and treated with certain circumspection and "wait and watch" attitude. But equally importantly, should India allow itself to be swamped by a sense of *déjà vu*—cutting itself off the emerging debate on the nuclear disarmament? Or, should India emulate China's stance of waiting for other four NWS to reduce their arsenals to its own level, before going for any serious negotiations? As for India, contrary to whatever the critics might say, it will continue to strive for non-discriminatory nuclear disarmament discourse, as it has consistently done since the late 1940s. A case for universal nuclear disarmament on grounds of morality, environmental considerations and humanitarian reasons has always existed. While this logic shall hold eternally and universally, in these times of the predominance of realpolitik, a case for disarmament can be grounded even in the realm of national security paradigm. It is pertinent to recall that India remained an NNWS for decades on end till it was compelled by the national security imperatives to go nuclear. To put it simply, India will not hesitate to abjure nuclear weapons if its national security is not jeopardised. It is only in this context that the issue need to be studied keeping in mind India's nuclear-armed neighbours—both bent upon hobbling India's efforts to realize its dreams of reaching its potential as not only a regional power but also a superpower along with China by 2035, or latest by 2050.

India has long campaigned for nuclear disarmament on non-discriminatory basis. Having gone nuclear in 1998, India does not consider the 'bomb' as an asset for its national security imperatives. So, it still wants to push for the old desideratum with a renewed vigour. However, in order to contribute meaningfully to the evolving debate on disarmament issues, India must amplify its own understanding of concept of the universal nuclear disarmament. This unambiguity is essential as the concept has lent itself to different interpretations in different countries over the years. As India has accused the NWS of imposing a discriminatory NPT regime on the world, it follows that its definition of world without nuclear weapons will involve all countries renouncing their right to possess or use nuclear weapons, and accepting verifiable compliance. In a word, it is a state of zero nuclear weapons—not of fewer (nuclear) weapons, or in fewer hands. That concept explains India's insistence to link non-proliferation with disarmament, because the former is dependent on the latter for its sustainability. It must be clearly understood that non-proliferation is not disarmament. Even the NPT has two important parts: initial, non-proliferation and final, disarmament. By way of an obfuscation, the NWS—the hegemons—have overemphasized the non-proliferation and almost forgotten the disarmament provisions of the NPT. Their aim is very simple, i.e. to bar the entry of new entrants to their 'elite' club. Hence, the need for India to caution the world against the real designs of the five hegemons. India must continue to remind the world that the goal of disarmament calls for steps beyond mere reduction of nuclear arms and arms control through Comprehensive Nuclear Test Ban Treaty (CTBT) or Fissile Material Cut-off Treaty (FMCT). In fact, like the NPT, other non-proliferation treaties (such as CTBT and FMCT) will also be found wanting in controlling proliferation unless linked to disarmament.

Some critics assert India has not thought through the consequences of universal nuclear disarmament on its national security and strategic interests. But, it does not seem to be well-founded averment. India had long criticized the NPT for being a discriminatory document. India has always demanded a level playing field for all states. It was only when India descried a threat to its national security under the prevalent nuclear regime that it went for nuclear tests in 1998. The aim obviously was to create a level playing field. India is equally certain that its national security will not be jeopardized in a nuclear weapons free world. In such a world, India will be confident to square off with its menacing rivals like China, not to speak of noisy ones like Pakistan. India's conventional might too is substantial.

Another interim measure could be the avoidance of nuclear accidents and unauthorized use of such weapons. Even if the world has not travelled much on the road to nuclear disarmament, the fact remains that the weapon has not been used since 1945. This non-use has given us the term 'nuclear taboo', and it is important to ensure that this taboo is not violated, even through an unintended accident. To ensure this, NWS must put these weapons in a de-alerted state. Some NWS are believed to have adopted such measures in full or part. The U.S. and Russia are known such nuclear powers. If all NWS were to adopt such a posture, it would be a significant step in both delegitimizing these weapons and also ensuring that the nuclear taboo stands unbroken.

The West generally equates disarmament with arms reduction rather than arms elimination. During the Cold War, arms control was an important item on the agenda of two leading nuclear powers. The INF, CFE, CWC and ABM were examples of successful arms control negotiations between the two superpowers, and of multilateral negotiations.

After the Cold War ended, the U.S. and Russia concluded, signed, ratified and implemented Strategic Arms Reduction Treaty I (START I) with an expiry date of 5 December 2009. They also signed START II which was not ratified by the Russian Duma. Some discussions had also taken place on START III, but it was not signed. In 2002, the two nations signed Strategic Offensive Reductions Treaty (SORT) without any negotiations. SORT commits both sides to reduce their nuclear weapons to 1700-2200 range by 2010. The verification rules of START I apply. The SORT declaration was tied up with START I, and expired on 5 December 2009.

Nuclear disarmament is a complex issue, so think the NWS who have made these weapons an important part in their national security architecture—forgetting that they came into existence only in mid-1940s. The experts have asserted that nuclear wars are not winnable. The most important factor in this field is political will. Security establishments and strategic experts state that their elimination will jeopardize the security of their countries. So ran the arguments when banning and proscription of the chemical weapons were under discussion. As in that case, so in the case of nuclear weapons, what is required is the change in the mindsets. The rest will follow. In any case, a view needs to be taken of the different countries' position on the issue. Even if most analysts feel the lead must come from the two major stockpile holders of this 'abomination', it is only the collective will of the international community that will nudge these two towards the final elimination of their stocks.

Another important issue is nuclear terrorism. Carlos Marighella, an inveterate espouser of terrorism says, "Terrorism is an arm the revolutionary can never relinquish". Its implication is rather simple: The terrorist will not stop at anything, and try to lay his hand at any arms, means, and methods that will serve his purpose, nuclear devices not excluded. And the disgraced Pakistani nuclear scientist A.Q. Khan having run an open nuclear Wal-Mart for years, till he was grounded in 2003, says that any interested entity—an individual, a group, or a country—can lay its hands on a quantity of fissile material, if not a crude nuclear device itself. The consequences will be too frightening even to imagine.

The web of disarmament issues is quite complex. Since NPT encompasses the major concerns, viz. nuclear disarmament, non-proliferation, and harnessing nuclear energy for peaceful use, the NPT Review Conference popularly known as RevCon is held early five years. It undertakes a review of progress in nuclear non-proliferation during the period and suggests measures to supplement the NPT which remains the lynch pin to securing nuclear symmetry globally. The Final Document of Eighth RevCon held in New York on 28 May 2010, which was issued by consensus, reaffirmed the intent of the state parties towards implementation of the Treaty and underlined the role in promoting peace and stability globally. The three arms of nuclear disarmament covered in the RevCon included disarmament with progress made lauded upon during the various meetings, particularly the U.S. and Russian Prague agreement which promises to reduce their warheads to 1550 within a reasonable time. The RevCon Document called upon accelerated progress by the nuclear weapon states (NWS) and not just the U.S. and Russia in this direction.

An analysis of the Final Document and the debate of the Eighth RevCon would indicate that the trend of the previous Conferences has been continued in this one as well for there has been an abiding commitment of all signatories towards the provisions of the Treaty per se, which is encouraging.

There was some progress on control of fissile material with a call for negotiating an FMCT thus: "The Conference reaffirms the urgent necessity of negotiating and bringing to a conclusion a non-discriminatory, multilateral and internationally and effectively verifiable treaty banning the production of fissile material for nuclear weapons or other nuclear explosive devices".

It would not be out of place to suggest that while there is a general consensus of the global community on the requirement and the effectiveness of the NPT as an instrument of control of growth of nuclear weapons, it has not restricted in providing options to states which have determined by their security needs to obtain nuclear weapons capability. These states have also not been motivated to rejoin the Treaty despite some exceptional waivers accorded in some cases such as India, for sufficient incentives to join the same are not evident. While there are attempts to strengthen the verification powers of the IAEA, the organization is seen by some as Iran as the handmaiden of the West. There are credibility problems as well. Notwithstanding these issues, a sense can be gained from a survey of the nuclear documents that the non-proliferation regime has ensured that the world does not become a nuclear armoury, howsoever large an arsenal a few selected states may have. It is right to believe that by facilitating restrictions of the politics of nations on the whole, proliferation can be controlled. Therein perhaps lies the strength of the nuclear non-proliferation system. But disarmament is a far cry. That is how things are as of now.

The book *Disarmament Issues* in two volumes has a wide coverage. Volume I presents various treaties including Comprehensive Nuclear Test-Ban Treaty (CTBT), Strategic Offensive Treaty (SOT); agreements, conventions, statements, speeches, remarks, etc. by eminent international leaders on disarmament issues. Volume II contains resolutions, remarks, statements and working papers on nuclear disarmament, non-proliferation, nuclear tests, prevention of war, etc. The book offers a comprehensive Introduction that analyses various disarmament issues with special reference to nuclear weapon states and their role in bringing about nuclear disarmament, India's stance on Non-proliferation Treaty (NTP), efforts to create a nuclear weapon free world, threat of nuclear terrorism and other disarmament issues.

It will be useful to the students and teachers of international relations, political science and scholars in these fields. It will also benefit policymakers, parliamentarians, government officials, etc. To those concerned with world peace and security the book will provide for an enriching and intellectually stimulating reading.

Brig. Rahul K. Bhonsle
Col. Ved Prakash
K.R. Gupta

Contents

VOLUME II

Introduction

Nuclear, biological and chemical (NBC) arms are the most inhumane of all weapons. Designed to terrify as well as to destroy, they can, in the hands of either states or non-state actors, cause destruction on a vastly greater scale than any conventional weapons, and their impact is far more indiscriminate and long-lasting. So long as any state has such weapons, especially nuclear arms, others will want them—for the same reasons as the ones offered by the former. So long as any such weapons remain in any state's arsenal, there is high risk that they will one day be used, by design or accident. Any such use will be catastrophic.

The Second World War wreaked untold destruction on humanity. Not only conventional arms of higher destructive power were used but also two one-sided nuclear inflictions were made by the U.S. on Japan. Although conventional weapons have done more damage to humanity—which took a toll of around 23 million people killed on wounded in wars upto 1990, the nuclear weapons are much more dangerous as they have the capacity to wipe out entire humanity from the earth. A brief account of making and using atomic weapons by America towards the end of Second World War, and the short- and long-term cousequences therefore are given below.

How It All Started

Project Manhattan came to a successful conclusion with the testing of the first atomic bomb "Trinity" in the U.S. on 16 July 1945. It is the same project in which Dr. Joseph Rotblat, Nobel Prize Laureate (1995), an ardent advocate of total nuclear disarmament, refused to participate.

Two atomic bombs were subsequently dropped on Hiroshima and Nagasaki using a B-29 Bomber on 6 and 9 August 1945, respectively named "Little Boy" and "Fat Man". It was all over within a week, starting on Monday and ending on Thursday. The consequences were horrendous: 2,10,000 humans were killed, 1,40,000 in Hiroshima and 70,000 in Nagasaki. The shear physical destruction in the two areas and subsequent suffering of people due to nuclear fall-out remain beyond description.

Obvious gain to the Allies was the end of a protracted war as Japan, which totally baffled and bewildered, readily agreed to an unconditional surrender. But at what cost to humanity? War was coming to an end anyway. Was the attack really undertaken to test the destructive potential of the new weapon rather than bringing the war to an end? It needs emphasis that it was a Far Eastern country, Japan, that was targeted, and not a European country, Germany, that had wrought greater havoc on the U.S. and its European Allies and their troops. Critics saw racial consideration behind selection of Japan for testing a newly-invented nuclear monster. Yet again, where was the justification for second "test" on Nagasaki? As the well-known strategist, Jasjit Singh of India, says: "Dropping of the bomb over Hiroshima and Nagasaki has less military logic than the perceived need to define the nature of the post cold war international order."

So the U.S. became the first country in the human history to deploy this deadly weapon, and an Asian nation was the victim. But the former was not destined—or expected—to be a lone occupant of the nuclear summit. In the succeeding years, scientific research continued and the technology was harnessed to perfect the Fission and Thermonuclear Fusion devices. The Fission Bomb was developed and tested by other nations in the following order:

The Soviet Union	1949
The United Kingdom	1952
France	1960

Meanwhile, the U.S. had set its sight to go beyond the Fission—to the Thermonuclear Fusion devices. As was only to be expected, the US was the leader in this field too. It developed and tested it in 1952. Expectedly, yet again, the three European nations followed suit in the field of the Fusion Bomb, and interestingly, in the same order as was the case with the Fission Bomb:

The Soviet Union	1953
The United Kingdom	1957
France	1968

The four nuclear powers, with the most potent weapon in their arsenal, got an edge over the rest—'the lesser mortals'. This weapon emerged as a currency of power and became a status symbol. So these four powers—all European—were a class apart, an exclusive, elite club. For these powers, the value of this weapon lay in its providing a mutual 'deterrence'. Meantime, post-World War II, the Soviet Union had emerged as the second superpower. This 'deterrence' factor had gained salience in the U.S.-USSR relations. It is generally believed that the possession of the nuclear power (read, warheads) helped in avoiding total war between the two superpowers, even if they continued adding conventional weapons to their stocks and struggling for economic supremacy and gaining of areas of ideological influence. So it was a race for supremacy between Moscow and Washington for drawing adherents to their respective economic models of development, viz. Communist and Capitalist. This approach of direct confrontation is best remembered by the 1962 nuclear stand-off between the two superpowers over Cuba, when the USSR is believed to have blinked. The other two examples of this confrontationist posturing involved North Korea and Vietnam. This one-up-manship continued till 1969. But the U.S. defeat in Vietnam was the watershed, marking a shift in the U.S. policy.[1]

Today, a determined nation with a reasonably advanced scientific and technical capability and infrastructure can build an arsenal of relatively simple nuclear weapons without detection and testing. Before the CTBT comes into force, such a proliferation could be facilitated significantly if anyone of the NWS was willing to provide a testing ground to such nations covertly on its soil. The case of North Korea is rather unique: a nation which cannot feed its populace has invested hugely to produce a nuclear arsenal, defying a mighty U.S.A. and compelling it to negotiations on its terms.

The above formulations and averments are enough to show that achieving the objective of nuclear non-proliferation is neither realistic nor a just or justified aim. So, only fair and logical answer lies in the total elimination of nuclear weapons. Coming in the way of achieving this desideratum are the five NWS, who are determined to check horizontal proliferation and least interested in the elimination of their huge nuclear stockpiles. They could not be unaware of the inevitable consequences of their stubborn refusal to see the light. Denied the means and possibilities of ensuring their national security with nuclear weapons, they (some nations) might revert to building requisite stocks of other varieties of the weapons of mass destruction (WMDs), including biological and chemical, even if they stand banned. This is bound to happen if these nations perceive a serious threat to their national security. Proliferation of WMDs, including the nuclear weapons, cannot be stopped through treaties and conventions only, "they also need a global security paradigm free of political and economic exploitation; and it should be based on fair play that ensures socio-economic justice internationally".

Nuclear Versus Conventional Arms: Prioritising the Issue

The emphasis on elimination of nuclear weapons *ad nauseam* over the last so many decades ignoring altogether the control—if not the elimination—of conventional weapons is rather misplaced—even pervert, as will be seen later on this discussion. This also has been a point of disagreement in proceedings of various committees of CD where the allocation of time and resources between conventional and nuclear weapons control was debated.

This huge, disproportionate allocation of resources on discussing nuclear weapons, their proliferation and elimination is inexplicable. After all, nuclear weapons were used in 1945 in two attacks, which took a toll of around a quarter million people who were either killed or injured. Compared to this, in 140 conflicts between 1945 and 1990s, at least 23 million people perished, essentially due to the use of conventional weapons, as stated earlier. Another estimate has it that some 45 million people have died since 1945 through the use of conventional weapons. Forty-five per cent of these casualties were civilians—not military men. It is obvious that the conventional weapons have been the main killers of humankind, and hence, should be the focus of CD.

The lack of interest in controlling the conventional weapons, in fact exposes the "real thinking and grand design" of the West. The aim of the NWS till date has been to thwart the horizontal spread of nuclear weapons, thus allowing them to maintain their monopoly of the deadly weapons. Even if India and Pakistan have gatecrashed into the nuclear club, the fact remains they have done so at a huge cost to their economy and political standing. They had to face sanctions of all kinds. India has gained some redress via the Indo-U.S. civilian nuclear deal, but still has not been included in the nuclear weapons states; there are only five recognized NWS—whether it be under NPT or CTBT. All their exertions till date have been aimed at ensuring their national security through their possession of nuclear weapons, simultaneously denying the same to 'lesser' nations. Both the CTBT and Fissile Materials Ban Treaty (FMBT), while contributing towards the achieving of commitments made in the NPT Principles and Objectives agreed in May 1995, primarily served the interests of NWS as these distinctly ensure continuing their monopoly in the field of nuclear arsenal by further denying any new comer entry into the "exclusive nuclear weapons club".

Some analysts ascribe ulterior motives to developed countries for not allotting appropriate share of time and resources to control the production of conventional weapons. As the empirical data shows, all the wars/conflicts after the World War II have been fought in and between the poor Third World countries—generally underdeveloped and mostly poor. Even more importantly, the rich and developed countries are the main producers and suppliers of the conventional weapons to the combatant countries. It is the rich cartels in the developed countries that are making huge profits through the arms trail. It is generally believed that these countries, through their political and economic decision, create demands for the arms. Besides these official channels, there are huge private players in the field who indulge in Narco trade-related arms supplies.

Professor Joseph Rotblat, who became an ardent advocate of total nuclear disarmament, is acclaimed throughout the world for his achievement in mobilizing opposition to nuclear weapons. He asserts that elimination of nuclear weapons alone is not enough to guarantee to save this world from a nuclear disaster. He says: "If humanity is to survive...it would take more than elimination of nuclear weapons—it will require abolition of all wars." Yet again, why should elimination of war be emphasized from the nuclear weapons point of view only? As stated above, conventional weapons have inflicted far more death and destruction on the world as compared to the nuclear weapons. So, elimination of wars and conflicts is equally important from the point of view of conventional weapons, if not more, as from one of the weapons of mass destruction. But elimination of wars is a desirable idea, ideal perhaps, that should be assigned to a distant future. More important is to work for immediate aim. For last over 60 years, international community has worked single-mindedly on elimination of nuclear weapons and achieved little tangible results. Certain powers, with vested interests, have successfully skewed the nuclear agenda. Instead of elimination, all energy has been invested on the non-proliferation of nuclear weapons.

Nuclear Disarmament and Control of Production of Fissile Materials are Intertwined

The erstwhile Soviet Union maintained that the fissile material cut-off should be coupled with the total nuclear disarmament. Needless to say, this was when the Soviet Union had not tested its fission bomb. It needs to be noted that the main difference between the previous (year 1946, when the U.S. was the sole nuclear power) and the present (mid-1990s, when India was deemed to be keen to join the elitist NWS club, or some would say, "knocking at its door") cut-off proposals is that current version is packaged as a nuclear non-proliferation measures primarily designed to place a check on the weapons program of Israel, India and Pakistan. U.S. officials (like Steve Aoki of

President Clinton's National Security Council Staff on 30 March 1995) had publicly stated that the U.S. would not participate in a cut-off that did not include India and Pakistan, at a minimum. "India and Pakistan are willing to negotiate a cut-off but with a stipulation that it be non-discriminatory—as called for in the 1993 U.N. General Assembly resolution." Their stance was: "If NWS are allowed to keep a stockpile of fissile nuclear material, so should they be! Likewise, if some nations are allowed to commercially reprocess and/or enrich these materials, all nations should too be."

Egypt believed that the exclusion of existing stockpiles would consolidate the status quo for NWS and also reward the undeclared NWS. It also emphasized that the ban would have to address all fissile materials, civilian and military, that could be used in nuclear weapons or nuclear explosive devices. India's position was: The convention should focus on future production of fissile material, permit production for civilian purposes and not be applicable retrospectively. No resolution had been adopted as of April 1997 by the U.N. on the cut-off of fissile material.

The cut-off proposal had implicit in it an effective verification system which could not be ensured absolutely—beyond any doubts and flaws—with the technologies then available. The non nuclear weapon states (NNWS), which are parties to the NPT are already committed to not producing fissile materials. Some are of the view that the cost of implementing cut-off, especially against cheating, will be too high, and will outweigh its benefits. Further, the fissile material cut-off proposal aims at achieving a nuclear non-proliferation level which falls below the aims of NPT, as such it has potential to damage the NPT by creating a new, less restrictive arms control accord that other nations may eventually prefer.

Emphasizing the seriousness of proliferation of WMDs, General Errera, on behalf of the EU, said: "The 15 countries of the European Union, like so many others, are convinced that proliferation of WMD represents one of the most serious threats to peace and international security. The risk to humanity from such proliferation goes beyond straightforward division between North and South, between countries with nuclear capability and those without. This was recognized at the highest level by the

Security Council in its statement on 31 January 1992. Non-proliferation is a common cause, just as the NPT is common property."

Moving Towards Nuclear Disarmament

Over the last couple of years, there has been a resurgence of interest in the subject of nuclear disarmament. It is known that the desire for a nuclear weapon free world (NWFW) had disappeared from the radar of the international community after 1995, until 2007. Of course, there were reasons for this phenomenon. Once the indefinite and unconditional extension of the NPT had been obtained at the NPT Extension and Review Conference in 1995, the NWS, having ensured against any further proliferation, went back to reinforcing nuclear deterrence as the bedrock of their national security strategies. In the decade following this seminal event, the NWS retreated to their comfort zones, having shut the door against the NNWS. Consequently, the issue of universal nuclear disarmament was either paid mere lip service or completely ignored by the policymakers in the NWS. Meanwhile, sudden end of the U.S.-U.S.S.R. confrontation, consequent to the demise of the Cold War era in 1991 and as a result, the unravelling of the Soviet Union, meant a reduction in the fear of a nuclear Armageddon. As a natural corollary to all this, NNWS and NGOs that had been at the forefront of the cause of the nuclear disarmament through the years of Cold War, were also lulled into a state of comfort.

A fresh look at the nuclear disarmament was dictated by the emergence of two new nuclear damages: (i) acquisition of nuclear weapons by 'states of proliferation concern' that perceive an asymmetric advantage in this weapon against a more powerful adversary; and (ii) the possibility of non-state actors acquiring the nuclear capability and unleashing nuclear terrorism on the unwary world. The second danger results from the realization of inadequacy of deterrence against these new, novel threats posed by the non-state actors harbouring suicidal tendencies and are of extremist persuation. Classical deterrence, built on sheer numbers, will not work against these irrational actors. After all, success of deterrence in the past has been premised on the rationality of the players.

Indian Initiatives in More Specific Context

In order to translate its concept of nuclear disarmament into reality, India has tried to make use of every opportunity in multilateral fora to get the international community to pursue it consensually. Within the U.N. and outside it, through appeals, proposals and action plans, India has constantly and consistently striven to realize an UWFW. Some are briefly summed up here:

- Indian initiatives on the subject can be traced back to the very time of the country's birth as an independent nation. As early as 1948, at the time of consideration of the report of the newly created U.N. Atomic Energy Commission, India had proposed limiting the use of atomic energy to peaceful purposes and elimination of nuclear weapons from national arsenals.
- In 1950, India used its voice in the U.N. to draw world attention to the fact that the arms race was not only a threat to international peace and security but was also a drain on human and economic resources that could be better deployed in other developmental activities. It pleaded for creation of a U.N. Peace Fund formed through a progressive reduction of arms and directing the amount thus released towards development. This proposal sought to establish and give a practical form to the linkage that India had drawn between disarmament and development.
- In 1953, Krishna Menon speaking at the First Committee of the United Nation's General Assembly (UNGA), categorically rejected a mere regulation of atomic weapons through arms control. He was rather emphatic: "There is only one thing to do with atomic weapons and that is to do away with them."
- A year later (in 1954) and soon after the U.S. first tested hydrogen weapons in Marshall Islands, Jawaharlal Nehru appealed for suspension of all nuclear testing until the use of the bomb was prohibited. Speaking in the Parliament on 2 April 1954, he said: "We have advocated prohibition of all such weapons (nuclear,

thermonuclear, chemical and biological) by common consent and immediately by agreement among those concerned." A year later, this appeal found an echo at the 1955 Bandung Conference of the Non-aligned nation, when 29 Asian and African countries expressed their support for the prohibition of nuclear weapons.

- In 1955, yet again, Krishna Menon speaking in the U.N., called for discontinuance of testing and absolute prohibition of the use of atomic weapons. Expressing his frustration at the whole process of disarmament negotiations and their inability to reach any conclusion, he said: "We are in the ninth year of this disarmament debate...and has a single weapon of war abandoned consequent to there discussions?... And the answer is no."
- In 1956, to streamline efforts towards nuclear disarmament, India presented a memorandum to the Disarmament Commission, suggesting certain concrete steps: (i) cessation of experimental nuclear explosion; (ii) dismantling of at least some of the nuclear weapons as a measure to reverse the arms race; (iii) declaration by nations not to manufacture any more nuclear weapons; and (iv) prohibition of export or transfer of nuclear weapons to other countries by the then declared NWS. Incidentally, by then less than 100 nuclear tests had been conducted and only three countries had emerged as NWS. Unfortunately, none of these measures received the attention they deserved.
- In 1957, the Indian delegation to the 12th session of the UNGA put forth a draft resolution appealing to "the states to agree without delay to suspend tests of nuclear and thermonuclear weapons". The resolution was defeated by a vote of 34 to 24 with 24 abstentions.[2] India informed the Secretary General about "the growing impatience among the neutral nations over the fruitless procedures in Disarmament Commission".

Nuclear Disarmament and the Credible Nuclear Deterrence

Post-1998, there was a perceptible waning of interest in disarmament. Even if some critics find it curious, this shift in India's passion for disarmament after the 1998 tests, Indian analysts say, is demanded by country's national security parameters in the changed strategic environment post-indefinite extension of the NPT. Even if critics see greater evidence of the predominance of realpolitik with a shift in focus to building of a credible nuclear deterrence, the Indians ask simply: Is not this shift unavoidable in the changed security situation created by nuclearised neighbourhood, particularly an unpredictable China? Yet again, a strong nuclear India is also demanded by its emerging power status.

There is certain cynicism within the nation about the lack of seriousness on the part of NWS about the objective of universal nuclear abolition—given the past Indian experience and the entangled web of present international relations. Consequently, recent initiatives, including the one by President Obama, are seen and treated with certain circumspection and "wait and watch" attitude. But equally importantly, should India allow itself to be swamped by a sense of *déjà vu*—cutting itself off the emerging debate on the nuclear disarmament? Or, should India emulate China's stance of waiting for other four NWS to reduce their arsenals to its own level, before going any serious negotiations? As for India, contrary to whatever the critics might say, it will continue to strive for non-discriminatory nuclear disarmament discourse, as it has consistently done since the late 1940s. A case for universal nuclear disarmament on grounds of morality, environmental considerations and humanitarian reasons has always existed. While this logic shall hold eternally and universally, in these times of the predominance of realpolitik, a case for disarmament can be grounded even in the realm of national security paradigm. As has been stressed earlier in these pages, India remained a NNWS for decades on end till it was compelled by the national security imperatives to go nuclear. To put it simply, India will not hesitate to abjure nuclear weapons if its national security is not jeopardised. It is only in this context that the issue is examined keeping in mind both of India's nuclear-armed neighbours—both bent upon hobbling India's efforts to realize its dreams of reaching its potential as not only a regional power but also a superpower along with China by 2035, or latest by 2050!

As for Pakistan, India's superiority in the field of conventional arms is widely acknowledged. In fact, Pakistan's quest for and acquisition of nuclear weapons was impelled by a desire to find an effective 'strategic equaliser' to somehow offset the Indian domination in the field of conventional weaponry—besides, of course, in regard to its size, population and economic might. Pakistan has, therefore, used its nuclear weapons to defend itself against the possibility of having to fight a superior army, which it would have had to since its military strategy is premised on waging a sub-conventional conflict against India.[3]

It bears emphasis to say that Pakistan decided to change course after failing to achieve its objective of wresting Kashmir from India through repeated conventional wars. After its disastrous misadventure of 1971, when it lost half of its territory in the East, Pakistan decided on the policy of bleeding India through 'a thousand cuts'—an euphemism for sub-conventional or low-intensity conflict, popularly known as terrorism. For a decade and a half, it trained extremist fundamentalists/Islamist militants with the help of Pak military and the ISI, in particular for cross-border terrorism. Initially for a decade or so, it was periodic or episodic phenomenon, but it—cross-border terrorism—became a torrent by the late 1980s. And there were shrewd calculations behind it. By 1987, Pakistan was in possession of nuclear weapons. It was confirmed by no less a person than A.Q. Khan in his interview with India's former High Commissioner to U.K., Kuldip Nayar. With it, Islamabad had cancelled out India's conventional military might. How? Pakistan's nuclear weapons capability allowed it to perpetrate cross-border terrorism even as it curtailed India's retaliatory options by playing up the fears of a conventional response possibly escalating to the nuclear level. No one can be sure of the nuclear threshold of a country like Pakistan—always at war within between its various actors (military and civilian politicians). In any case, Islamabad fuelled these apprehensions by projecting a low threshold. Even though Indian planners have catered for a conventional war of limited proportions, even when in possession of nuclear weapons, it is still a fact that the country is deterred by Pakistani nuclear arsenal from taking any decisive action of the kind it could in 1965, or 1971. It is then logical to conclude that the elimination of Pakistan's nuclear weapons would severely constrain its ability to indulge in sub-conventional provocations for fear of retaliation by a superior military force. It is easy to see that Pakistan's nuclear capability complicates India's national security problems and its disappearance under universal nuclear disarmament plan would not adversely impact India's security calculations, it would rather strengthen its defences against Pakistan's 'pinpricks'. Pakistan under the circumstances, would be extremely mindful of India's retaliatory capabilities.

As of today, China's preponderance of nuclear weapons exposes India to its nuclear coercion and blackmail. Even when India must be seriously engaged in enhancing the credibility of its nuclear deterrence to cancel out, to an extent, Chinese threat of blackmail, still the presence of superior Chinese arsenal renders India weak to face the dangers of existential risks from those quarters. But with a sustained and intelligent modernization of India's conventional capabilities, a non-nuclear China would not enjoy any substantial advantage over India. This would be particularly true of limited local wars that are thought likely between nations in future, as the U.N. and international community almost certainly are bound to pressurize the combatants to come to a ceasefire arrangements. The days of the wars stretching over years, like the Korean or Iraq-Iran conflicts, are almost certainly over. Short-duration wars between China and India, given their territorial disputes still unresolved, are not ruled out. Any war that may have to be fought over the North-East region, or further up in the disputed Himalayan reaches, would not be a disastrous repeat of the 1962 variety as India has learnt its lessons. If China has improved its strategic infrastructure in border regions of its Tibetan region, so has India—even if not to the same level. Maintaining a technological edge in (conventional) weapon systems, besides training, and raising a few more mountain divisions and combat squadrons of the Indian Army and Air Force, if considered necessary, should serve as a credible deterrent.[4] Therefore, it is reasonable to conclude that in a non-nuclear environment—meaning a conflict with conventional weapons ranged on either side—India could face a Chinese threat with certain confidence. Rather, it is the presence of nuclear weapons that tilts the balance in favour of China, given its larger and more capable nuclear arsenal. So it is in India's national interest that it continues its long-standing campaign for nuclear disarmament in the councils of the world.

So it is obvious that from its national security perspective, vis-à-vis its two nuclear-armed immediate neighbours, India needs an NWFW. Such a world is also desirable, far beyond its neighbourhood, for the good of the international community. In a wider context, the stress of India's leaders, beginning with its independence, on the nuclear disarmament and ultimately the elimination of this destructive weapon, as a matter of principle, holds good even in the changed circumstance of India possessing the weapon itself. If India went nuclear, it was by way of a defensive measure. Hence its adoption of no-first-use policy. For a country "that perceives a narrow/limited role for nuclear weapons, only for nuclear deterrence, and not as a war fighting weapon, or a tool to influence the scope and conduct of a superior conventional force, or an instrument to change the foreign policy of another...the attachment towards nuclear weapon is limited." So, it is obvious that if steps and mechanism could be devised to verify nuclear disarmament, and consequent abolition of the 'evil', India would have little to object to and would show a willingness to shed its nuclear baggage without any sense of loss of security. That, in fact, will be a concern, which many other nations that use nuclear weapons for their multi-role capability, well beyond mere nuclear deterrence, would be obliged to address.

How Can India Push for an NWFW?

India has long campaigned for nuclear disarmament on non-discriminatory basis. Having gone nuclear in 1998, India does not consider the 'bomb' as an asset for its national security imperatives. So, it still wants to push for the old desideratum with a renewed vigour. An important question is: What could New Delhi contribute to the evolving debate on the subject?

First and foremost, India must amplify its own understanding of concept of the universal nuclear disarmament. This unambiguity is essential as the concept has lent itself to different interpretations in different countries over the years. As India has accused the NWS of imposing a discriminatory NPT regime on the world, it follows that its definition of world without nuclear weapons will involve all countries renouncing their right to possess or use nuclear weapons, and accepting verifiable compliance. In a word, it is a state of zero nuclear weapons—not of fewer (nuclear) weapons, or in fewer hands. That concept explains India's insistence to link non-proliferation with disarmament, because the former is dependent on the latter for its sustainability. It must be clearly understood that non-proliferation is not disarmament. Even the NPT has two important parts: initial, non-proliferation and final, disarmament. By way of an obfuscation, the NWS—the hegemons—have over-emphasized the non-proliferation and almost forgotten the disarmament provisions of the NPT. Their aim is very simple: to bar the entry of new entrants to their 'elite' club. Hence, the need for India to caution the world against the real designs of the five hegemons. India must continue to remind the world that the goal of disarmament calls for steps beyond mere reduction of nuclear arms and/or arms control through CTBT or FMCT. In fact, like the NPT, other non-proliferation treaties (like the CTBT and FMCT) will also be found wanting in controlling proliferation unless linked to disarmament. Some nations are bound to perceive a threat to their security if some NWS is located in their vicinity—or even beyond. The world cannot afford to have two classes of nations: 'haves' and 'have-nots'. But the sad reality is that the five hegemons have shown no inclination to create level playing fields. No wonder that most recent initiatives have stopped short of recommending measures beyond mere arms control and non-proliferation. The result is the situation just depicted above.

Deterioration of Nuclear Environment

The year 1995 marked a watershed in international nuclear environment. By forcing the unconditional and indefinite extension of the NPT on the international community, India was left with no option but to go in far overt nuclear weaponisation. The Sino-Pakistan nuclear weapon collaboration continued in violation of the NPT and it was obvious that the NPT regime in India's neighbourhood had collapsed. China was, at this stage, assisting Pakistan in setting up plutonium production reactor at Khushal.

Presumably influenced by these considerations, the then Prime Minister Narasimha Rao decided to hold the tests towards the end of 1995; unfortunately, that was discovered by the Americans and, therefore, was called off. Now that the legitimization of the nuclear weapons was a given fact with the unconditional extension of the NPT, India could have lived with the nuclear option without overt weaponisation in a world where the nuclear weapons had a not been legitimized, but that course was no more viable in a world of legitimized nuclear weapons. Unfortunately, the full implications of the legitimization of the nuclear weapons were not debated either in this country or abroad. This fatal setback to nuclear disarmament and progress towards delegitimization of nuclear weapons was hailed by most of the peace movements abroad as a great victory.

By this time the NWS had consolidated the international nuclear hegemonic order to cover most of the globe. "The entire industrial world came under the Organisation of Security and Cooperation in Europe (OSCE) protected by the nuclear deterrence of the U.S., Russia, U.K., and France. So were the members of the Commonwealth of Independent States (CIS). The U.S. nuclear security cover protected Organization of American States in the Western hemisphere; and South Korea, Japan, Australia and New Zealand had bilateral security treaties with the U.S. bringing them under the U.S. extended deterrent protection. China had its own nuclear security. Africa, South Pacific nations, and the ASEAN chose to accept the nuclear overlordship and protectorate status of nuclear hegemonic powers and their security guarantees by accepting Nuclear-Weapons-Free Zone (NWFZ). West and South-West Asia came under the jurisdiction of the Central Command of the US and its Fifth Fleet." Thus, the entire globe, except for the Indian subcontinent, was covered by the international nuclear hegemonic order.

This obviously showed a grave deterioration in the security architecture of India during the three-year-period of 1995-98, along with the legitimization of the nuclear weapons through unconditional extension of the NPT. "Indian Parliament, politicians, academic and media with some exceptions did not pay adequate attention to it."

The U.S. and other NWS decided to impose the CTBT to ensure that there would be no more new NWS—thus closing the doors of this powerful, elite club. For the first time the Indian Ambassador's statement on 20 June 1996 in CD stated that the nuclear issue is a national security concern for India and advanced it as one of the reasons why India was unable to accede to CTBT. Presumably, this tipped off the hegemonic NWS like China and the U.K. who in turn introduced a clause at the last moment that India along with 43 other nations should sign the Treaty to bring it into force. This clause was coercive and a violation of the Vienna Convention on Treaties which stipulates that a nation not willing to be a party to a treaty cannot be imposed obligations arising out of the treaty. It bears emphasis that this clause was put in at the insistence of China—itself a nuclear proliferator to Pakistan. The international community approved that coercive CTBT—which signalled a major deterioration in our security environment.

Arms Control to Nuclear Disarmament: Landmarks En Route

A flurry of initiatives in the field of arms control and nuclear disarmament have been briefly mentioned earlier. President Obama's call for nuclear disarmament in April 2009 gave a fillip to these initiatives. A closer examination of Obama's rhetoric hid a somewhat baser and narrow national interest. It did not stem from urge for international peace following total elimination of nuclear weapons. What is not able about this sudden emphasis and concern on nuclear disarmament? Much of this concern piggybacks on apprehensions about nuclear proliferation and potential nuclear terrorism. All these recent arguments about nuclear disarmament, including the ones by the so-called 'gang of four' (Shultz, Perry, Kissinger and Nunn) flow from their concern about the possibility that proliferation might render the

U.S. more vulnerable to nuclear attack from terrorists, or from 'rogue' states or third world dictators.

There is nothing necessarily wrong with security concerns driving nuclear disarmament. But there is a flip side to it. The fact that today's nuclear disarmament rhetoric is not driven by the moral revulsion about the nuclear weapons that had motivated Nehru, Rajiv Gandhi, and even Ronald Reagan, raises the suspicion that if American security concerns are addressed, say, through a rejuvenated NPT, then nuclear disarmament would again be placed on the invisible tap of a distant mountain—discussed *ad nauseam* at the slightly left-wing academic conferences. Such apprehensions are not the result of a fervid imagination. There is a history to it. Ever since the NPT came into force, the NWS led by the same U.S. have shown excessive zeal for non-proliferation and completely ignored nuclear disarmament—knowing well that NPT mandates both! If the U.S. and Russia have reduced their nuclear arsenals, it is because their national interests demand it. There is nothing altruistic about this reduction. They have never linked such arms controls, achieved through Strategic Arms Limitation Talk (SALT) and Strategic Arms Reduction Treaty (START), with ultimate elimination of nuclear weapons.

Analysts have no doubt that the soaring rhetoric was nothing more that the opening salvo of public relations campaign aimed at rebuilding and perfecting the non-proliferation regime, and even more specifically, it is aimed at burnishing American credentials in time for the 2010 NPT Review Conference (RevCon). This RevCon is already looking like it would be stormy. The NWS led by the U.S. had a smooth sailing when NPT was extended unconditionally. NNWS have been emboldened by the adverse opinion of the ICJ on the legitimacy of the nuclear weapons. The NNWS would definitely push for laying down the road map for elimination and delegitimisation of these weapons. All this window-dressing was deemed necessary by the U.S. in the run-up to the RevCon.

Moving Towards Nuclear Disarmament: Future Steps

Some critics assert that India has not thought through the consequences of universal nuclear disarmament on its national security and strategic interests. It does not seem to be well-founded averment. India had long criticized the NPT for being a discriminatory document. India has always demanded level playing fields for all states. It was only when India descried a threat to its national security under the prevalent nuclear regime that it went for nuclear tests in 1998. The aim obviously was to create level playing fields. India is equally certain that its national security will not be jeopardized in a NWFW. The issue has been examined earlier. In such a world, India will be confident to square off with its menacing rivals like China, not to speak of noisy ones like Pakistan. India's conventional might cannot be laughed at.

At the world stage, India and several other countries have called for NWS along the lines of BWC and CWC, which successfully banned biological and chemical weapons in the past, respectively. In fact, some NGO groups have already proposed models for such a NWC. The argument that a NWC would be more difficult to conclude than the BWC or the CWC does not seem to hold water. Chemical weapons technology is far more widespread and far more easily available as compared to the nuclear one and is possessed by far fewer nations. Given these facts, an NWC should be far easier. CWC has been a success, of course, there is no doubt the CWC conclusion required courage and political commitment, and so will the NWD—and both in equal measures. All that stands in the way are self-serving and vested interests of the NWS.

There are other measures that can facilitate the final denouement. Abolition of the nuclear weapons demands that they must first be delegitimized. The advisory opinion of the International Court of Justice in 1996 on the illegality of nuclear weapons was a step in the right direction—even if a minor one, since that ruling is not binding in nature on the nations. But delegitimizing these weapons depends upon the political will of the powers that be, the NWS. For example, their nuclear doctrines need to be reframed to reduce the salience of these weapons in them. The same view is pedalled by some analysts in a more direct manner: They must renounce the 'first use' of nuclear weapon in their doctrines, claiming that this 'artificial' reliance on the 'first use' has no practical significance. Why the use of term 'artificial'? Because in reality it would be difficult for any political leader to order a nuclear strike ever pre-emptively. Consequently, these analysts argue, irrespective of what they might say in their muscular-sounding doctrinal statements, 'most' states are likely to practise NFU principle. By extension, acknowledging this reality translates into all NWS offering an NFU pledge which would *ipso facto* lead to the delegitimization process.

The scenario painted above by some analysts may be too rational, pragmatic—even simplistic. 'Most' countries may not resort to pre-emptive strike, but the term still leaves some which may. More importantly, only one country (India) till date has adopted a declaratory NFU. The only other country in this field, China, has offered a conditional NFU. So, the possibility of all NWS adopting NFU policy is rather over-enthusiastic prognosis.

Another interim measure could be the avoidance of nuclear accidents and unauthorized use of such weapons. Even if the world has not travelled much on the road to nuclear disarmament, the fact remains the weapon has not been used since 1945. This non-use has given us the term 'nuclear taboo', and it is important to ensure that this taboo is not violated, even through an unintended accident. To ensure this, NWS must put these weapons in a de-alerted state. Some NWS are believed to have adopted such measures in full or part. The U.S. and Russia are known such nuclear powers. If all NWS were to adopt such a posture, it would be a significant step in both delegitimizing these weapons and also ensuring that the nuclear taboo stands unbroken.

In India, an international conference was organized by the Centre for Strategic and International Studies and the International Council of World Affair, in 2009, to hold discussion on the theme of "A World Free of Nuclear Weapons".[5]

The U.S. and Russia hold huge stockpiles of the nuclear weapons—95 per cent of the world arsenal. The two have special responsibility in articulating their commitment to a NWFW, and taking steps to achieve the goal. They have effected certain reductions under SALT and START treaties. Critics say that was done more under compulsions of their narrow national interests rather than a genuine push towards NWFW. George Perkovich and Acton scripted the practical aspects of total disarmament in an Adelphi Paper of 2008.[6] Their paper was discussed worldwide. "The debate showed that most people felt that nuclear disarmament is an extremely complex issue with many political and technical hurdles in its path." These are sort of self-serving arguments often preferred by the vested interests. That the argument cited here and often cited by the NWS for their inability to proceed towards the NWFW, has been found wanting.

Reduction in Nuclear Arms

The West generally equates disarmament with arms reduction rather than arms elimination. During the Cold War, arms control was an important item on the agenda of two leading nuclear powers. The INF, CFE, CWC and ABM were examples of successful arms control negotiations between the U.S. and Russia, and of multilateral negotiations.

After the Cold War ended, the U.S. and Russia concluded, signed, ratified and implemented START I with an expiry date of 5 December 2009. They also signed START II which was not ratified by the Russian Duma. Some discussions had also taken place on START III, but it was not signed. In 2002, the two nations signed Strategic Offensive Reductions Treaty (SORT) without any negotiations. SORT commits both sides to reduce their nuclear weapons to 1700-2200 range by 2010. The verification rules of START I apply. The SORT declaration was tied up with START I, expired 5 December 2009 (Table 1).

Despite the success of START I, Russia and the U.S. continue to have 95 per cent of the world's nuclear arsenal.

The 2009 estimates of the U.S. National Nuclear Security Administration place the current nuclear holdings of the two powers as given in Table 2.

Table 1

Nuclear Assenal of the U.S. and Russia

Total	US	Russia
Strategic operational	4,700	4,100
Non-strategic operational	500	3,800
In reserve	4,200	5,100
Total	9,400	13,000

Thus, the two between them still have 22,400 weapons, of which some 13,100 are operational. This, when they do not face Cold War types of threats from each other.

Other types of nuclear capabilities are given in Table 2.

Table 2

Other Nuclear Capabilities of U.S. and Russia

	Delivery	System/launders		Fissile material (civil + military stockpiles in metric tonnes)	
	ICBMs	SLBMs	Bombers	HEm	Plutonium
U.S.	450	288	113	1073 ± 300	186 ± 25
Russia	383	160	77	703 ± 50	92

President Obama and President Madvedev in their meeting in London in April 2001 gave a political push to fresh arms control negotiations. After several rounds of START negotiations in May, June and July, the two principals held a summit in Moscow on 6 July 2009, each agreeing to reduce his nuclear warheads to 1500-1675 range and delivery vehicles to 500-1100 range. The promised reductions (some 25 per cent over SORT) are rather modest, still they constitute a positive step forward. "More reductions have been promised in future negotiations".

A Look at the Future Prospects

Nuclear disarmament is a complex issue, so think the NWS who have made these weapons an important part in their national security architecture—forgetting that they came into existence only in mid-1940s. In the recent years, the experts had asserted that nuclear wars are not winnable. What is most important factor in this field is political will. Security establishments and strategic experts will assert that their elimination will jeopardize the security of their countries. So ran the arguments when banning and proscription of the chemical weapons were under discussion. As in that case, so in the case of nuclear weapons, what is required is the change in the mindsets. The rest will follow. In any case, a view needs to be taken of the different countries position on the issue. Even if most analysts feel the lead must come from the two major stockpile holders of this 'abomination', it is only the collective will of the international community that will nudge these two towards the final elimination of their stocks.

Interestingly, the Bush era 2002 Nuclear Posture Review regards the nuclear weapons usable in certain contingencies. Russia is known to be embarking on an ambitious plan to renovate its strategic and missile forces. In Russian security strategy, nuclear weapons and ballistic missiles have assumed greater salience in recent years, particularly the post-Cold War period. There is a reason for this change. Soviet Union/Russia collapsed as a superpower after 1991. Unfortunately, its conventional forces failed to keep pace with their counterparts, which can be deployed against it by the sole superpower. With SALT and START reductions in their respective nuclear arsenals, the two powers pinned their hopes on the conventional forces for their security. Russia became painfully aware of inadequacy in the field of conventional forces. Hence, the decision to fall back upon nuclear forces—or whatever balance is left in its arsenal—to safeguard its strategic interests. Russia also regards the proposed U.S. ballistic missile defence system in Poland as a major hurdle in the U.S.-Russia rapprochement and also to arms control negotiations. But of late, things are moving in the latter field.

For China too, nuclear weapons remain a currency of power. It will take up the issue only if the big two make some progress in the nuclear disarmament. India is surrounded by two nuclear powers. The dynamics of nuclear weapons in the West Asia is dictated by the geopolitical 'realities' as perceived by Israel and Iran.

Some analysts and vested interests 'perceive' certain technical hurdles in the way of nuclear disarmament, besides the political ones mentioned above—mainly concerning the monitoring and verification problems. How do we deal with the cheaters? Can the cheating be abolished? Then there is the question/possibility of terrorists laying their hands on the fissile materials and cobbling together a crude nuclear device. Some feel there are no foolproof solutions. Still others assert these fears are overdone and overplayed for the gullible. START I verification methods are fairly credible, if the powers-that-be mean business. Large numbers of nuclear weapons indeed have been eliminated. Then, why is this obfuscation now?

Some analysts are sanguine that these difficulties notwithstanding, the nuclear disarmament destination will be reached only through a normative and legalistic approach in which nuclear weapons are completely banned.[7] In this regard, there is already a ruling by the ICJ, even if it is non-binding, which has declared the nuclear bomb illegal.

A report by a U.S. Congressional Commission on the Strategic Posture of the U.S. chaired by William J. Perry is of greater relevance to the issue of nuclear disarmament. It argues that "both the U.S. and Russia should be seen by other countries as seriously moving towards reducing the salience of nuclear weapons in their force postures". Only then will other countries extend cooperation in checking nuclear proliferation. Interestingly, it is U.S. Commission and its recommendations are informed by narrow U.S. national interests: Russia and the U.S. "should be 'seen' by other countries...". This recommendation does not suggest a single step towards the elimination of nuclear weapon, rather it is a ploy to extract from other countries (essentially meaning majority of NNWS and countries like India) some more cooperation on the issue. The rest of recommendations, summarized here, too are steps in the same direction, not towards universal disarmament:

- Signing of a new START with Russia.
- A broader strategic dialogue with Russia on nuclear energy, ballistic missile defence, space, etc.
- The U.S. should seek an international FMCT.
- Should the U.S. ratify CTBT?

On the last point, there were differences within the Commission. Those favouring ratification argued that it would not affect the maintenance of a safe, secure and reliable nuclear weapons stockpile without additional nuclear testing. Opponents argued that CTBT would require signature and ratification of countries like North Korea, Iran, Pakistan, India, China, Israel and Egypt—a proposition deemed difficult. Therefore, the U.S. should not be bound by restrictions which other countries ignored.

They also argued that a 'zero-yield' prohibition contained in the Treaty was essentially unverifiable and, therefore, several countries could cheat. The opponents of the CTBT also noted that Russia and China are possibly conducting low-yield tests needed for tactical nuclear war fighting. More importantly, skeptics felt that maintaining a safe and reliable nuclear stockpile in the absence of testing was risky.[8]

Arms control, and reduction in nuclear arsenals of NWS can contribute to the goal of disarmament in a rather limited way. They may no longer succeed in pushing the NNWS towards greater perfection in the field of non-proliferation to check the nuclear spread horizontally but ignoring to take even minor steps in the direction of elimination of nuclear weapons. This ploy may work no longer.

Nuclear Terrorism

Carlos Marighella, a passionate student and an inveterate espouser of terrorism says, "Terrorism is an arm the revolutionary can never relinquish". Its implication is rather simple: The terrorist will not stop at anything, and try to lay his hand at any arms, means, and methods that will serve his purpose, nuclear devices not excluded. And the disgraced Pakistani metallurgist A.Q. Khan having run an open nuclear Wal-Mart for years, till he was grounded in 2003, any interested entity—an individual, a group, or a country—can lay its hands on a quantity of fissile material, if not a crude nuclear device itself. The consequences will be too frightening even to imagine. But first, a little about the debate on the issue.

Brian Jenkins of the RAND Corporation likened the terrorism to the theatre. Following the theatre metaphor, a serious question arises concerning this prospective variant of the macro-terrorism, the nuclear threat.

The Ford Foundation study of Mason Willrich and Theodore Taylor is the leading work in the field that has heightened the public attention on the possibility of nuclear terror. Even the field of fiction has drawn many authors into capturing this theme.

There are two schools of thought on the issue. The realistic school examines motives, feasibility and historical evidence. It is not so sure and certain as is the 'faith bloc' that seems to accept the likelihood of nuclear terrorism as a matter of fatalistic faith, or at least as a concession to expert opinions.

The faith bloc sees the possibility of acquisition of fissile materials, hence nuclear explosive devices provide the motive for terrorist to find or compile the capabilities to carry out the threat of nuclear terrorism. This line of reasoning conceives the prospective nuclear terrorist as a mountain climber who will climb the plutonium hill simply because it is there.

Louis Rene Beres says the design of a nuclear bomb is not very difficult—in fact nuclear weapons are relatively easy to make. Forest Frank stated: "The amount of expertise needed to construct a bomb is perhaps no greater than that derived from a college physics, chemistry and perhaps engineering." Willrich and Taylor are certain that a determined terrorist group could acquire nuclear weapon manufacturing capability once it had the required fissile materials. Taylor holds consistently that just one person could accomplish the task.

But it is equally true that the whole thing has been made to look so simple—involving denigration of sophistication required. Even in a null-planned effort, many months of intense work would be required to produce a weapon; and then, there is good chance that the device would fail to detonate or that there could be fatal accidents during the construction. The view is shared by Robert Kupperman, Chief Scientist, Arms Control and Disarmament Agency.

Several experts posit that nuclear terrorists place modern society at great risk because the logic of threat of nuclear retaliation would be futile against the elusive terrorists. In order to deter a terrorist who is not already dissuaded by organizational costs from the nuclear path, we should think of imposing unacceptable and credible costs, viz. capture, death or destruction of the organization, and not nuclear retaliation. But in the present-day scenario, even the effectiveness or deterrence value of the former variety of costs/punishment loses all its value because there are any number of frenzied youth willing and ready to offer themselves as suicide bombers—attaching no value to human life.

Putting the Macro-terrorism in Perspective

The entity most likely to engage in nuclear terrorism could be a national government. Actually, a suggestive model of nuclear terrorism is the one case in history that occurred. It was used by a government in dreadful urgency to bring a bitter and costly war to an end. It was the nation that enjoyed the luxury of being alone to possess such dreadful things.

Since that unilateral 'terrorism', what has prevailed is the passive kind of terrorism, commonly known as 'deterrence'. The most passive deterrence of all would be just letting it be known that a government or other organization simply had nuclear weapons, letting every potential addressee of the 'deterrent threat' reach his own conclusions about what kind of misbehaviour, if any, might provoke nuclear activity. It is obvious that the 'nuclear blackmail' that might be practiced by a non-government organization, by a front organization set up by some government, or even by a government itself, would be more effective than the small acts of individual terrorism that may first come to mind.

It would probably look more like diplomacy than terrorism, attached to a 'just' cause. The strategists might be concerned about avoiding harm to bystanders, but well-aware of practice of nuclear-weapon states which threaten nuclear destruction to the people whose leaders 'misbehave'. And they might be no more transient in world politics than most liberation movements, governments in exile, or ethnic communities.

A nuclear bomb has come to attain a unique status and importance of its own. Not only major nations, aspiring to be counted among the influential players in the international community, want to possess it, even smaller ones like North Korea, Iraq, Pakistan, Israel, Libya, etc. were determined in their intent. If P-5 thought they could prevent others following in their foot steps by concluding the NPT, they must have been suitably chastened by now. If India and Pakistan have publicly declared their assets in May 1998, Israel is known to possess nuclear bombs. North Korea too seems to have crossed the Rubicon. After the states, now we have individuals—non-state or state actors and more alarmingly, terrorists—who are single-mindedly chasing the dream. But first a brief narrative of birth of the nuclear device and subsequent developments.

The key questions are: How real is the threat of the terrorists laying their hands on the real thing? Is a successful theft of the fissile material from the nuclear power industry, in private or public sector, possible? Are such materials, present in the industry, in forms and quantities, liable to be used for an illicit manufacture of a nuclear device—even in crude form? If a terrorist succeeds in making such a weapon, what are the consequences? It must be admitted that any science graduate interested in it can make a bomb since the formula is available in the relevant books, as also on the ubiquitous internet. To wit, a number of terrorists today are highly qualified technocrats and professionals. The danger of nucler terrorism is thus real, and grave at that.

Nuclear Terrorism: The Only One Way to Counter It

The loudest and most strident critics of Indo-U.S. Civil Nuclear Deal are anti-proliferation activists—dubbed as proliferation Ayatollahs by some Indian analysts. Such criticism is hypocritical. Even a man like Stroke Talbot, who held numerous rounds of talks with India's then External Affairs Minister Jaswant Singh all over the globe and indeed laid down the parameters of Indo-U.S. strategic relationship from which grew this Deal, now expresses worry that making an exception in the case of India would encourage other nations to acquire nuclear weapons. However, it can be argued that equating India to other nations is fallacious, and ignoring its impeccable record of responsibility in this field is being naive. Nations like North Korea which has already gone nuclear or Iran, at the brink do not need India's exception to proceed on the nuclear path. More importantly, if the Americans seriously believe that the NPT is still relevant, they are mistaken.

"After tacit complicity in the nuclear proliferation initiated by China and aided by Pakistan, it is brazen of American to sermonise on the dangers of nuclear proliferation."[9] Sitting on piles of nuclear weapons, the US and other of the N-5 members are not only guilty of being duplicitous but are also guilty of practicing double standards if they preach abstinence to others.

Seen as currency of power, there will always be certain irresistible temptation for some major/middling nations to go nuclear. There are already declared or otherwise four nuclear powers outside the NPT, and more will be joining them sooner rather than later.

Thus, nothing short now of total nuclear disarmament, which India has stood for long years, non-discriminatory in its scope and to be monitored by a recognized world authority, can become a safeguard against future nuclear terrorism.

Pakistan and Nuclear Terrorism

Pakistan and India are two nuclear-weapons powers in the subcontinent. For the last decade or so, Pakistan has painted the region as dangerous flash point because of unresolved Kashmir 'dispute'—Pakistan's term. Since the 1998 nuclear test, Pakistan has upgraded it to the nuclear flash point. It has occasionally indulged in nuclear sabre-rattling, encouragingly played up by the western, and particularly the U.S., media.

Some analysts believe there is slim but finite probability that Pakistan would use the Kashmir issue to resort to acts of nuclear terrorism, or nuclear blackmail at the very least. Some Indian strategists have analysed the subject, but not deeply enough. This aspect certainly deserves much more national and international attention and subsequent serious research than has been the case so far.

There has been comments that in an upheaval, the Pak nuclear weapons could fall in the hands of the Islamic fundamentalist elements. Such fears have given birth to occasional reports in the press that Israel and India "are planning joint operation to take out or destroy the Pak nuclear arsenal's launching facilities". Israeli bombing of Iraq's nuclear facility is cited to bolster such a proposition by India, though both countries have denied any such plans.

But what has never been doubted or questioned is the American concern in October 2001 about 'loss of control' in Pakistan over its nuclear weapon cores and trigger sub-assemblies after the 9/11 Al Qaeda attacks. What had further deepened U.S. fears was the fact that some senior Pakistani nuclear scientists and engineers had links with Kandahar. The fear was that such sub-assemblies or the sensitive technologies for making nuclear weapons could end up in the hands of Pakistani jihadi outfits through raids on nuclear bases or through collusion of sympathetic, Islamised elements of the Pakistani Army. These fears were not unfounded.

The Pyramid of Nuclear Geopolitics

A seminal event in the paradigm of nuclear non-proliferation, the Treaty on the Non-Proliferation of Nuclear Weapons (NPT) Review Conference popularly known as the RevCon has just concluded in New York on 28 May 2010. Held once in five years, the RevCon undertakes a review of progress in nuclear non-proliferation during the period and suggests measures to supplement the NPT which remains the lynch pin to securing nuclear symmetry globally. The Final Document which was issued by consensus reaffirmed the intent of the state parties towards implementation of the treaty and underlined the role in promoting peace and stability globally. The three arms of nuclear disarmament covered included disarmament with progress made lauded upon during the various meetings, particularly the U.S. and Russian Prague agreement which promises to reduce their warheads to 1550 within a reasonable time. The RevCon Document has called upon accelerated progress by the nuclear-weapon states (NWS) and not just the U.S. and Russia in this direction.

One of the related recommendations is a call to reduce the salience of nuclear weapons in geopolitics, something on which there is likely to be limited progress despite the commitments being made by the NWS. Moreover, there were no concrete recommendations made in this direction. While a survey of the international scene would reveal that more and more countries are wanting to join the nuclear 'club'. With three proxy NWS, India, Pakistan and Israel out of the NPT loop, one alleged nuclear weapons holder North Korea, a declared pariah, and allegations of others such as Iran, and now even Myanmar wanting to join the nuclear 'haves', the NPT's credibility is at stake, though this issue was not discussed in the RevCon, which after the experience of the 2005 RevCon, where there was lack of consensus in drafting a final document, seemed to be more intent on signing one this time around than in recommending decisions to control the spread of nuclear weapons and encourage exploitation of peaceful uses of nuclear energy.

This failure can be attributed to a simple geometrical model represented by a pyramid. The triangular pyramid has two connotations in nuclear geopolitics. The large base and narrow apex represent the structure of utilization of nuclear energy. At the top are the five NWS, the United States, Russia, China, United Kingdom and France. At the lower level are the three "proxy" NWS India, Pakistan and Israel, below that would be North Korea a suspected NWS followed by states which are said to be aspiring for a nuclear weapon such as Iran though Tehran has completely denied such an intent, then those which have ambitions to acquire weapons status but have not expressly worked towards the same, and finally the large base of nations of the 189 countries party to the NPT which have mainly restricted their interest to peaceful use of nuclear energy.

The NWS pyramid is the second structure of geopolitics. There are a series of triangular configurations in this model. The first is the three western allies, United States, Britain and France which are likely to co join their policies to mutual advantage against any possible future global configuration against or competing with them. This is the traditional geopolitical configuration of the West versus the Rest, the latter being primarily Russia and China. With France and Britain seriously considering continuance of their respective nuclear arsenals, it is now left to the United States to carry the burden of the West.

This in turn has created the second subset in this model and perhaps the most significant one of the United States, Russia and China. These three nations will continue to use their nuclear arsenal for gaining advantage in the global geo-polity and retain their own sphere of influence. The reduction of weapons stockpile of one will be related to the other two. While Russia and the United States have decided to do so, it is not clear how China seeks to view reduction in its nuclear stockpile. This creates the third pyramidical subset that of China, India and Pakistan. Thus, as China retains its arsenal, India finds justified reasons to hold to its weapons and this is linked to Pakistan's weapon aspirations as well. To the latter it also provides deterrence against conventional adventure by India and a cover to carry on a proxy war against it. Thus, the China-Pakistan axis can be seen drawing maximum benefit from the nuclear weapons per se and may be least interested in going for any arms control or disarmament.

Then there are other outsiders in this geopolitical theatre. For instance, for Israel, holding nuclear weapons covertly is an existential security issue that guarantees that its rivals in the Middle East view it with caution and are prevented from any offensive designs either conventional or nuclear, as and when one of the powers acquires such a capability. Wary of the loss of face as well as military reputation suffered in the Yom Kippur war of 1973, nuclear weapons provide Tel Aviv the guarantee of survival.

North Korea is another outsider so to say for which nuclear weapons give the advantage of a "respected pariah" whatever that term may come to mean. For the otherwise bankrupt regime gets enormous clout internally, while in the global field it is able to engage with the high and the mighty by flaunting nuclear weapons capability rules, sharing the table with the United States, Russia and Japan. Many also suspect that North Korea is a protégé of China.

Then there are the aspirants, Iran which was recently sanctioned by the United Nations for the fourth time is one of the main suspects in this category. How far it has progressed in this direction depends on position and perception. Iran's rivals feel that it is very close to acquiring nuclear capability, while its supporters including Brazil of late and Turkey which have, "grandfathered" a deal to swap nuclear fuel for 20 per cent enrichment for Tehran are also amongst the latter category.

Turkey and Brazil have their own political agenda. Turkey is host to ninety U.S. tactical nuclear weapons as part of NATO's nuclear umbrella. While Brazil which entered the NPT in 1997 is reported to have an active program of its own and it did not allow IAEA inspectors inside an uranium enrichment facility near Rio de Janeiro on grounds of protecting proprietary information.

Such is the challenge before the NPT RevCon, i.e. that of global geopolitics of various interlocking pyramids, that it was not quite unusual for no major progress in disarmament emerging.

However, the NPT is not just the only treaty dictating the geopolitics of nuclear weapons. Comprehensive Test Ban Treaty

(CTBT), and Fissile Material Cut-Off Treaty (FMCT) are even more complex and have seen uncompromising stands by various countries including the NWS, thereby a consensus has not been forthcoming.

In this survey of geo-polity, where does the extensive documentation and debate on nuclear energy, non proliferation, weapons control, test and fissile material bans stand? In global political discourse the largest bank of documents remains that in the field of nuclear disarmament and arms control. Despite the skepticism expressed thus far, there is near universal adherence to the parameters of control laid down for instance of the 189 parties to the NPT, almost all are adhering to its precepts in letter and spirit, while just a handful are outside its purview and a couple suspected to be making advances to either reject or flout its norms. This certainly denotes the successful evolution of an international debate and consensus on peaceful uses of nuclear energy and abhorrence of nuclear weapons as currency of power.

Current Issues in Nuclear Non-proliferation including the Geopolitics

A perspective on the current issues in nuclear non-proliferation against the backdrop of the Eighth NPT Review Conference held in New York from 3 to 18 May 2010 will provide an effective matrix for assessment of implementation of the global NPT regime. It will be particularly important for an Indian audience since India is a non signatory of the NPT and as an observer can see if the Treaty really works to attain the results that is intended to achieve. So what the documents will permit you to address is the following vital questions in relation to the nuclear issue:

- Is the global nuclear disarmament regime working?
- Is there a commitment of the NWS towards disarmament?
- Is sufficient progress being made towards test ban and fissile material control?
- Can NNWS hope to obtain full benefits from peaceful use of nuclear energy and are NWS committed to support them?

- Are there sufficient incentives for proxy NWS as India, Pakistan and Israel to join the NPT?

The NPT

The NPT opened for signature in 1968 and entered into force in 1970. It categorizes states as nuclear weapon states (NWS) and non-nuclear weapon states (NNWS). The former are those who have carried out a weapons test before 1 January 1967 and thus includes the United States, Soviet Union (now Russia), United Kingdom, France and China. While the latter category includes all other states including ironically those who have tested afterwards, India and Pakistan in 1998, Israel on an unspecified date and Democratic People's Republic of Korea which withdrew from the treaty in 2003 presumably with an intent to carry out tests.

Under the NPT, the NWS are permitted to retain their nuclear arsenals but cannot transfer or assist any NNWS from acquiring nuclear weapons, a clause which is suspected to have been flouted by some states as China which is said to have helped Pakistan and possibly even North Korea in acquiring some elements of nuclear weapons capability. China is also accused of carrying out a nuclear weapons test on behalf of Pakistan and is also said to be now, "grandfathering" a program for providing Islamabad two nuclear reactors, though these will be primarily used for generating energy in an electricity starved Pakistan.

The NNWS are proscribed from acquiring nuclear weapons in any form or even aspiring for the same as Iran is now discovering, but are permitted to use nuclear energy for peaceful purposes under full-scope safeguards administered by the International Atomic Energy Agency (IAEA).

Article VII (3) of the NPT requires that, "five years after the entry into force of this Treaty, a (review) conference of parties to the Treaty shall be held in Geneva, Switzerland, in order to review the operation of this Treaty with a view to assuring that the purposes of the Preamble and the provisions of the Treaty are being realized." The first RevCon was held in 1975 and one is now held subsequently every five years.

The RevCons

The first RevCon had 91 state parties which urged the NWS to continue to be committed to disarmament and sought their compliance to these obligations. The second RevCon held in Geneva from 11 August to 7 September 1980 had 112 state participants and no consensus was reached on the final declaration due to lack of agreement on implementation of Article VI as it was felt that the NWS did not commit themselves to halting the arms race. The third RevCon was held again at Geneva, from 27 August-21 September 1985 with 131 state parties to the treaty where a final declaration for establishing nuclear weapon free zones was adopted. Discussion was also held on Comprehensive Test Ban Treaty (CTBT).

The fourth RevCon held in Geneva from 20 August to 14 September 1990 once again failed to adopt a final declaration on a series of disagreements over disarmament, CTBT, and assurances for assistance in peaceful use of nuclear energy. The fifth RevCon in 1995 was held in New York from 17 April to 12 May with 178 states signatorics to the treaty attending, China and France joined the NPT as NWS. State parties agreed to extend the treaty indefinitely under Article X.2 of the Treaty. The sixth RevCon from 24 April to 19 May in New York in 2000 finally adopted a final document with, "Thirteen Practical Steps" towards nuclear disarmament. The seventh RevCon in 2005 in New York from 2 May to 27 May had 188 state parties in attendance and no consensus was reached towards a final declaration, primarily because a number of issues were highly contentious such as status of North Korea and Iran, nuclear terrorism and so on. Of the seven RevCons only three succeeded in attaining consensus on a final document indicating the level of differences in this debate in the international community per se.

The Eighth RevCon

The Eight Revcon in 2010 was held in New York from 3 to 28 May. Three Preparatory Conferences or PrepComs were held prior to the same in 2007 in Vienna, a year later in Geneva, and in New York in 2009. While there was no substantial agreement during these PrepComs, the impetus provided by the Obama Administration certainly had an impact on the Eighth RevCon and there was a joint statement which has reinforced commitment of the state parties to disarmament. Part I of the Final Document on which consensus was obtained highlights,

"1. The Conference reaffirms that the full and effective implementation of the Treaty on the Non-Proliferation of Nuclear Weapons and the regime of Non-proliferation in all its aspects has a vital role in promoting international peace and security. The Conference reaffirms that every effort should be made to implement the Treaty in all its aspects and to prevent the proliferation of nuclear weapons and other nuclear explosive devices, without hampering the peaceful uses of nuclear energy by states parties to the Treaty. The Conference remains convinced that universal adherence to the Treaty and full compliance of all parties with all its provisions are the best way to prevent the spread of nuclear weapons and other nuclear explosive devices.

2. The Conference recalls that the overwhelming majority of states entered into legally binding commitments not to receive, manufacture or otherwise acquire nuclear weapons or other nuclear explosive devices in the context, inter alia, of the corresponding legally binding commitments by the nuclear-weapon States to nuclear disarmament in accordance with the Treaty.

3. The Conference notes that the nuclear-weapon states reaffirmed their commitment not to transfer to any recipient whatsoever, nuclear weapons or other nuclear explosive devices, or control over such weapons or explosive devices directly, or indirectly, and not in any way to assist, encourage or induce any non-nuclear-weapon state to manufacture or otherwise acquire nuclear weapons or other nuclear explosive devices, or control over such weapons or explosive devices.

4. The Conference notes that the non-nuclear-weapon states parties to the Treaty reaffirmed their commitment not to receive the transfer from any transferor whatsoever of nuclear weapons or other nuclear explosive devices, or of control over such weapons or explosive devices directly, or indirectly, not to manufacture or otherwise acquire nuclear weapons or other nuclear explosive devices, and not to seek or receive any assistance in the manufacture of nuclear weapons or other nuclear explosive devices".

Making a specific reference to South Asia, the Conference Document states,

"107. The Conference urges India and Pakistan to accede to the Treaty on the Non-Proliferation of Nuclear Weapons as non-nuclear-weapon states and to place all their nuclear facilities under comprehensive IAEA safeguards promptly and without conditions. The Conference further urges both states to strengthen their non-proliferation export control measures over technologies, material and equipment that can be used for the production of nuclear weapons and their delivery systems".

The Conference has also called upon India, Pakistan and Israel to, "accede to it without further delay and without any conditions, and to bring into force the required comprehensive safeguards agreements and additional protocols consistent with the model additional protocol."

On issues of test ban, the Conference reaffirmed that, "cessation of all nuclear test explosions and all other nuclear explosions, by constraining the development and qualitative improvement of nuclear weapons and ending the development of advanced new types of nuclear weapons, constitutes an effective measure of nuclear disarmament and non-proliferation in all its aspects" towards which the role of entry into force of CTBT is considered of, vital importance, "including abidance by NWS on nuclear testing".

Issues in Perspective

Are We Serious on Nuclear Disarmament?

An analysis of the Final document and the debate of the Eight RevCon would indicate that the trend of the previous Conferences has been continued in this one as well, for there has been an abiding commitment of all signatories towards the provisions of the Treaty per se, which is encouraging.

There is some progress on control of fissile material with a call for negotiating an FMCT thus, "The Conference reaffirms the urgent necessity of negotiating and bringing to a conclusion a non-discriminatory, multilateral and internationally and effectively verifiable treaty banning the production of fissile material for nuclear weapons or other nuclear explosive devices". Also of significance was the demand by the Conference on the

Secretary-General of the United Nations to convene a high-level meeting in September 2010 in support of the work of the Conference on Disarmament to address this specific issue.

However, apart from this and due to the fact that the record of arriving at a consensus on the Final Document has been now balanced with the same agreed upon in four of the eight conferences held, there has been no substantial progress. For instance, critical issues such as nuclear terrorism have not received the level of attention desired except a perfunctory mention in the Final Document as, "The Conference encourages all states parties that have not yet done so to become party to the International Convention for the Suppression of Acts of Nuclear Terrorism as soon as possible." There are 115 signatories to the International Convention for the Suppression of Acts of Nuclear Terrorism and 66 states have ratified the Convention, including India that leaves a large block of over 70 countries which are not signatories of this important document, some possibly due to bureaucratic inertia and others which may not consider this important enough to devote their attention.

Related to this is the issue of illegal trafficking. Surprisingly, even though the International Atomic Energy Agency has released data on the number of incidents of illegal trafficking in nuclear material at 15 cases in 2008 and 1266 cases in the past 12 years involving 99 countries with highly enriched uranium and plutonium reportedly involved in 18 incidents, this issue has not received due attention in the Document apart from a call, "upon all states parties to improve their national capabilities to detect, deter and disrupt illicit trafficking in nuclear materials throughout their territories, in accordance with their relevant international legal obligations, and calls upon those states parties in a position to do so to work to enhance international partnerships and capacity-building in this regard".

Also importantly, there has been no tangible progress on the establishment of a universal nuclear disarmament regime or at least establishing a framework for provisions for the same. No measures to discourage non compliance or prevent defection have been devised even though North Korea left the Treaty. The overall tenor of the debate thus remains at the philosophical rather than tangible level with goals for universal disarmament remaining only in the realms of discussion by policy planners than implementation through universal acceptance.

Is the Global Nuclear Disarmament Regime Working?

The efficacy of the global nuclear disarmament regime would appear to be working if the level of weaponisation is assessed. For, apart from North Korea there have been no known proliferators in the past decade or so. North Korea is said to have tested in October 2006 and May 2009 after it walked out of the Treaty while the other three states which are out of the regime—India, Pakistan and Israel—had tested before. There are a number of countries as South Africa and Libya who had forsaken the nuclear weapons option, the former voluntarily, but that was part of the larger geopolitics rather than a commitment towards the Treaty. Brazil is also seen to be capable of but not opting for a nuclear weapons capability, clearly it is in Brazilian interest to keep South America free from this menace.

Countries such as Iran seem to be working towards acquisition of nuclear weapons. The jury is still out on whether Iran, which has been sanctioned for the fourth time recently, is opting to weaponise or is a victim of its rivalry with the United States of America and the West. Iran's supporters state that unlike India and Pakistan or Israel, Tehran is a signatory of the NPT, its facilities are being inspected regularly by the IAEA and no less a leader than the Supreme Authority Ayatollah Khamanei has denied that Iran is seeking nuclear weapons. The right of Iran for access to nuclear fuel and technology for peaceful civilian purposes is however being denied as claimed by its supporters as well as Tehran itself.

A U.N. Security Council resolution on Iran recently placed extensive sanctions. The resolution per se targets mainly military and nuclear cooperation. The U.N. Secretary-General is required to create a panel of experts to monitor implementation of the sanctions but how effectively this can be done and the net result of the same will determine the effectiveness of the sanctions on the country. In the 41 new named entities and individuals, including one scientist and enterprises linked to the Islamic Revolutionary Guard Corps, these sanctions have been followed by those by the United States and European Union which are targeting the commercial entities.

In the case of Iran the IAEA is also playing an active role in encouraging non-proliferation. Thus, a Report on Iran, Implementation of the NPT Safeguards Agreement and Relevant Provisions of Security Council Resolutions 1737 (2006), 1747 (2007), 1803 (2008) and 1835 (2008) in the Islamic Republic of Iran was also submitted recently just before the sanctions.

At a second level, the Vienna Group (Russia, France, and the United States) is examining an Iranian proposal for fuel swap for enrichment up to 20 per cent for use in the Tehran medical facilities. The controversy over where and how the swap takes place due to apprehensions of Iran that it would be denied the fuel once it leaves the country is leading to an impasse. How this will be resolved remains to be seen.

While the larger global nuclear disarmament regime seems to be working, the specific cases as Iran and North Korea determine that there are many flaws in its functioning with bilateral and multilateral geo-polity playing an important role in the determinations being made by each country.

Is There a Commitment of the NWS Towards Disarmament?

The goals for a, "global zero" have been expressed by President Obama most recently and the commitment was made jointly by the United States and Russia at Prague in April 2009. President Obama sought to reassure the world of commitment of the United States to see a nuclear free world and stated, "America's commitment is to seek the peace and security of a world without nuclear weapons." Despite these commitments there has been very limited progress on actual curtailing of nuclear weapons globally. Thus, while the total warheads have been restricted by the U.S. and Russia to 1550, there are concerns of lack of any commitment made for curtailing development of capabilities.

The Treaty to come into effect once again requires ratification by the respective parliaments or the U.S. Senate and the Russian Duma. There are objections to provisions of the restrictions for arming inter-continental ballistic missiles (ICBMs) or submarine-launched ballistic missiles with missile interceptors and also missile defence options which will not allow the Bill to be passed by either the Senate or the Duma, thereby restricting the Obama-Medvedev initiative.

Moreover, states which ostensibly should have no need for nuclear weapons such as France and Britain continue to hold huge stockpiles, thereby denoting lack of commitment. Coming back to the pyramid model, unless the United States and Russia reduce and come to a global zero, China is not likely to do so. Unless China reduces its arsenal, India, and *ipso facto*, Pakistan will avoid doing so. Some have even linked China and North Korea wherein Pyongyang is being utilized by Beijing to play familiar power politics with the United States as well as former rival Japan. Then there are concerns about the Israeli weapons arsenal which is in being with the so-called, "Islamic" bomb with Pakistan and something which can be, "loaned" to other states in case the necessity arises? So it appears sadly that the commitment of the NWS and the proxy NWS towards disarmament is weak, given that these serve each a definite political purpose. For Pakistan it provides a screen for proxy war against India, for China a vast leverage against the United States, Russia, Japan and not to forget its southern neighbour, India, for the U.S.A. and Russia it is the logic of the Cold War that will prevent reduction of the nuclear arsenal and so on. Thus, it is evident that the commitment of the NWS towards disarmament remains weak and has not motivated states that have acquired this capability to forsake it, given that it provides them exceptional powers and that it requires collective bargaining of the legislative authorities which is always a difficult process in democracies like the United States.

Is Sufficient Progress Being Made Towards Test Ban and Fissile Material Control?

While the Eighth RevCon has called for greater commitment of the world powers towards a Test Ban and Fissile Material Control Treaty, there is once again not much progress on this account. One treaty that is the CTBT is not likely to come into place in a hurry for the United States is not likely to ratify the Treaty. The Democrats though committed to the Treaty, lack the 67 out of 100 votes or the two-thirds majority in the U.S. Senate for such a vote to pass. Given the past experience, there is limited likelihood of such an agreement being reached by the U.S. senators which may set into motion the process of others joining the CTBT including India.

The FMCT proposes to ban the production of fissile material for nuclear weapons or other nuclear explosive devices and is applicable to plutonium and high efficiency uranium (HEU) but does not apply to non-fissile materials, like tritium or the existing stockpiles. Even though a universal FMCT is long way off that the entry into force is proposed to be automatic after NWS have acceded to the same makes it unviable for countries as India which will see the same as discriminatory.

Can NNWS Hope to Obtain Full Benefits from Peaceful Use of Nuclear Energy?, and are NWS Committed to Support Them?

While a large number of countries in the world have acquired nuclear energy and reactors, there are considerable hindrances to acquisition of such energy—be these political, technical or financial—which somehow make these sources vulnerable and unattractive. Developing countries having growing energy needs are also most vulnerable and sensitive to political pressure and dependence on large states for regular supply of nuclear fuel and other technology needs. This subordination restricts their options of acquiring nuclear energy plants unhindered. With the development of alternate energy options from non-conventional and renewable sources, the nuclear energy has become even more unattractive. What happens in case of a nuclear accident is also a danger faced by those who are not fully prepared to bear all the consequences of these acts. Thus, there is a need for a global approach to provide investment and technology for adoption of the nuclear pathway by all nations, particularly the developing ones, thereby providing sufficient incentives for this purpose. Till this happens, those developing countries which are within the ambit of the NPT NNWS category may not fully benefit from the provisions of the same for acquiring nuclear energy.

Are There Sufficient Incentives for Proxy NWS—India, Pakistan and Israel—to Join the NPT?

India, Pakistan, Israel and North Korea are the proxy NWS which are outside the ambit of the NPT. India is not likely to join the NPT as a NNWS. Grant of such a status would not be acceptable to countries as China. Pakistan will not join the NPT if India remains out or it too is granted the NNWS, Israel does not acknowledge it has nuclear weapons but has restrained from joining the NPT and thus *ipso facto* accepts its status. These states at present have no incentive to join the NPT. With the Indo-U.S. nuclear deal it appears that India may not have any incentive to join the NPT for it may have attained all the advantages of the NWS through this bilateral treaty, particularly after the enactment of Nuclear Liability Act, which has also opened the doors for nuclear commerce with other countries ranging from Russia, France, Canada to Kazakhstan. Pakistan is also on the verge of getting a similar arrangement though under the IAEA safeguards, with China. North Korea will only join the NPT in case of a regime change which does not appear to be a likely scenario despite the abject poverty and underdevelopment in the country. Thus, lack of sufficient incentives may not lead to India, Pakistan or Israel joining the NPT in the near future.

Another important aspect of nuclear power is its great potential for peaceful uses. In a world that is struggling both for developing alternative sources of energy to coal and petroleum, and to mitigate the adverse impacts of using fossil fuels on environment, nuclear energy assumes great importance. India has not only been raising its voice against piling up nuclear weapons by many countries, particularly the advanced countries, but is also now playing a leading role in exploring the possibilities of using nuclear energy for a number of positive uses on a large scale. The Indo-U.S. civil nuclear deal is an example of India's recognition as a country which has the warewithal of harnessing nuclear energy for peaceful purposes and open it for trade so that other countries may also draw benefit out of it.

Having got the necessary clearance from the IAEA, India can now get much-needed nuclear fuel to be used in the nuclear reactors. It has signed agreements with many countries of the Nuclear Suppliers Group including France, Russia, Kazakhstan, England, Argentina for regular supply of nuclear fuel and equipment. India also enacted the Civil Liability for the Nuclear Damages Act 2010 in August 2010 which was necessary to put in place a compensation regime that limited the liabilities of companies in case of a nuclear accident. The legislation was critical for India's energy security and will facilitate the building of nuclear plants.

In October 2010, India signed another document, the Convention on Supplementary Compensation for Nuclear Damage (CSC), which will facilitate its international nuclear commerce. The CSC provides for additional compensation a signatory country can draw in case of a nuclear accident. It intends to establish an international fund to increase the amount available to compensate nuclear victims, and also allows for providing relief for civil damages occurring within a nation's economic zone.

The CSC has now been signed by 14 countries—including India, though only four countries—the U.S., Argentina, Morocco and Romania-have ratified it so far. It can come into force only after a minimum of five countries, each having at least 400,000 units of installed nuclear capacity, ratify it. Most nuclear suppliers have been unhappy with the stringent provisions of India's nuclear liabilities act. Signing the CSC will assuage international fears of doing nuclear business with India.

It is hoped that with these developments, international attention will focus on using nuclear energy for the progress of society rather than making more deadlier nuclear weapons and building arsenals.

Conclusion

In conclusion it would not be out of place to suggest that while there is a general consensus of the global community on the requirement and the effectiveness of the NPT as an instrument of control of growth of nuclear weapons, it has not restricted in providing options to states which have determined by their security needs to obtain nuclear weapons capability. These states have also not been motivated to rejoin the Treaty despite some exceptional waivers accorded in some cases as that by India, for sufficient incentives to join the same are not evident. Moreover, the pyramid theory comes into effect and hence, it becomes strategically unviable to join the Treaty without being declared an NWS. While there are attempts to strengthen the verification powers of the IAEA, the organization is seen by some like Iran as the hand maiden of the West. There are credibility problems as well. Notwithstanding these issues, a sense can be gained from a survey of the nuclear documents that the non-proliferation regime has ensured that the world does not become a nuclear armoury, howsoever large an arsenal a few selected states may have, by facilitating restrictions of the politics to these that on the whole proliferation can be controlled. Therein perhaps lies the strength of the nuclear non-proliferation system.

NOTES

1. Fasahat H. Sayed (ed.), *Nuclear Disarmament and Conventional Arms Control*, Friends Publication, Islamabad, Pakistan, p. 8.
2. J.P. Murray, *From Yalta to Disarmament: Cold War Debate*, New York: M.R. Press, 1961, pp. 264, 275.
3. Manpreet Sethi, "Pakistan's Nuclear Doctrine and Strategy", *Air Power Journal*, Vol. 2, No. 3, Monsoon 2007, July-September, pp. 27-56.
4. India is known to have raised two mountain divisions and based a fighter jet squadron in its North-East, around the turn of the year 2009—if press reports are to be believed.
5. Manpreet Sethi, *Towards a Nuclear Weapon Free World*, New Delhi: K.W. Publishers Pvt. Ltd., 2009.
6. George Perkovich and James M. Acton, *Abolishing Nuclear Weapons*, Adelphi Paper 296, London: International Institute for Strategic Studies, 2008.
7. Zia Mian, "Beyond the Security Debate: Moral and Legal Dimensions of Abolition", in George Perkovich and James Acton (eds.), *Abolishing Nuclear Weapons: A Debate*, Carnegie Endowment, 2009, pp. 295-303.
8. The full text of the Commission's report is available at www.usip.org
9. Rajinder Puri, *The Statesman*, 15 November 2006.

1

Comprehensive Nuclear-Test-Ban Treaty

PREAMBLE

The States Parties to this Treaty (hereinafter referred to as "the States Parties"),

Welcoming the international agreements and other positive measures of recent years in the field of nuclear disarmament, including reductions in arsenals of nuclear weapons, as well as in the field of the prevention of nuclear proliferation in all its aspects,

Underlining the importance of the full and prompt implementation of such agreements and measures,

Convinced that the present international situation provides an opportunity to take further effective measures towards nuclear disarmament and against the proliferation of nuclear weapons in all its aspects, and declaring their intention to take such measures,

Stressing therefore the need for continued systematic and progressive efforts to reduce nuclear weapons globally, with the ultimate goal of eliminating those weapons, and of general and complete disarmament under strict and effective international control,

Recognizing that the cessation of all nuclear weapon test explosions and all other nuclear explosions, by constraining the development and qualitative improvement of nuclear weapons and ending the development of advanced new types of nuclear weapons, constitutes an effective measure of nuclear disarmament and nonproliferation in all its aspects,

Further recognizing that an end to all such nuclear explosions will thus constitute a meaningful step in the realization of a systematic process to achieve nuclear disarmament,

Convinced that the most effective way to achieve an end to nuclear testing is through the conclusion of a universal and internationally and effectively verifiable comprehensive nuclear test-ban treaty, which has long been one of the highest priority objectives of the international community in the field of disarmament and non-proliferation,

Noting the aspirations expressed by the Parties to the 1963 Treaty Banning Nuclear Weapon Tests in the Atmosphere, in Outer Space and Under Water to seek to achieve the discontinuance of all test explosions of nuclear weapons for all time,

Noting also the views expressed that this Treaty could contribute to the protection of the environment,

Affirming the purpose of attracting the adherence of all States to this Treaty and its objective to contribute effectively to the prevention of the proliferation of nuclear weapons in all its aspects, to the process of nuclear disarmament and therefore to the enhancement of international peace and security,

Have agreed as follows:

ARTICLE I—BASIC OBLIGATIONS

1. Each State Party undertakes not to carry out any nuclear weapon test explosion or any other nuclear explosion, and to prohibit and prevent any such nuclear explosion at any place under its jurisdiction or control.

2. Each State Party undertakes, furthermore, to refrain from causing, encouraging, or in any way participating in the carrying out of any nuclear weapon test explosion or any other nuclear explosion.

ARTICLE II—THE ORGANIZATION

A. GENERAL PROVISIONS

1. The States Parties hereby establish the Comprehensive Nuclear Test-Ban Treaty Organization (hereinafter referred to as "the Organization") to achieve the object and purpose of this Treaty, to ensure the implementation of its provisions, including those for international verification of compliance with it, and to provide a forum for consultation and cooperation among States Parties.

2. All States Parties shall be members of the Organization. A State Party shall not be deprived of its membership in the Organization.

3. The seat of the Organization shall be Vienna, Republic of Austria.

4. There are hereby established as organs of the Organization: the Conference of the States Parties, the Executive Council and the Technical Secretariat, which shall include the International Data Centre.

5. Each State Party shall cooperate with the Organization in the exercise of its functions in accordance with this Treaty. States Parties shall consult, directly among themselves, or through the Organization or other appropriate international procedures, including procedures within the framework of the United Nations and in accordance with its Charter, on any matter which may be raised relating to the object and purpose, or the implementation of the provisions, of this Treaty.

6. The Organization shall conduct its verification activities provided for under this Treaty in the least intrusive manner possible consistent with the timely and efficient accomplishment of their objectives. It shall request only the information and data necessary to fulfil its responsibilities under this Treaty. It shall take every precaution to protect the confidentiality of information on civil and military activities and facilities coming to its knowledge in the implementation of this Treaty and, in particular, shall abide by the confidentiality provisions set forth in this Treaty.

7. Each State Party shall treat as confidential and afford special handling to information and data that it receives in confidence from the Organization in connection with the implementation of this Treaty. It shall treat such information and data exclusively in connection with its rights and obligations under this Treaty.

8. The Organization, as an independent body, shall seek to utilize existing expertise and facilities, as appropriate, and to maximize cost efficiencies, through cooperative arrangements with other international organizations such as the International Atomic Energy Agency. Such arrangements, excluding those of a minor and normal commercial and contractual nature, shall be set out in agreements to be submitted to the Conference of the States Parties for approval.

9. The costs of the activities of the Organization shall be met annually by the States Parties in accordance with the United Nations scale of assessments adjusted to take into account differences in membership between the United Nations and the Organization.

10. Financial contributions of States Parties to the Preparatory Commission shall be deducted in an appropriate way from their contributions to the regular budget.

11. A member of the Organization which is in arrears in the payment of its assessed contribution to the Organization shall have no vote in the Organization if the amount of its arrears equals or exceeds the amount of the contribution due from it for the preceding two full years. The Conference of the States Parties may, nevertheless, permit such a member to vote if it is satisfied that the failure to pay is due to conditions beyond the control of the member.

B. THE CONFERENCE OF THE STATES PARTIES

Composition, Procedures and Decision-making

12. The Conference of the States Parties (hereinafter referred to as "the Conference") shall be composed of all States Parties. Each State Party shall have one representative in the Conference, who may be accompanied by alternates and advisers.

13. The initial session of the Conference shall be convened by the Depositary no later than 30 days after the entry into force of this Treaty.

14. The Conference shall meet in regular sessions, which shall be held annually, unless it decides otherwise.

15. A special session of the Conference shall be convened:

(a) When decided by the Conference;

(b) When requested by the Executive Council; or

(c) When requested by any State Party and supported by a majority of the States Parties.

The special session shall be convened no later than 30 days after the decision of the Conference, the request of the Executive Council, or the attainment of the necessary support, unless specified otherwise in the decision or request.

16. The Conference may also be convened in the form of an Amendment Conference, in accordance with Article VII.

17. The Conference may also be convened in the form of a Review Conference, in accordance with Article VIII.

18. Sessions shall take place at the seat of the Organization unless the Conference decides otherwise.

19. The Conference shall adopt its rules of procedure. At the beginning of each session, it shall elect its President and such other officers as may be required. They shall hold office until a new President and other officers are elected at the next session.

20. A majority of the States Parties shall constitute a quorum.

21. Each State Party shall have one vote.

22. The Conference shall take decisions on matters of procedure by a majority of members present and voting. Decisions on matters of substance shall be taken as far as possible by consensus. If consensus is not attainable when an issue comes up for decision, the President of the Conference shall defer any vote for 24 hours and during this period of deferment shall make every effort to facilitate achievement of consensus, and shall report to the Conference before the end of this period. If consensus is not possible at the end of 24 hours, the Conference shall take

a decision by a two-thirds majority of members present and voting unless specified otherwise in this Treaty. When the issue arises as to whether the question is one of substance or not, that question shall be treated as a matter of substance unless otherwise decided by the majority required for decisions on matters of substance.

23. When exercising its function under paragraph 26 (k), the Conference shall take a decision to add any State to the list of States contained in Annex 1 to this Treaty in accordance with the procedure for decisions on matters of substance set out in paragraph 22. Notwithstanding paragraph 22, the Conference shall take decisions on any other change to Annex 1 to this Treaty by consensus.

Powers and Functions

24. The Conference shall be the principal organ of the Organization. It shall consider any questions, matters or issues within the scope of this Treaty, including those relating to the powers and functions of the Executive Council and the Technical Secretariat, in accordance with this Treaty. It may make recommendations and take decisions on any questions, matters or issues within the scope of this Treaty raised by a State Party or brought to its attention by the Executive Council.

25. The Conference shall oversee the implementation of, and review compliance with, this Treaty and act in order to promote its object and purpose. It shall also oversee the activities of the Executive Council and the Technical Secretariat and may issue guidelines to either of them for the exercise of their functions.

26. The Conference shall:

(a) Consider and adopt the report of the Organization on the implementation of this Treaty and the annual programme and budget of the Organization, submitted by the Executive Council, as well as consider other reports;

(b) Decide on the scale of financial contributions to be paid by States Parties in accordance with paragraph 9;

(c) Elect the members of the Executive Council;

(d) Appoint the Director-General of the Technical Secretariat (hereinafter referred to as "the Director-General");

(e) Consider and approve the rules of procedure of the Executive Council submitted by the latter;

(f) Consider and review scientific and technological developments that could affect the operation of this Treaty. In this context, the Conference may direct the Director-General to establish a Scientific Advisory Board to enable him or her, in the performance of his or her functions, to render specialized advice in areas of science and technology relevant to this Treaty to the Conference, to the Executive Council, or to States Parties. In that case, the Scientific Advisory Board shall be composed of independent experts serving in their individual capacity and appointed, in accordance with terms of reference adopted by the Conference, on the basis of their expertise and experience in the particular scientific fields relevant to the implementation of this Treaty;

(g) Take the necessary measures to ensure compliance with this Treaty and to redress and remedy any situation that contravenes the provisions of this Treaty, in accordance with Article V;

(h) Consider and approve at its initial session any draft agreements, arrangements, provisions, procedures, operational manuals, guidelines and any other documents developed and recommended by the Preparatory Commission;

(i) Consider and approve agreements or arrangements negotiated by the Technical Secretariat with States Parties, other States and international organizations to be concluded by the Executive Council on behalf of the Organization in accordance with paragraph 38 (h);

(j) Establish such subsidiary organs as it finds necessary for the exercise of its functions in accordance with this Treaty; and

(k) Update Annex 1 to this Treaty, as appropriate, in accordance with paragraph 23.

C. THE EXECUTIVE COUNCIL

Composition, Procedures and Decision-making

27. The Executive Council shall consist of 51 members. Each State Party shall have the right, in accordance with the provisions of this Article, to serve on the Executive Council.

28. Taking into account the need for equitable geographical distribution, the Executive Council shall comprise:

(a) Ten States Parties from Africa;

(b) Seven States Parties from Eastern Europe;

(c) Nine States Parties from Latin America and the Caribbean;

(d) Seven States Parties from the Middle East and South Asia;

(e) Ten States Parties from North America and Western Europe; and

(f) Eight States Parties from South-East Asia, the Pacific and the Far East.

All States in each of the above geographical regions are listed in Annex 1 to this Treaty. Annex 1 to this Treaty shall be updated, as appropriate, by the Conference in accordance with paragraphs 23 and 26 (k). It shall not be subject to amendments or changes under the procedures contained in Article VII.

29. The members of the Executive Council shall be elected by the Conference. In this connection, each geographical region shall designate States Parties from that region for election as members of the Executive Council as follows:

(a) At least one-third of the seats allocated to each geographical region shall be filled, taking into account political and security interests, by States Parties in that region designated on the basis of the nuclear capabilities relevant to the Treaty as determined by international data as well as all or any of the following indicative criteria in the order of priority determined by each region:

(i) Number of monitoring facilities of the International Monitoring System;

(ii) Expertise and experience in monitoring technology; and

(iii) Contribution to the annual budget of the Organization;

(b) One of the seats allocated to each geographical region shall be filled on a rotational basis by the State Party that is first in the English alphabetical order among the States Parties in that region that have not served as members of the Executive Council for the longest period of time since becoming States Parties or since their last term, whichever is shorter. A State Party designated on this basis may decide to forgo its seat. In that case, such a State Party shall submit a letter of renunciation to the Director-General, and the seat shall be filled by the State Party following next-in-order according to this sub-paragraph; and

(c) The remaining seats allocated to each geographical region shall be filled by States Parties designated from among all the States Parties in that region by rotation or elections.

30. Each member of the Executive Council shall have one representative on the Executive Council, who may be accompanied by alternates and advisers.

31. Each member of the Executive Council shall hold office from the end of the session of the Conference at which that member is elected until the end of the second regular annual session of the Conference thereafter, except that for the first election of the Executive Council, 26 members shall be elected to hold office until the end of the third regular annual session of the Conference, due regard being paid to the established numerical proportions as described in paragraph 28.

32. The Executive Council shall elaborate its rules of procedure and submit them to the Conference for approval.

33. The Executive Council shall elect its Chairman from among its members.

34. The Executive Council shall meet for regular sessions. Between regular sessions it shall meet as may be required for the fulfilment of its powers and functions.

35. Each member of the Executive Council shall have one vote.

36. The Executive Council shall take decisions on matters of procedure by a majority of all its members. The Executive Council shall take decisions on matters of substance by a two-thirds majority of all its members unless specified otherwise in this Treaty. When the issue arises as to whether the question is one of substance or not, that question shall be treated as a matter of substance unless otherwise decided by the majority required for decisions on matters of substance.

Powers and Functions

37. The Executive Council shall be the executive organ of the Organization. It shall be responsible to the Conference. It shall carry out the powers and functions entrusted to it in accordance with this Treaty. In so doing, it shall act in conformity with the recommendations, decisions and guidelines of the Conference and ensure their continuous and proper implementation.

38. The Executive Council shall:

(a) Promote effective implementation of, and compliance with, this Treaty;

(b) Supervise the activities of the Technical Secretariat;

(c) Make recommendations as necessary to the Conference for consideration of further proposals for promoting the object and purpose of this Treaty;

(d) Cooperate with the National Authority of each State Party;

(e) Consider and submit to the Conference the draft annual programme and budget of the Organization, the draft report of the Organization on the implementation of this Treaty, the report on the performance of its own activities and such other reports as it deems necessaiy or that the Conference may request;

(f) Make arrangements for the sessions of the Conference, including the preparation of the draft agenda;

(g) Examine proposals for changes, on matters of an administrative or technical nature, to the Protocol or the Annexes thereto, pursuant to Article VII, and make recommendations to the States Parties regarding their adoption;

(h) Conclude, subject to prior approval of the Conference, agreements or arrangements with States Parties, other States and international organizations on behalf of the Organization and supervise their implementation, with the exception of agreements or arrangements referred to in sub-paragraph (i);

(i) Approve and supervise the operation of agreements or arrangements relating to the implementation of verification activities with States Parties and other States; and

(j) Approve any new operational manuals and any changes to the existing operational manuals that may be proposed by the Technical Secretariat.

39. The Executive Council may request a special session of the Conference.

40. The Executive Council shall:

(a) Facilitate cooperation among States Parties, and between States Parties and the Technical Secretariat, relating to the implementation of this Treaty through information exchanges;

(b) Facilitate consultation and clarification among States Parties in accordance with Article IV; and

(c) Receive, consider and take action on requests for, and reports on, on-site inspections in accordance with Article IV.

41. The Executive Council shall consider any concern raised by a State Party about possible non-compliance with this Treaty and abuse of the rights established by this Treaty. In so doing, the Executive Council shall consult with the States Parties involved

and, as appropriate, request a State Party to take measures to redress the situation within a specified time. To the extent that the Executive Council considers further action to be necessary, it shall take, inter alia, one or more of the following measures:

(a) Notify all States Parties of the issue or matter;

(b) Bring the issue or matter to the attention of the Conference;

(c) Make recommendations to the Conference or take action, as appropriate, regarding measures to redress the situation and to ensure compliance in accordance with Article V.

D. THE TECHNICAL SECRETARIAT

42. The Technical Secretariat shall assist States Parties in the implementation of this Treaty. The Technical Secretariat shall assist the Conference and the Executive Council in the performance of their functions. The Technical Secretariat shall carry out the verification and other functions entrusted to it by this Treaty, as well as those functions delegated to it by the Conference or the Executive Council in accordance with this Treaty. The Technical Secretariat shall include, as an integral part, the International Data Centre.

43. The functions of the Technical Secretariat with regard to verification of compliance with this Treaty shall, in accordance with Article IV and the Protocol, include inter alia:

(a) Being responsible for supervising and coordinating the operation of the International Monitoring System;

(b) Operating the International Data Centre;

(c) Routinely receiving, processing, analysing and reporting on International Monitoring System data;

(d) Providing technical assistance in, and support for, the installation and operation of monitoring stations;

(e) Assisting the Executive Council in facilitating consultation and clarification among States Parties;

(f) Receiving requests for on-site inspections and processing them, facilitating Executive Council consideration of such requests, carrying out the preparations for, and providing technical support during, the conduct of on-site inspections, and reporting to the Executive Council;

(g) Negotiating agreements or arrangements with States Parties, other States and international organizations and concluding, subject to prior approval by the Executive Council, any such agreements or arrangements relating to verification activities with States Parties or other States; and

(h) Assisting the States Parties through their National Authorities on other issues of verification under this Treaty.

44. The Technical Secretariat shall develop and maintain, subject to approval by the Executive Council, operational manuals to guide the operation of the various components of the verification regime, in accordance with Article IV and the Protocol. These manuals shall not constitute integral parts of this Treaty or the Protocol and may be changed by the Technical Secretariat subject to approval by the Executive Council. The Technical Secretariat shall promptly inform the States Parties of any changes in the operational manuals.

45. The functions of the Technical Secretariat with respect to administrative matters shall include:

(a) Preparing and submitting to the Executive Council the draft programme and budget of the Organization;

(b) Preparing and submitting to the Executive Council the draft report of the Organization on the implementation of this Treaty and such other reports as the Conference or the Executive Council may request;

(c) Providing administrative and technical support to the Conference, the Executive Council and other subsidiary organs;

(d) Addressing and receiving communications on behalf of the Organization relating to the implementation of this Treaty; and

(e) Carrying out the administrative responsibilities related to any agreements between the Organization and other international organizations.

46. All requests and notifications by States Parties to the Organization shall be transmitted through their National Authorities to the Director-General. Requests and notifications shall be in one of the official languages of this Treaty. In response the Director-General shall use the language of the transmitted request or notification.

47. With respect to the responsibilities of the Technical Secretariat for preparing and submitting to the Executive Council the draft programme and budget of the Organization, the Technical Secretariat shall determine and maintain a clear accounting of all costs for each facility established as part of the International Monitoring System. Similar treatment in the draft programme and budget shall be accorded to all other activities of the Organization.

48. The Technical Secretariat shall promptly inform the Executive Council of any problems that have arisen with regard to the discharge of its functions that have come to its notice in the performance of its activities and that it has been unable to resolve through consultations with the State Party concerned.

49. The Technical Secretariat shall comprise a Director-General, who shall be its head and chief administrative officer, and such scientific, technical and other personnel as may be required. The Director-General shall be appointed by the Conference upon the recommendation of the Executive Council for a term of four years, renewable for one further term, but not thereafter. The first Director-General shall be appointed by the Conference at its initial session upon the recommendation of the Preparatory Commission.

50. The Director-General shall be responsible to the Conference and the Executive Council for the appointment of the staff and for the organization and functioning of the Technical Secretariat. The paramount consideration in the employment of the staff and in the determination of the conditions of service shall be the necessity of securing the highest standards of

professional expertise, experience, efficiency, competence and integrity. Only citizens of States Parties shall serve as the Director-General, as inspectors or as members of the professional and clerical staff. Due regard shall be paid to the importance of recruiting the staff on as wide a geographical basis as possible. Recruitment shall be guided by the principle that the staff shall be kept to the minimum necessary for the proper discharge of the responsibilities of the Technical Secretariat.

51. The Director-General may, as appropriate, after consultation with the Executive Council, establish temporary working groups of scientific experts to provide recommendations on specific issues.

52. In the performance of their duties, the Director-General, the inspectors, the inspection assistants and the members of the staff shall not seek or receive instructions from any Government or from any other source external to the Organization. They shall refrain from any action that might reflect adversely on their positions as international officers responsible only to the Organization. The Director-General shall assume responsibility for the activities of an inspection team.

53. Each State Party shall respect the exclusively international character of the responsibilities of the Director-General, the inspectors, the inspection assistants and the members of the staff and shall not seek to influence them in the discharge of their responsibilities.

E. PRIVILEGES AND IMMUNITIES

54. The Organization shall enjoy on the territory and in any other place under the jurisdiction or control of a State Party such legal capacity and such privileges and immunities as are necessary for the exercise of its functions.

55. Delegates of States Parties, together with their alternates and advisers, representatives of members elected to the Executive Council, together with their alternates and advisers, the Director-General, the inspectors, the inspection assistants and the members of the staff of the Organization shall enjoy such privileges and immunities as are necessary in the independent exercise of their functions in connection with the Organization.

56. The legal capacity, privileges and immunities referred to in this Article shall be defined in agreements between the Organization and the States Parties as well as in an agreement between the Organization and the State in which the Organization is seated. Such agreements shall be considered and approved in accordance with paragraph 26 (h) and (i).

57. Notwithstanding paragraphs 54 and 55, the privileges and immunities enjoyed by the Director-General, the inspectors, the inspection assistants and the members of the staff of the Technical Secretariat during the conduct of verification activities shall be those set forth in the Protocol.

ARTICLE III—NATIONAL IMPLEMENTATION MEASURES

1. Each State Party shall, in accordance with its constitutional processes, take any necessary measures to implement its obligations under this Treaty. In particular, it shall take any necessary measures:

(a) To prohibit natural and legal persons anywhere on its territory or in any other place under its jurisdiction as recognized by international law from undertaking any activity prohibited to a State Party under this Treaty;

(b) To prohibit natural and legal persons from undertaking any such activity anywhere under its control; and

(c) To prohibit, in conformity with international law, natural persons possessing its nationality from undertaking any such activity anywhere.

2. Each State Party shall cooperate with other States Parties and afford the appropriate form of legal assistance to facilitate the implementation of the obligations under paragraph 1.

3. Each State Party shall inform the Organization of the measures taken pursuant to this Article.

4. In order to fulfil its obligations under the Treaty, each State Party shall designate or set up a National Authority and shall so inform the Organization upon entry into force of the Treaty for it. The National Authority shall serve as the national focal point for liaison with the Organization and with other States Parties.

ARTICLE IV—VERIFICATION

A. GENERAL PROVISIONS

1. In order to verify compliance with this Treaty, a verification regime shall be established consisting of the following elements:

(a) An International Monitoring System;

(b) Consultation and clarification;

(c) On-site inspections; and

(d) Confidence-building measures.

At entry into force of this Treaty, the verification regime shall be capable of meeting the verification requirements of this Treaty.

2. Verification activities shall be based on objective information, shall be limited to the subject matter of this Treaty, and shall be carried out on the basis of full respect for the sovereignty of States Parties and in the least intrusive manner possible consistent with the effective and timely accomplishment of their objectives. Each State Party shall refrain from any abuse of the right of verification.

3. Each State Party undertakes in accordance with this Treaty to cooperate, through its National Authority established pursuant to Article III, paragraph 4, with the Organization and with other States Parties to facilitate the verification of compliance with this Treaty by, inter alia:

(a) Establishing the necessary facilities to participate in these verification measures and establishing the necessary communication;

(b) Providing data obtained from national stations that are part of the International Monitoring System;

(c) Participating, as appropriate, in consultation and clarification process;

(d) Permitting the conduct of on-site inspections; and

(e) Participating, as appropriate, in confidence-building measures.

4. All States Parties, irrespective of their technical and financial capabilities, shall enjoy the equal right of verification and assume the equal obligation to accept verification.

5. For the purposes of this Treaty, no State Party shall be precluded from using information obtained by national technical means of verification in a manner consistent with generally recognized principles of international law, including that of respect for the sovereignty of States.

6. Without prejudice to the right of States Parties to protect sensitive installations, activities or locations not related to this Treaty, States Parties shall not interfere with elements of the verification regime of this Treaty or with national technical means of verification operating in accordance with paragraph 5.

7. Each State Party shall have the right to take measures to protect sensitive installations and to prevent disclosure of confidential information and data not related to this Treaty.

8. Moreover, all necessary measures shall be taken to protect the confidentiality of any information related to civil and military activities and facilities obtained during verification activities.

9. Subject to paragraph 8, information obtained by the Organization through the verification regime established by this Treaty shall be made available to all States Parties in accordance with the relevant provisions of this Treaty and the Protocol.

10. The provisions of this Treaty shall not be interpreted as restricting the international exchange of data for scientific purposes.

11. Each State Party undertakes to cooperate with the Organization and with other States Parties in the improvement of the verification regime, and in the examination of the verification potential of additional monitoring technologies such as electromagnetic pulse monitoring or satellite monitoring, with a view to developing, when appropriate, specific measures to enhance the efficient and cost-effective verification of this Treaty. Such measures shall, when agreed, be incorporated in existing provisions in this Treaty, the Protocol or as additional sections of the Protocol, in accordance with Article VII, or, if

appropriate, be reflected in the operational manuals in accordance with Article II, paragraph 44.

12. The States Parties undertake to promote cooperation among themselves to facilitate and participate in the fullest possible exchange relating to technologies used in the verification of this Treaty in order to enable all States Parties to strengthen their national implementation of verification measures and to benefit from the application of such technologies for peaceful purposes.

13. The provisions of this Treaty shall be implemented in a manner which avoids hampering the economic and technological development of the States Parties for further development of the application of atomic energy for peaceful purposes.

Verification Responsibilities of the Technical Secretariat

14. In discharging its responsibilities in the area of verification specified in this Treaty and the Protocol, in cooperation with the States Parties the Technical Secretariat shall, for the purpose of this Treaty:

(a) Make arrangements to receive and distribute data and reporting products relevant to the verification of this Treaty in accordance with its provisions, and to maintain a global communications infrastructure appropriate to this task;

(b) Routinely through its International Data Centre, which shall in principle be the focal point within the Technical Secretariat for data storage and data processing:

(i) Receive and initiate requests for data from the International Monitoring System;

(ii) Receive data, as appropriate, resulting from the process of consultation and clarification, from on-site inspections, and from confidence-building measures; and

(iii) Receive other relevant data from States Parties and international organizations in accordance with this Treaty and the Protocol;

(c) Supervise, coordinate and ensure the operation of the International Monitoring System and its component elements, and of the International Data Centre, in accordance with the relevant operational manuals;

(d) Routinely process, analyse and report on International Monitoring System data according to agreed procedures so as to permit the effective international verification of this Treaty and to contribute to the early resolution of compliance concerns;

(e) Make available all data, both raw and processed, and any reporting products, to all States Parties, each State Party taking responsibility for the use of International Monitoring System data in accordance with Article II, paragraph 7, and with paragraphs 8 and 13 of this Article;

(f) Provide to all States Parties equal, open, convenient and timely access to all stored data;

(g) Store all data, both raw and processed, and reporting products;

(h) Coordinate and facilitate requests for additional data from the International Monitoring System;

(i) Coordinate requests for additional data from one State Party to another State Party;

(j) Provide technical assistance in, and support for, the installation and operation of monitoring facilities and respective communication means, where such assistance and support are required by the State concerned;

(k) Make available to any State Party, upon its request, techniques utilized by the Technical Secretariat and its International Data Centre in compiling, storing, processing, analysing and reporting on data from the verification regime; and

(l) Monitor, assess and report on the overall performance of the International Monitoring System and of the International Data Centre.

15. The agreed procedures to be used by the Technical Secretariat in discharging the verification responsibilities referred to in paragraph 14 and detailed in the Protocol shall be elaborated in the relevant operational manuals.

B. THE INTERNATIONAL MONITORING SYSTEM

16. The International Monitoring System shall comprise facilities for seismological monitoring, radionuclide monitoring including certified laboratories, hydroacoustic monitoring, infrasound monitoring, and respective means of communication, and shall be supported by the International Data Centre of the Technical Secretariat.

17. The International Monitoring System shall be placed under the authority of the Technical Secretariat. All monitoring facilities of the International Monitoring System shall be owned and operated by the States hosting or otherwise taking responsibility for them in accordance with the Protocol.

18. Each State Party shall have the right to participate in the international exchange of data and to have access to all data made available to the International Data Centre. Each State Party shall cooperate with the International Data Centre through its National Authority.

Funding the International Monitoring System

19. For facilities incorporated into the International Monitoring System and specified in Tables 1-A, 2-A, 3 and 4 of Annex 1 to the Protocol, and for their functioning, to the extent that such facilities are agreed by the relevant State and the Organization to provide data to the International Data Centre in accordance with the technical requirements of the Protocol and relevant operational manuals, the Organization, as specified in agreements or arrangements pursuant to Part I, paragraph 4 of the Protocol, shall meet the costs of:

(a) Establishing any new facilities and upgrading existing facilities, unless the State responsible for such facilities meets these costs itself;

(b) Operating and maintaining International Monitoring System facilities, including facility physical security if appropriate, and application of agreed data authentication procedures;

(c) Transmitting International Monitoring System data (raw or processed) to the International Data Centre by the most direct and cost-effective means available, including, if necessary, via appropriate communications nodes, from monitoring stations, laboratories, analytical facilities or from national data centres; or such data (including samples where appropriate) to laboratory and analytical facilities from monitoring stations; and

(d) Analysing samples on behalf of the Organization.

20. For auxiliary network seismic stations specified in Table 1-B of Annex 1 to the Protocol the Organization, as specified in agreements or arrangements pursuant to Part I, paragraph 4 of the Protocol, shall meet the costs only of:

(a) Transmitting data to the International Data Centre;

(b) Authenticating data from such stations;

(c) Upgrading stations to the required technical standard, unless the State responsible for such facilities meets these costs itself;

(d) If necessary, establishing new stations for the purposes of this Treaty where no appropriate facilities currently exist, unless the State responsible for such facilities meets these costs itself; and

(e) Any other costs related to the provision of data required by the Organization as specified in the relevant operational manuals.

21. The Organization shall also meet the cost of provision to each State Party of its requested selection from the standard range of International Data Centre reporting products and services, as specified in Part I, Section F of the Protocol. The cost of preparation and transmission of any additional data or products shall be met by the requesting State Party.

22. The agreements or, if appropriate, arrangements concluded with States Parties or States hosting or otherwise taking responsibility for facilities of the International Monitoring

System shall contain provisions for meeting these costs. Such provisions may include modalities whereby a State Party meets any of the costs referred to in paragraphs 19 (a) and 20 (c) and (d) for facilities which it hosts or for which it is responsible, and is compensated by an appropriate reduction in its assessed financial contribution to the Organization. Such a reduction shall not exceed 50 per cent of the annual assessed financial contribution of a State Party, but may be spread over successive years. A State Party may share such a reduction with another State Party by agreement or arrangement between themselves and with the concurrence of the Executive Council. The agreements or arrangements referred to in this paragraph shall be approved in accordance with Article II, paragraphs 26 (h) and 38 (i).

Changes to the International Monitoring System

23. Any measures referred to in paragraph 11 affecting the International Monitoring System by means of addition or deletion of a monitoring technology shall, when agreed, be incorporated into this Treaty and the Protocol pursuant to Article VII, paragraphs 1 to 6.

24. The following changes to the International Monitoring System, subject to the agreement of those States directly affected, shall be regarded as matters of an administrative or technical nature pursuant to Article VII, paragraphs 7 and 8:

- (a) Changes to the number of facilities specified in the Protocol for a given monitoring technology; and
- (b) Changes to other details for particular facilities as reflected in the Tables of Annex 1 to the Protocol (including, inter alia, State responsible for the facility; location; name of facility; type of facility; and attribution of a facility between the primary and auxiliary seismic networks).

If the Executive Council recommends, pursuant to Article VII, paragraph 8 (d), that such changes be adopted, it shall as a rule also recommend pursuant to Article VII, paragraph 8 (g), that such changes enter into force upon notification by the Director-General of their approval.

25. The Director-General, in submitting to the Executive Council and States Parties information and evaluation in accordance with Article VII, paragraph 8 (b), shall include in the case of any proposal made pursuant to paragraph 24:

(a) A technical evaluation of the proposal; (b) A statement on the administrative and financial impact of the proposal; and

(c) A report on consultations with States directly affected by the proposal, including indication of their agreement.

Temporary Arrangements

26. In cases of significant or irretrievable breakdown of a monitoring facility specified in the Tables of Annex 1 to the Protocol, or in order to cover other temporary reductions of monitoring coverage, the Director-General shall, in consultation and agreement with those States directly affected, and with the approval of the Executive Council, initiate temporary arrangements of no more than one year's duration, renewable if necessary by agreement of the Executive Council and of the States directly affected for another year. Such arrangements shall not cause the number of operational facilities of the International Monitoring System to exceed the number specified for the relevant network; shall meet as far as possible the technical and operational requirements specified in the operational manual for the relevant network; and shall be conducted within the budget of the Organization. The Director-General shall furthermore take steps to rectify the situation and make proposals for its permanent resolution. The Director-General shall notify all States Parties of any decision taken pursuant to this paragraph.

Cooperating National Facilities

27. States Parties may also separately establish cooperative arrangements with the Organization, in order to make available to the International Data Centre supplementary data from national monitoring stations that are not formally part of the International Monitoring System.

28. Such cooperative arrangements may be established as follows:

(a) Upon request by a State Party, and at the expense of that State, the Technical Secretariat shall take the steps required to certify that a given monitoring facility meets the technical and operational requirements specified in the relevant operational manuals for an International Monitoring System facility, and make arrangements for the authentication of its data. Subject to the agreement of the Executive Council, the Technical Secretariat shall then formally designate such a facility as a cooperating national facility. The Technical Secretariat shall take the steps required to revalidate its certification as appropriate;

(b) The Technical Secretariat shall maintain a current list of cooperating national facilities and shall distribute it to all States Parties; and

(c) The International Data Centre shall call upon data from cooperating national facilities, if so requested by a State Party, for the purposes of facilitating consultation and clarification and the consideration of on-site inspection requests, data transmission costs being borne by that State Party.

The conditions under which supplementary data from such facilities are made available, and under which the International Data Centre may request further or expedited reporting, or clarifications, shall be elaborated in the operational manual for the respective monitoring network.

C. CONSULTATION AND CLARIFICATION

29. Without prejudice to the right of any State Party to request an on-site inspection, States Parties should, whenever possible, first make every effort to clarify and resolve, among themselves or with or through the Organization, any matter which may cause concern about possible non-compliance with the basic obligations of this Treaty.

30. A State Party that receives a request pursuant to paragraph 29 directly from another State Party shall provide the clarification to the requesting State Party as soon as possible, but in any case no later than 48 hours after the request. The requesting and

requested States Parties may keep the Executive Council and the Director-General informed of the request and the response.

31. A State Party shall have the right to request the Director-General to assist in clarifying any matter which may cause concern about possible non-compliance with the basic obligations of this Treaty. The Director-General shall provide appropriate information in the possession of the Technical Secretariat relevant to such a concern. The Director-General shall inform the Executive Council of the request and of the information provided in response, if so requested by the requesting State Party.

32. A State Party shall have the right to request the Executive Council to obtain clarification from another State Party on any matter which may cause concern about possible non-compliance with the basic obligations of this Treaty. In such a case, the following shall apply:

(a) The Executive Council shall forward the request for clarification to the requested State Party through the Director-General no later than 24 hours after its receipt;
(b) The requested State Party shall provide the clarification to the Executive Council as soon as possible, but in any case no later than 48 hours after receipt of the request;
(c) The Executive Council shall take note of the clarification and forward it to the requesting State Party no later than 24 hours after its receipt;
(d) If the requesting State Party deems the clarification to be inadequate, it shall have the right to request the Executive Council to obtain further clarification from the requested State Party.

The Executive Council shall inform without delay all other States Parties about any request for clarification pursuant to this paragraph as well as any response provided by the requested State Party.

33. If the requesting State Party considers the clarification obtained under paragraph 32 (d) to be unsatisfactory, it shall have the right to request a meeting of the Executive Council in

which States Parties involved that are not members of the Executive Council shall be entitled to take part. At such a meeting, the Executive Council shall consider the matter and may recommend any measure in accordance with Article V.

D. ON-SITE INSPECTIONS

Request for an On-Site Inspection

34. Each State Party has the right to request an on-site inspection in accordance with the provisions of this Article and Part II of the Protocol in the territory or in any other place under the jurisdiction or control of any State Party, or in any area beyond the jurisdiction or control of any State.

35. The sole purpose of an on-site inspection shall be to clarify whether a nuclear weapon test explosion or any other nuclear explosion has been carried out in violation of Article I and, to the extent possible, to gather any facts which might assist in identifying any possible violator.

36. The requesting State Party shall be under the obligation to keep the on-site inspection request within the scope of this Treaty and to provide in the request information in accordance with paragraph 37. The requesting State Party shall refrain from unfounded or abusive inspection requests.

37. The on-site inspection request shall be based on information collected by the International Monitoring System, on any relevant technical information obtained by national technical means of verification in a manner consistent with generally recognized principles of international law, or on a combination thereof. The request shall contain information pursuant to Part II, paragraph 41 of the Protocol.

38. The requesting State Party shall present the on-site inspection request to the Executive Council and at the same time to the Director-General for the latter to begin immediate processing.

Follow-up After Submission of an On-Site Inspection Request

39. The Executive Council shall begin its consideration immediately upon receipt of the on-site inspection request.

40. The Director-General, after receiving the on-site inspection request, shall acknowledge receipt of the request to the requesting State Party within two hours and communicate the request to the State Party sought to be inspected within six hours. The Director-General shall ascertain that the request meets the requirements specified in Part II, paragraph 41 of the Protocol, and, if necessary, shall assist the requesting State Party in filing the request accordingly, and shall communicate the request to the Executive Council and to all other States Parties within 24 hours.

41. When the on-site inspection request fulfils the requirements, the Technical Secretariat shall begin preparations for the on-site inspection without delay.

42. The Director-General, upon receipt of an on-site inspection request referring to an inspection area under the jurisdiction or control of a State Party, shall immediately seek clarification from the State Party sought to be inspected in order to clarify and resolve the concern raised in the request.

43. A State Party that receives a request for clarification pursuant to paragraph 42 shall provide the Director-General with explanations and with other relevant information available as soon as possible, but no later than 72 hours after receipt of the request for clarification.

44. The Director-General, before the Executive Council takes a decision on the on-site inspection request, shall transmit immediately to the Executive Council any additional information available from the International Monitoring System or provided by any State Party on the event specified in the request, including any clarification provided pursuant to paragraphs 42 and 43, as well as any other information from within the Technical Secretariat that the Director-General deems relevant or that is requested by the Executive Council.

45. Unless the requesting State Party considers the concern raised in the on-site inspection request to be resolved and withdraws the request, the Executive Council shall take a decision on the request in accordance with paragraph 46.

Executive Council Decisions

46. The Executive Council shall take a decision on the on-site inspection request no later than 96 hours after receipt of the request from the requesting State Party. The decision to approve the on-site inspection shall be made by at least 30 affirmative votes of members of the Executive Council. If the Executive Council does not approve the inspection, preparations shall be stopped and no further action on the request shall be taken.

47. No later than 25 days after the approval of the on-site inspection in accordance with paragraph 46, the inspection team shall transmit to the Executive Council, through the Director-General, a progress inspection report. The continuation of the inspection shall be considered approved unless the Executive Council, no later than 72 hours after receipt of the progress inspection report, decides by a majority of all its members not to continue the inspection. If the Executive Council decides not to continue the inspection, the inspection shall be terminated, and the inspection team shall leave the inspection area and the territory of the inspected State Party as soon as possible in accordance with Part II, paragraphs 109 and 110 of the Protocol.

48. In the course of the on-site inspection, the inspection team may submit to the Executive Council, through the Director-General, a proposal to conduct drilling. The Executive Council shall take a decision on such a proposal no later than 72 hours after receipt of the proposal. The decision to approve drilling shall be made by a majority of all members of the Executive Council.

49. The inspection team may request the Executive Council, through the Director-General, to extend the inspection duration by a maximum of 70 days beyond the 60-day time-frame specified in Part II, paragraph 4 of the Protocol, if the inspection team considers such an extension essential to enable it to fulfil its mandate. The inspection team shall indicate in its request which of the activities and techniques listed in Part II, paragraph 69 of the Protocol it intends to carry out during the extension period. The Executive Council shall take a decision on the extension request no later than 72 hours after receipt of the request. The

decision to approve an extension of the inspection duration shall be made by a majority of all members of the Executive Council.

50. Any time following the approval of the continuation of the on-site inspection in accordance with paragraph 47, the inspection team may submit to the Executive Council, through the Director-General, a recommendation to terminate the inspection. Such a recommendation shall be considered approved unless the Executive Council, no later than 72 hours after receipt of the recommendation, decides by a two-thirds majority of all its members not to approve the termination of the inspection. In case of termination of the inspection, the inspection team shall leave the inspection area and the territory of the inspected State Party as soon as possible in accordance with Part II, paragraphs 109 and 110 of the Protocol.

51. The requesting State Party and the State Party sought to be inspected may participate in the deliberations of the Executive Council on the on-site inspection request without voting. The requesting State Party and the inspected State Party may also participate without voting in any subsequent deliberations of the Executive Council related to the inspection.

52. The Director-General shall notify all States Parties within 24 hours about any decision by and reports, proposals, requests and recommendations to the Executive Council pursuant to paragraphs 46 to 50.

Follow-up After Executive Council Approval of an On-Site Inspection

53. An on-site inspection approved by the Executive Council shall be conducted without delay by an inspection team designated by the Director-General and in accordance with the provisions of this Treaty and the Protocol. The inspection team shall arrive at the point of entry no later than six days following the receipt by the Executive Council of the on-site inspection request from the requesting State Party.

54. The Director-General shall issue an inspection mandate for the conduct of the on-site inspection. The inspection mandate shall contain the information specified in Part II, paragraph 42 of the Protocol.

55. The Director-General shall notify the inspected State Party of the inspection no less than 24 hours before the planned arrival of the inspection team at the point of entry, in accordance with Part II, paragraph 43 of the Protocol.

The Conduct of an On-Site Inspection

56. Each State Party shall permit the Organization to conduct an on-site inspection on its territory or at places under its jurisdiction or control in accordance with the provisions of this Treaty and the Protocol. However, no State Party shall have to accept simultaneous on-site inspections on its territory or at places under its jurisdiction or control.

57. In accordance with the provisions of this Treaty and the Protocol, the inspected State Party shall have:

(a) The right and the obligation to make every reasonable effort to demonstrate its compliance with this Treaty and, to this end, to enable the inspection team to fulfil its mandate;

(b) The right to take measures it deems necessary to protect national security interests and to prevent disclosure of confidential information not related to the purpose of the inspection;

(c) The obligation to provide access within the inspection area for the sole purpose of determining facts relevant to the purpose of the inspection, taking into account sub-paragraph (b) and any constitutional obligations it may have with regard to proprietary rights or searches and seizures;

(d) The obligation not to invoke this paragraph or Part II, paragraph 88 of the Protocol to conceal any violation of its obligations under Article I; and

(e) The obligation not to impede the ability of the inspection team to move within the inspection area and to carry out inspection activities in accordance with this Treaty and the Protocol.

Access, in the context of an on-site inspection, means both the physical access of the inspection team and the inspection equipment to, and the conduct of inspection activities within, the inspection area.

58. The on-site inspection shall be conducted in the least intrusive manner possible, consistent with the efficient and timely accomplishment of the inspection mandate, and in accordance with the procedures set forth in the Protocol. Wherever possible, the inspection team shall begin with the least intrusive procedures and then proceed to more intrusive procedures only as it deems necessary to collect sufficient information to clarify the concern about possible non-compliance with this Treaty. The inspectors shall seek only the information and data necessary for the purpose of the inspection and shall seek to minimize interference with normal operations of the inspected State Party.

59. The inspected State Party shall assist the inspection team throughout the on-site inspection and facilitate its task.

60. If the inspected State Party, acting in accordance with Part II, paragraphs 86 to 96 of the Protocol, restricts access within the inspection area, it shall make every reasonable effort in consultations with the inspection team to demonstrate through alternative means its compliance with this Treaty.

Observer

61. With regard to an observer, the following shall apply:

(a) The requesting State Party, subject to the agreement of the inspected State Party, may send a representative, who shall be a national either of the requesting State Party or of a third State Party, to observe the conduct of the on-site inspection;

(b) The inspected State Party shall notify its acceptance or non-acceptance of the proposed observer to the Director-General within 12 hours after approval of the on-site inspection by the Executive Council;

(c) In case of acceptance, the inspected State Party shall grant access to the observer in accordance with the Protocol;

(d) The inspected State Party shall, as a rule, accept the proposed observer, but if the inspected State Party exercises a refusal, that fact shall be recorded in the inspection report.

There shall be no more than three observers from an aggregate of requesting States Parties.

Reports of an On-Site Inspection

62. Inspection reports shall contain:

(a) A description of the activities conducted by the inspection team;

(b) The factual findings of the inspection team relevant to the purpose of the inspection;

(c) An account of the cooperation granted during the on-site inspection;

(d) A factual description of the extent of the access granted, including the alternative means provided to the team, during the on-site inspection; and

(e) Any other details relevant to the purpose of the inspection.

Differing observations made by inspectors may be attached to the report.

63. The Director-General shall make draft inspection reports available to the inspected State Party. The inspected State Party shall have the right to provide the Director-General within 48 hours with its comments and explanations, and to identify any information and data which, in its view, are not related to the purpose of the inspection and should not be circulated outside the Technical Secretariat. The Director-General shall consider the proposals for changes to the draft inspection report made by the inspected State Party and shall wherever possible incorporate them. The Director-General shall also annex the comments and explanations provided by the inspected State Party to the inspection report.

64. The Director-General shall promptly transmit the inspection report to the requesting State Party, the inspected State Party, the Executive Council and to all other States Parties. The Director-General shall further transmit promptly to the Executive Council and to all other States Parties any results of

sample analysis in designated laboratories in accordance with Part II, paragraph 104 of the Protocol, relevant data from the International Monitoring System, the assessments of the requesting and inspected States Parties, as well as any other information that the Director-General deems relevant. In the case of the progress inspection report referred to in paragraph 47, the Director-General shall transmit the report to the Executive Council within the time-frame specified in that paragraph.

65. The Executive Council, in accordance with its powers and functions, shall review the inspection report and any material provided pursuant to paragraph 64, and shall address any concerns as to:

(a) Whether any non-compliance with this Treaty has occurred; and

(b) Whether the right to request an on-site inspection has been abused.

66. If the Executive Council reaches the conclusion, in keeping with its powers and functions, that further action may be necessary with regard to paragraph 65, it shall take the appropriate measures in accordance with Article V.

Frivolous or Abusive On-Site Inspection Requests

67. If the Executive Council does not approve the on-site inspection on the basis that the on-site inspection request is frivolous or abusive, or if the inspection is terminated for the same reasons, the Executive Council shall consider and decide on whether to implement appropriate measures to redress the situation, including the following:

(a) Requiring the requesting State Party to pay for the cost of any preparations made by the Technical Secretariat;

(b) Suspending the right of the requesting State Party to request an on-site inspection for a period of time, as determined by the Executive Council; and

(c) Suspending the right of the requesting State Party to serve on the Executive Council for a period of time.

E. CONFIDENCE-BUILDING MEASURES

68. In order to:

(a) Contribute to the timely resolution of any compliance concerns arising from possible misinterpretation of verification data relating to chemical explosions; and

(b) Assist in the calibration of the stations that are part of the component networks of the International Monitoring System, each State Party undertakes to cooperate with the Organization and with other States Parties in implementing relevant measures as set out in Part III of the Protocol.

ARTICLE V—MEASURES TO REDRESS A SITUATION AND TO ENSURE COMPLIANCE, INCLUDING SANCTIONS

1. The Conference, taking into account, inter alia, the recommendations of the Executive Council, shall take the necessary measures, as set forth in paragraphs 2 and 3, to ensure compliance with this Treaty and to redress and remedy any situation which contravenes the provisions of this Treaty.

2. In cases where a State Party has been requested by the Conference or the Executive Council to redress a situation raising problems with regard to its compliance and fails to fulfil the request within the specified time, the Conference may, inter alia, decide to restrict or suspend the State Party from the exercise of its rights and privileges under this Treaty until the Conference decides otherwise.

3. In cases where damage to the object and purpose of this Treaty may result from non-compliance with the basic obligations of this Treaty, the Conference may recommend to States Parties collective measures which are in conformity with international law.

4. The Conference, or alternatively, if the case is urgent, the Executive Council, may bring the issue, including relevant information and conclusions, to the attention of the United Nations.

ARTICLE VI—SETTLEMENT OF DISPUTES

1. Disputes that may arise concerning the application or the interpretation of this Treaty shall be settled in accordance with the relevant provisions of this Treaty and in conformity with the provisions of the Charter of the United Nations.

2. When a dispute arises between two or more States Parties, or between one or more States Parties and the Organization, relating to the application or interpretation of this Treaty, the parties concerned shall consult together with a view to the expeditious settlement of the dispute by negotiation or by other peaceful means of the parties' choice, including recourse to appropriate organs of this Treaty and, by mutual consent, referral to the International Court of Justice in conformity with the Statute of the Court. The parties involved shall keep the Executive Council informed of actions being taken.

3. The Executive Council may contribute to the settlement of a dispute that may arise concerning the application or interpretation of this Treaty by whatever means it deems appropriate, including offering its good offices, calling upon the States Parties to a dispute to seek a settlement through a process of their own choice, bringing the matter to the attention of the Conference and recommending a time-limit for any agreed procedure.

4. The Conference shall consider questions related to disputes raised by States Parties or brought to its attention by the Executive Council. The Conference shall, as it finds necessary, establish or entrust organs with tasks related to the settlement of these disputes in conformity with Article II, paragraph 26 (j).

5. The Conference and the Executive Council are separately empowered, subject to authorization from the General Assembly of the United Nations, to request the International Court of Justice to give an advisory opinion on any legal question arising within the scope of the activities of the Organization. An agreement between the Organization and the United Nations shall be concluded for this purpose in accordance with Article II, paragraph 38 (h).

6. This Article is without prejudice to Articles IV and V.

ARTICLE VII—AMENDMENTS

1. At any time after the entry into force of this Treaty, any State Party may propose amendments to this Treaty, the Protocol, or the Annexes to the Protocol. Any State Party may also propose changes, in accordance with paragraph 7, to the Protocol or the Annexes thereto. Proposals for amendments shall be subject to the procedures in paragraphs 2 to 6. Proposals for changes, in accordance with paragraph 7, shall be subject to the procedures in paragraph 8.

2. The proposed amendment shall be considered and adopted only by an Amendment Conference.

3. Any proposal for an amendment shall be communicated to the Director-General, who shall circulate it to all States Parties and the Depositary and seek the views of the States Parties on whether an Amendment Conference should be convened to consider the proposal. If a majority of the States Parties notify the Director-General no later than 30 days after its circulation that they support further consideration of the proposal, the Director-General shall convene an Amendment Conference to which all States Parties shall be invited.

4. The Amendment Conference shall be held immediately following a regular session of the Conference unless all States Parties that support the convening of an Amendment Conference request that it be held earlier. In no case shall an Amendment Conference be held less than 60 days after the circulation of the proposed amendment.

5. Amendments shall be adopted by the Amendment Conference by a positive vote of a majority of the States Parties with no State Party casting a negative vote.

6. Amendments shall enter into force for all States Parties 30 days after deposit of the instruments of ratification or acceptance by all those States Parties casting a positive vote at the Amendment Conference.

7. In order to ensure the viability and effectiveness of this Treaty, Parts I and III of the Protocol and Annexes 1 and 2 to the

Protocol shall be subject to changes in accordance with paragraph 8, if the proposed changes are related only to matters of an administrative or technical nature. All other provisions of the Protocol and the Annexes thereto shall not be subject to changes in accordance with paragraph 8.

8. Proposed changes referred to in paragraph 7 shall be made in accordance with the following procedures:

(a) The text of the proposed changes shall be transmitted together with the necessary information to the Director-General. Additional information for the evaluation of the proposal may be provided by any State Party and the Director-General. The Director-General shall promptly communicate any such proposals and information to all States Parties, the Executive Council and the Depositary;

(b) No later than 60 days after its receipt, the Director-General shall evaluate the proposal to determine all its possible consequences for the provisions of this Treaty and its implementation and shall communicate any such information to all States Parties and the Executive Council;

(c) The Executive Council shall examine the proposal in the light of all information available to it, including whether the proposal fulfils the requirements of paragraph 7. No later than 90 days after its receipt, the Executive Council shall notify its recommendation, with appropriate explanations, to all States Parties for consideration. States Parties shall acknowledge receipt within 10 days;

(d) If the Executive Council recommends to all States Parties that the proposal be adopted, it shall be considered approved if no State Party objects to it within 90 days after receipt of the recommendation. If the Executive Council recommends that the proposal be rejected, it shall be considered rejected if no State Party objects to the rejection within 90 days after receipt of the recommendation;

(e) If a recommendation of the Executive Council does not meet with the acceptance required under subparagraph (d), a decision on the proposal, including whether it fulfils the requirements of paragraph 7, shall be taken as a matter of substance by the Conference at its next session;

(f) The Director-General shall notify all States Parties and the Depositary of any decision under this paragraph;

(g) Changes approved under this procedure shall enter into force for all States Parties 180 days after the date of notification by the Director-General of their approval unless another time period is recommended by the Executive Council or decided by the Conference.

ARTICLE VIII—REVIEW OF THE TREATY

1. Unless otherwise decided by a majority of the States Parties, ten years after the entry into force of this Treaty a Conference of the States Parties shall be held to review the operation and effectiveness of this Treaty, with a view to assuring itself that the objectives and purposes in the Preamble and the provisions of the Treaty are being realized. Such review shall take into account any new scientific and technological developments relevant to this Treaty. On the basis of a request by any State Party, the Review Conference shall consider the possibility of permitting the conduct of underground nuclear explosions for peaceful purposes. If the Review Conference decides by consensus that such nuclear explosions may be permitted, it shall commence work without delay, with a view to recommending to States Parties an appropriate amendment to this Treaty that shall preclude any military benefits of such nuclear explosions. Any such proposed amendment shall be communicated to the Director-General by any State Party and shall be dealt with in accordance with the provisions of Article VII.

2. At intervals of ten years thereafter, further Review Conferences may be convened with the same objective, if the Conference so decides as a matter of procedure in the preceding

year. Such Conferences may be convened after an interval of less than ten years if so decided by the Conference as a matter of substance.

3. Normally, any Review Conference shall be held immediately following the regular annual session of the Conference provided for in Article II.

ARTICLE IX—DURATION AND WITHDRAWAL

1. This Treaty shall be of unlimited duration.

2. Each State Party shall, in exercising its national sovereignty, have the right to withdraw from this Treaty if it decides that extraordinary events related to the subject matter of this Treaty have jeopardized its supreme interests.

3. Withdrawal shall be effected by giving notice six months in advance to all other States Parties, the Executive Council, the Depositary and the United Nations Security Council. Notice of withdrawal shall include a statement of the extraordinary event or events which a State Party regards as jeopardizing its supreme interests.

ARTICLE X—STATUS OF THE PROTOCOL AND THE ANNEXES

The Annexes to this Treaty, the Protocol, and the Annexes to the Protocol form an integral part of the Treaty. Any reference to this Treaty includes the Annexes to this Treaty, the Protocol and the Annexes to the Protocol.

ARTICLE XI—SIGNATURE

This Treaty shall be open to all States for signature before its entry into force.

ARTICLE XII—RATIFICATION

This Treaty shall be subject to ratification by States Signatories according to their respective constitutional processes.

ARTICLE XIII—ACCESSION

Any State which does not sign this Treaty before its entry into force may accede to it at any time thereafter.

ARTICLE XIV—ENTRY INTO FORCE

1. This Treaty shall enter into force 180 days after the date of deposit of the instruments of ratification by all States listed in Annex 2 to this Treaty, but in no case earlier than two years after its opening for signature.

2. If this Treaty has not entered into force three years after the date of the anniversary of its opening for signature, the Depositary shall convene a Conference of the States that have already deposited their instruments of ratification upon the request of a majority of those States. That Conference shall examine the extent to which the requirement set out in paragraph 1 has been met and shall consider and decide by consensus what measures consistent with international law may be undertaken to accelerate the ratification process in order to facilitate the early entry into force of this Treaty.

3. Unless otherwise decided by the Conference referred to in paragraph 2 or other such conferences, this process shall be repeated at subsequent anniversaries of the opening for signature of this Treaty, until its entry into force.

4. All States Signatories shall be invited to attend the Conference referred to in paragraph 2 and any subsequent conferences as referred to in paragraph 3, as observers.

5. For States whose instruments of ratification or accession are deposited subsequent to the entry into force of this Treaty, it shall enter into force on the 30th day following the date of deposit of their instruments of ratification or accession.

ARTICLE XV—RESERVATIONS

The Articles of and the Annexes to this Treaty shall not be subject to reservations. The provisions of the Protocol to this Treaty and the Annexes to the Protocol shall not be subject to reservations incompatible with the object and purpose of this Treaty.

ARTICLE XVI—DEPOSITARY

1. The Secretary-General of the United Nations shall be the Depositary of this Treaty and shall receive signatures, instruments of ratification and instruments of accession.

2. The Depositary shall promptly inform all States Signatories and acceding States of the date of each signature, the date of deposit of each instrument of ratification or accession, the date of the entry into force of this Treaty and of any amendments and changes thereto, and the receipt of other notices.

3. The Depositary shall send duly certified copies of this Treaty to the Governments of the States Signatories and acceding States.

4. This Treaty shall be registered by the Depositary pursuant to Article 102 of the Charter of the United Nations.

ARTICLE XVII—AUTHENTIC TEXTS

This Treaty, of which the Arabic, Chinese, English, French, Russian and Spanish texts are equally authentic, shall be deposited with the Secretary-General of the United Nations.

ANNEX 1 TO THE TREATY—LIST OF STATES PURSUANT TO ARTICLE II, PARAGRAPH 28

Africa

Algeria, Angola, Benin, Botswana, Burkina Faso, Burundi, Cameroon, Cape Verde, Central African Republic, Chad, Comoros, Congo, Côte d'Ivoire, Djibouti, Egypt, Equatorial Guinea, Eritrea, Ethiopia, Gabon, Gambia, Ghana, Guinea, Guinea-Bissau, Kenya, Lesotho, Liberia, Libyan Arab Jamahiriya, Madagascar, Malawi, Mali, Mauritania, Mauritius, Morocco, Mozambique, Namibia, Niger, Nigeria, Rwanda, Sao Tome & Principe, Senegal, Seychelles, Sierra Leone, Somalia, South Africa, Sudan, Swaziland, Togo, Tunisia, Uganda, United Republic of Tanzania, Zaire, Zambia, Zimbabwe.

Eastern Europe

Albania, Armenia, Azerbaijan, Belarus, Bosnia and Herzegovina, Bulgaria, Croatia, Czech Republic, Estonia, Georgia, Hungary, Latvia, Lithuania, Poland, Republic of Moldova, Romania, Russian Federation, Slovakia, Slovenia, The former Yugoslav Republic of Macedonia, Ukraine, Yugoslavia.

Latin America and the Caribbean

Antigua and Barbuda, Argentina, Bahamas, Barbados, Belize, Bolivia, Brazil, Chile, Colombia, Costa Rica, Cuba, Dominica, Dominican Republic, Ecuador, El Salvador, Grenada, Guatemala, Guyana, Haiti, Honduras, Jamaica, Mexico, Nicaragua, Panama, Paraguay, Peru, Saint Kitts and Nevis, Saint Lucia, Saint Vincent and the Grenadines, Suriname, Trinidad and Tobago, Uruguay, Venezuela.

Middle East and South Asia

Afghanistan, Bahrain, Bangladesh, Bhutan, India, Iran (Islamic Republic of), Iraq, Israel, Jordan, Kazakstan, Kuwait, Kyrgyzstan, Lebanon, Maldives, Nepal, Oman, Pakistan, Qatar, Saudi Arabia, Sri Lanka, Syrian Arab Republic, Tajikistan, Turkmenistan, United Arab Emirates, Uzbekistan, Yemen.

North America and Western Europe

Andorra, Austria, Belgium, Canada, Cyprus, Denmark, Finland, France, Germany, Greece, Holy See, Iceland, Ireland, Italy, Liechtenstein, Luxembourg, Malta, Monaco, Netherlands, Norway, Portugal, San Marino, Spain, Sweden, Switzerland, Turkey, United Kingdom of Great Britain and Northern Ireland, United States of America.

South East Asia, the Pacific and the Far East

Australia, Brunei Darussalam, Cambodia, China, Cook Islands, Democratic People's Republic of Korea, Fiji, Indonesia, Japan, Kiribati, Lao People's Democratic Republic, Malaysia, Marshall Islands, Micronesia (Federated States of), Mongolia, Myanmar, Nauru, New Zealand, Niue, Palau, Papua New Guinea, Philippines, Republic of Korea, Samoa, Singapore, Solomon Islands, Thailand, Tonga, Tuvalu, Vanuatu, Viet Nam.

ANNEX 2 TO THE TREATY—LIST OF STATES PURSUANT TO ARTICLE XIV

List of States members of the Conference on Disarmament as at 18 June 1996 which formally participated in the work of the 1996 session of the Conference and which appear in Table 1 of the International Atomic Energy Agency's April 1996 edition of "Nuclear Power Reactors in the World", and of States members of the Conference on Disarmament as at 18 June 1996 which formally participated in the work of the 1996 session of the Conference and which appear in Table 1 of the International Atomic Energy Agency's December 1995 edition of "Nuclear Research Reactors in the World": Algeria, Argentina, Australia, Austria, Bangladesh, Belgium, Brazil, Bulgaria, Canada, Chile, China, Colombia, Democratic People's Republic of Korea, Egypt, Finland, France, Germany, Hungary, India, Indonesia, Iran (Islamic Republic of), Israel, Italy, Japan, Mexico, Netherlands, Norway, Pakistan, Peru, Poland, Romania, Republic of Korea, Russian Federation, Slovakia, South Africa, Spain, Sweden, Switzerland, Turkey, Ukraine, United Kingdom of Great Britain and Northern Ireland, United States of America, Viet Nam, Zaire.

PROTOCOL TO THE COMPREHENSIVE NUCLEAR TEST-BAN TREATY

PART I—THE INTERNATIONAL MONITORING SYSTEM AND INTERNATIONAL DATA CENTRE FUNCTIONS

A. GENERAL PROVISIONS

1. The International Monitoring System shall comprise monitoring facilities as set out in Article IV, paragraph 16, and respective means of communication.

2. The monitoring facilities incorporated into the International Monitoring System shall consist of those facilities specified in Annex 1 to this Protocol. The International Monitoring System shall fulfil the technical and operational requirements specified in the relevant operational manuals.

3. The Organization, in accordance with Article II, shall, in cooperation and consultation with the States Parties, with other States, and with international organizations as appropriate, establish and coordinate the operation and maintenance, and any future agreed modification or development of the International Monitoring System.

4. In accordance with appropriate agreements or arrangements and procedures, a State Party or other State hosting

or otherwise taking responsibility for International Monitoring System facilities and the Technical Secretariat shall agree and cooperate in establishing, operating, upgrading, financing, and maintaining monitoring facilities, related certified laboratories and respective means of communication within areas under its jurisdiction or control or elsewhere in conformity with international law. Such cooperation shall be in accordance with the security and authentication requirements and technical specifications contained in the relevant operational manuals. Such a State shall give the Technical Secretariat authority to access a monitoring facility for checking equipment and communication links, and shall agree to make the necessary changes in the equipment and the operational procedures to meet agreed requirements. The Technical Secretariat shall provide to such States appropriate technical assistance as is deemed by the Executive Council to be required for the proper functioning of the facility as part of the International Monitoring System.

5. Modalities for such cooperation between the Organization and States Parties or States hosting or otherwise taking responsibility for facilities of the International Monitoring System shall be set out in agreements or arrangements as appropriate in each case.

B. SEISMOLOGICAL MONITORING

6. Each State Party undertakes to cooperate in an international exchange of seismological data to assist in the verification of compliance with this Treaty. This cooperation shall include the establishment and operation of a global network of primary and auxiliary seismological monitoring stations. These stations shall provide data in accordance with agreed procedures to the International Data Centre.

7. The network of primary stations shall consist of the 50 stations specified in Table 1-A of Annex 1 to this Protocol. These stations shall fulfil the technical and operational requirements specified in the Operational Manual for Seismological Monitoring and the International Exchange of Seismological Data. Uninterrupted data from the primary stations shall be transmitted, directly or through a national data centre, on-line to the International Data Centre.

8. To supplement the primary network, an auxiliary network of 120 stations shall provide information, directly or through a national data centre, to the International Data Centre upon request. The auxiliary stations to be used are listed in Table 1-B of Annex 1 to this Protocol. The auxiliary stations shall fulfil the technical and operational requirements specified in the Operational Manual for Seismological Monitoring and the International Exchange of Seismological Data. Data from the auxiliary stations may at any time be requested by the International Data Centre and shall be immediately available through on-line computer connections.

C. RADIONUCLIDE MONITORING

9. Each State Party undertakes to cooperate in an international exchange of data on radionuclides in the atmosphere to assist in the verification of compliance with this Treaty. This cooperation shall include the establishment and operation of a global network of radionuclide monitoring stations and certified laboratories. The network shall provide data in accordance with agreed procedures to the International Data Centre.

10. The network of stations to measure radionuclides in the atmosphere shall comprise an overall network of 80 stations, as specified in Table 2-A of Annex 1 to this Protocol. All stations shall be capable of monitoring for the presence of relevant particulate matter in the atmosphere. Forty of these stations shall also be capable of monitoring for the presence of relevant noble gases upon the entry into force of this Treaty. For this purpose the Conference, at its initial session, shall approve a recommendation by the Preparatory Commission as to which 40 stations from Table 2-A of Annex 1 to this Protocol shall be capable of noble gas monitoring. At its first regular annual session, the Conference shall consider and decide on a plan for implementing noble gas monitoring capability throughout the network. The Director-General shall prepare a report to the Conference on the modalities for such implementation. All monitoring stations shall fulfil the technical and operational requirements specified in the Operational Manual for Radionuclide Monitoring and the International Exchange of Radionuclide Data.

11. The network of radionuclide monitoring stations shall be supported by laboratories, which shall be certified by the Technical Secretariat in accordance with the relevant operational manual for the performance, on contract to the Organization and on a fee-for-service basis, of the analysis of samples from radionuclide monitoring stations. Laboratories specified in Table 2-B of Annex 1 to this Protocol, and appropriately equipped, shall, as required, also be drawn upon by the Technical Secretariat to perform additional analysis of samples from radionuclide monitoring stations. With the agreement of the Executive Council, further laboratories may be certified by the Technical Secretariat to perform the routine analysis of samples from manual monitoring stations where necessary. All certified laboratories shall provide the results of such analysis to the International Data Centre, and in so doing shall fulfil the technical and operational requirements specified in the Operational Manual on Radionuclide Monitoring and the International Exchange of Radionuclide Data.

D. HYDROACOUSTIC MONITORING

12. Each State Party undertakes to cooperate in an international exchange of hydroacoustic data to assist in the verification of compliance with this Treaty. This cooperation shall include the establishment and operation of a global network of hydroacoustic monitoring stations. These stations shall provide data in accordance with agreed procedures to the International Data Centre.

13. The network of hydroacoustic stations shall consist of the stations specified in Table 3 of Annex 1 to this Protocol, and shall comprise an overall network of six hydrophone and five T-phase stations. These stations shall fulfil the technical and operational requirements specified in the Operational Manual for Hydroacoustic Monitoring and the International Exchange of Hydroacoustic Data.

E. INFRASOUND MONITORING

14. Each State Party undertakes to cooperate in an international exchange of infrasound data to assist in the verification of compliance with this Treaty. This cooperation

shall include the establishment and operation of a global network of infrasound monitoring stations. These stations shall provide data in accordance with agreed procedures to the International Data Centre.

15. The network of infrasound stations shall consist of the stations specified in Table 4 of Annex 1 to this Protocol, and shall comprise an overall network of 60 stations. These stations shall fulfil the technical and operational requirements specified in the Operational Manual for Infrasound Monitoring and the International Exchange of Infrasound Data.

F. INTERNATIONAL DATA CENTRE FUNCTIONS

16. The International Data Centre shall receive, collect, process, analyse, report on and archive data from International Monitoring System facilities, including the results of analysis conducted at certified laboratories.

17. The procedures and standard event screening criteria to be used by the International Data Centre in carrying out its agreed functions, in particular for the production of standard reporting products and for the performance of a standard range of services for States Parties, shall be elaborated in the Operational Manual for the International Data Centre and shall be progressively developed. The procedures and criteria developed initially by the Preparatory Commission shall be approved by the Conference at its initial session.

International Data Centre Standard Products

18. The International Data Centre shall apply on a routine basis automatic processing methods and interactive human analysis to raw International Monitoring System data in order to produce and archive standard International Data Centre products on behalf of all States Parties. These products shall be provided at no cost to States Parties and shall be without prejudice to final judgements with regard to the nature of any event, which shall remain the responsibility of States Parties, and shall include:

(a) Integrated lists of all signals detected by the International Monitoring System, as well as standard event lists and bulletins, including the values and associated uncertainties calculated for each event located by the

International Data Centre, based on a set of standard parameters;

(b) Standard screened event bulletins that result from the application to each event by the International Data Centre of standard event screening criteria, making use of the characterization parameters specified in Annex 2 to this Protocol, with the objective of characterizing, highlighting in the standard event bulletin, and thereby screening out, events considered to be consistent with natural phenomena or non-nuclear, man-made phenomena. The standard event bulletin shall indicate numerically for each event the degree to which that event meets or does not meet the event screening criteria. In applying standard event screening, the International Data Centre shall use both global and supplementary screening criteria to take account of regional variations where applicable. The International Data Centre shall progressively enhance its technical capabilities as experience is gained in the operation of the International Monitoring System;

(c) Executive summaries, which summarize the data acquired and archived by the International Data Centre, the products of the International Data Centre, and the performance and operational status of the International Monitoring System and International Data Centre; and

(d) Extracts or subsets of the standard International Data Centre products specified in sub-paragraphs (a) to (c), selected according to the request of an individual State Party.

19. The International Data Centre shall carry out, at no cost to States Parties, special studies to provide in-depth, technical review by expert analysis of data from the International Monitoring System, if requested by the Organization or by a State Party, to improve the estimated values for the standard signal and event parameters.

International Data Centre Services to States Parties

20. The International Data Centre shall provide States Parties with open, equal, timely and convenient access to all International Monitoring System data, raw or processed, all International Data Centre products, and all other International Monitoring System data in the archive of the International Data Centre or, through the International Data Centre, of International Monitoring System facilities. The methods for supporting data access and the provision of data shall include the following services:

(a) Automatic and regular forwarding to a State Party of the products of the International Data Centre or the selection by the State Party thereof, and, as requested, the selection by the State Party of International Monitoring System data;

(b) The provision of the data or products generated in response to ad hoc requests by States Parties for the retrieval from the International Data Centre and International Monitoring System facility archives of data and products, including interactive electronic access to the International Data Centre database; and

(c) Assisting individual States Parties, at their request and at no cost for reasonable efforts, with expert technical analysis of International Monitoring System data and other relevant data provided by the requesting State Party, in order to help the State Party concerned to identify the source of specific events. The output of any such technical analysis shall be considered a product of the requesting State Party, but shall be available to all States Parties.

The International Data Centre services specified in subparagraphs (a) and (b) shall be made available at no cost to each State Party. The volumes and formats of data shall be set out in the Operational Manual for the International Data Centre.

National Event Screening

21. The International Data Centre shall, if requested by a State Party, apply to any of its standard products, on a regular

and automatic basis, national event screening criteria established by that State Party, and provide the results of such analysis to that State Party. This service shall be undertaken at no cost to the requesting State Party. The output of such national event screening processes shall be considered a product of the requesting State Party.

Technical Assistance

22. The International Data Centre shall, where required, provide technical assistance to individual States Parties:

(a) In formulating their requirements for selection and screening of data and products;

(b) By installing at the International Data Centre, at no cost to a requesting State Party for reasonable efforts, computer algorithms or software provided by that State Party to compute new signal and event parameters that are not included in the Operational Manual for the International Data Centre, the output being considered products of the requesting State Party; and

(c) By assisting States Parties to develop the capability to receive, process and analyse International Monitoring System data at a national data centre.

23. The International Data Centre shall continuously monitor and report on the operational status of the International Monitoring System facilities, of communications links, and of its own processing systems. It shall provide immediate notification to those responsible should the operational performance of any component fail to meet agreed levels set out in the relevant operational manual.

PART II—ON-SITE INSPECTIONS

A. GENERAL PROVISIONS

1. The procedures in this Part shall be implemented pursuant to the provisions for on-site inspections set out in Article IV.

2. The on-site inspection shall be carried out in the area where the event that triggered the on-site inspection request occurred.

3. The area of an on-site inspection shall be continuous and its size shall not exceed 1,000 square kilometres. There shall be no linear distance greater than 50 kilometres in any direction.

4. The duration of an on-site inspection shall not exceed 60 days from the date of the approval of the on-site inspection request in accordance with Article IV, paragraph 46, but may be extended by a maximum of 70 days in accordance with Article IV, paragraph 49.

5. If the inspection area specified in the inspection mandate extends to the territory or other place under the jurisdiction or control of more than one State Party, the provisions on on-site inspections shall, as appropriate, apply to each of the States Parties to which the inspection area extends.

6. In cases where the inspection area is under the jurisdiction or control of the inspected State Party but is located on the territory of another State Party or where the access from the point of entry to the inspection area requires transit through the territory of a State Party other than the inspected State Party, the inspected State Party shall exercise the rights and fulfil the obligations concerning such inspections in accordance with this Protocol. In such a case, the State Party on whose territory the inspection area is located shall facilitate the inspection and shall provide for the necessary support to enable the inspection team to carry out its tasks in a timely and effective manner. States Parties through whose territory transit is required to reach the inspection area shall facilitate such transit.

7. In cases where the inspection area is under the jurisdiction or control of the inspected State Party but is located on the territory of a State not Party to this Treaty, the inspected State Party shall take all necessary measures to ensure that the inspection can be carried out in accordance with this Protocol. A State Party that has under its jurisdiction or control one or more areas on the territory of a State not Party to this Treaty shall take all necessary measures to ensure acceptance by the State on whose territory the inspection area is located of inspectors and inspection assistants designated to that State Party. If an inspected

State Party is unable to ensure access, it shall demonstrate that it took all necessary measures to ensure access.

8. In cases where the inspection area is located on the territory of a State Party but is under the jurisdiction or control of a State not Party to this Treaty, the State Party shall take all necessary measures required of an inspected State Party and a State Party on whose territory the inspection area is located, without prejudice to the rules and practices of international law, to ensure that the on-site inspection can be carried out in accordance with this Protocol. If the State Party is unable to ensure access to the inspection area, it shall demonstrate that it took all necessary measures to ensure access, without prejudice to the rules and practices of international law.

9. The size of the inspection team shall be kept to the minimum necessary for the proper fulfilment of the inspection mandate. The total number of members of the inspection team present on the territory of the inspected State Party at any given time, except during the conduct of drilling, shall not exceed 40 persons. No national of the requesting State Party or the inspected State Party shall be a member of the inspection team.

10. The Director-General shall determine the size of the inspection team and select its members from the list of inspectors and inspection assistants, taking into account the circumstances of a particular request.

11. The inspected State Party shall provide for or arrange the amenities necessary for the inspection team, such as communication means, interpretation services, transportation, working space, lodging, meals, and medical care.

12. The inspected State Party shall be reimbursed by the Organization, in a reasonably short period of time after conclusion of the inspection, for all expenses, including those mentioned in paragraphs 11 and 49, related to the stay and functional activities of the inspection team on the territory of the inspected State Party.

13. Procedures for the implementation of on-site inspections shall be detailed in the Operational Manual for On-Site Inspections.

B. STANDING ARRANGEMENTS

Designation of Inspectors and Inspection Assistants

14. An inspection team may consist of inspectors and inspection assistants. An on-site inspection shall only be carried out by qualified inspectors specially designated for this function. They may be assisted by specially designated inspection assistants, such as technical and administrative personnel, aircrew and interpreters.

15. Inspectors and inspection assistants shall be nominated for designation by the States Parties or, in the case of staff of the Technical Secretariat, by the Director-General, on the basis of their expertise and experience relevant to the purpose and functions of on-site inspections. The nominees shall be approved in advance by the States Parties in accordance with paragraph 18.

16. Each State Party, no later than 30 days after the entry into force of this Treaty for it, shall notify the Director-General of the names, dates of birth, sex, ranks, qualifications and professional experience of the persons proposed by the State Party for designation as inspectors and inspection assistants.

17. No later than 60 days after the entry into force of this Treaty, the Technical Secretariat shall communicate in writing to all States Parties an initial list of the names, nationalities, dates of birth, sex and ranks of the inspectors and inspection assistants proposed for designation by the Director-General and the States Parties, as well as a description of their qualifications and professional experience.

18. Each State Party shall immediately acknowledge receipt of the initial list of inspectors and inspection assistants proposed for designation. Any inspector or inspection assistant included in this list shall be regarded as accepted unless a State Party, no later than 30 days after acknowledgment of receipt of the list, declares its non-acceptance in writing. The State Party may include the reason for the objection. In the case of non-acceptance, the proposed inspector or inspection assistant shall not undertake or participate in on-site inspection activities on the territory or in any other place under the jurisdiction or control of the State

Party that has declared its non-acceptance. The Technical Secretariat shall immediately confirm receipt of the notification of objection.

19. Whenever additions or changes to the list of inspectors and inspection assistants are proposed by the Director-General or a State Party, replacement inspectors and inspection assistants shall be designated in the same manner as set forth with respect to the initial list. Each State Party shall promptly notify the Technical Secretariat if an inspector or inspection assistant nominated by it can no longer fulfil the duties of an inspector or inspection assistant.

20. The Technical Secretariat shall keep the list of inspectors and inspection assistants up to date and notify all States Parties of any additions or changes to the list.

21. A State Party requesting an on-site inspection may propose that an inspector from the list of inspectors and inspection assistants serve as its observer in accordance with Article IV, paragraph 61.

22. Subject to paragraph 23, a State Party shall have the right at any time to object to an inspector or inspection assistant who has already been accepted. It shall notify the Technical Secretariat of its objection in writing and may include the reason for the objection. Such objection shall come into effect 30 days after receipt of the notification by the Technical Secretariat. The Technical Secretariat shall immediately confirm receipt of the notification of the objection and inform the objecting and nominating States Parties of the date on which the inspector or inspection assistant shall cease to be designated for that State Party.

23. A State Party that has been notified of an inspection shall not seek the removal from the inspection team of any of the inspectors or inspection assistants named in the inspection mandate.

24. The number of inspectors and inspection assistants accepted by a State Party must be sufficient to allow for availability of appropriate numbers of inspectors and inspection assistants. If, in the opinion of the Director-General, the non-

acceptance by a State Party of proposed inspectors or inspection assistants impedes the designation of a sufficient number of inspectors and inspection assistants or otherwise hampers the effective fulfilment of the purposes of an on-site inspection, the Director-General shall refer the issue to the Executive Council.

25. Each inspector included in the list of inspectors and inspection assistants shall receive relevant training. Such training shall be provided by the Technical Secretariat pursuant to the procedures specified in the Operational Manual for On-Site Inspections. The Technical Secretariat shall co-ordinate, in agreement with the States Parties, a schedule of training for the inspectors.

Privileges and Immunities

26. Following acceptance of the initial list of inspectors and inspection assistants as provided for in paragraph 18 or as subsequently altered in accordance with paragraph 19, each State Party shall be obliged to issue, in accordance with its national procedures and upon application by an inspector or inspection assistant, multiple entry/exit and/or transit visas and other relevant documents to enable each inspector and inspection assistant to enter and to remain on the territory of that State Party for the sole purpose of carrying out inspection activities. Each State Party shall issue the necessary visa or travel documents for this purpose no later than 48 hours after receipt of the application or immediately upon arrival of the inspection team at the point of entry on the territory of the State Party. Such documents shall be valid for as long as is necessary to enable the inspector or inspection assistant to remain on the territory of the inspected State Party for the sole purpose of carrying out the inspection activities.

27. To exercise their functions effectively, members of the inspection team shall be accorded privileges and immunities as set forth in sub-paragraphs (a) to (i). Privileges and immunities shall be granted to members of the inspection team for the sake of this Treaty and not for the personal benefit of the individuals themselves. Such privileges and immunities shall be accorded to them for the entire period between arrival on and departure

from the territory of the inspected State Party, and thereafter with respect to acts previously performed in the exercise of their official functions.

(a) The members of the inspection team shall be accorded the inviolability enjoyed by diplomatic agents pursuant to Article 29 of the Vienna Convention on Diplomatic Relations of 18 April 1961;

(b) The living quarters and office premises occupied by the inspection team carrying out inspection activities pursuant to this Treaty shall be accorded the inviolability and protection accorded to the premises of diplomatic agents pursuant to Article 30, paragraph 1, of the Vienna Convention on Diplomatic Relations;

(c) The papers and correspondence, including records, of the inspection team shall enjoy the inviolability accorded to all papers and correspondence of diplomatic agents pursuant to Article 30, paragraph 2, of the Vienna Convention on Diplomatic Relations. The inspection team shall have the right to use codes for their communications with the Technical Secretariat;

(d) Samples and approved equipment carried by members of the inspection team shall be inviolable subject to provisions contained in this Treaty and exempt from all customs duties. Hazardous samples shall be transported in accordance with relevant regulations;

(e) The members of the inspection team shall be accorded the immunities accorded to diplomatic agents pursuant to Article 31, paragraphs 1, 2 and 3, of the Vienna Convention on Diplomatic Relations;

(f) The members of the inspection team carrying out prescribed activities pursuant to this Treaty shall be accorded the exemption from dues and taxes accorded to diplomatic agents pursuant to Article 34 of the Vienna Convention on Diplomatic Relations;

(g) The members of the inspection team shall be permitted to bring into the territory of the inspected State Party, without payment of any customs duties or related charges, articles for personal use, with the exception of articles the import or export of which is prohibited by law or controlled by quarantine regulations;

(h) The members of the inspection team shall be accorded the same currency and exchange facilities as are accorded to representatives of foreign Governments on temporary official missions; and

(i) The members of the inspection team shall not engage in any professional or commercial activity for personal profit on the territory of the inspected State Party.

28. When transiting the territory of States Parties other than the inspected State Party, the members of the inspection team shall be accorded the privileges and immunities enjoyed by diplomatic agents pursuant to Article 40, paragraph 1, of the Vienna Convention on Diplomatic Relations. Papers and correspondence, including records, and samples and approved equipment carried by them, shall be accorded the privileges and immunities set forth in paragraph 27 (c) and (d).

29. Without prejudice to their privileges and immunities the members of the inspection team shall be obliged to respect the laws and regulations of the inspected State Party and, to the extent that is consistent with the inspection mandate, shall be obliged not to interfere in the internal affairs of that State. If the inspected State Party considers that there has been an abuse of privileges and immunities specified in this Protocol, consultations shall be held between the State Party and the Director-General to determine whether such an abuse has occurred and, if so determined, to prevent a repetition of such an abuse.

30. The immunity from jurisdiction of members of the inspection team may be waived by the Director-General in those cases when the Director-General is of the opinion that immunity would impede the course of justice and that it can be waived without prejudice to the implementation of the provisions of this Treaty. Waiver must always be express.

31. Observers shall be accorded the same privileges and immunities accorded to members of the inspection team pursuant

to this section, except for those accorded pursuant to paragraph 27 (d).

Points of Entry

32. Each State Party shall designate its points of entry and shall supply the required information to the Technical Secretariat no later than 30 days after this Treaty enters into force for it. These points of entry shall be such that the inspection team can reach any inspection area from at least one point of entry within 24 hours. Locations of points of entry shall be provided to all States Parties by the Technical Secretariat. Points of entry may also serve as points of exit.

33. Each State Party may change its points of entry by giving notice of such change to the Technical Secretariat. Changes shall become effective 30 days after the Technical Secretariat receives such notification, to allow appropriate notification to all States Parties.

34. If the Technical Secretariat considers that there are insufficient points of entry for the timely conduct of inspections or that changes to the points of entry proposed by a State Party would hamper such timely conduct of inspections, it shall enter into consultations with the State Party concerned to resolve the problem.

Arrangements for Use of Non-Scheduled Aircraft

35. Where timely travel to the point of entry is not feasible using scheduled commercial flights, an inspection team may utilize non-scheduled aircraft. No later than 30 days after this Treaty enters into force for it, each State Party shall inform the Technical Secretariat of the standing diplomatic clearance number for non-scheduled aircraft transporting an inspection team and equipment necessary for inspection. Aircraft routings shall be along established international airways that are agreed upon between the State Party and the Technical Secretariat as the basis for such diplomatic clearance.

Approved Inspection Equipment

36. The Conference, at its initial session, shall consider and approve a list of equipment for use during on-site inspections.

Each State Party may submit proposals for the inclusion of equipment in the list. Specifications for the use of the equipment, as detailed in the Operational Manual for On-Site Inspections, shall take account of safety and confidentiality considerations where such equipment is likely to be used.

37. The equipment for use during on-site inspections shall consist of core equipment for the inspection activities and techniques specified in paragraph 69 and auxiliary equipment necessary for the effective and timely conduct of on-site inspections.

38. The Technical Secretariat shall ensure that all types of approved equipment are available for on-site inspections when required. When required for an on-site inspection, the Technical Secretariat shall duly certify that the equipment has been calibrated, maintained and protected. To facilitate the checking of the equipment at the point of entry by the inspected State Party, the Technical Secretariat shall provide documentation and attach seals to authenticate the certification.

39. Any permanently held equipment shall be in the custody of the Technical Secretariat. The Technical Secretariat shall be responsible for the maintenance and calibration of such equipment.

40. As appropriate, the Technical Secretariat shall make arrangements with States Parties to provide equipment mentioned in the list. Such States Parties shall be responsible for the maintenance and calibration of such equipment.

C. ON-SITE INSPECTION REQUEST, INSPECTION MANDATE AND NOTIFICATION OF INSPECTION

On-Site Inspection Request

41. Pursuant to Article IV, paragraph 37, the on-site inspection request shall contain at least the following information:

(a) The estimated geographical and vertical coordinates of the location of the event that triggered the request with an indication of the possible margin of error;

(b) The proposed boundaries of the area to be inspected, specified on a map and in accordance with paragraphs 2 and 3;

(c) The State Party or States Parties to be inspected or an indication that the area to be inspected or part thereof is beyond the jurisdiction or control of any State;

(d) The probable environment of the event that triggered the request;

(e) The estimated time of the event that triggered the request, with an indication of the possible margin of error;

(f) All data upon which the request is based;

(g) The personal details of the proposed observer, if any; and

(h) The results of a consultation and clarification process in accordance with Article IV, or an explanation, if relevant, of the reasons why such a consultation and clarification process has not been carried out.

Inspection Mandate

42. The mandate for an on-site inspection shall contain:

(a) The decision of the Executive Council on the onsite inspection request;

(b) The name of the State Party or States Parties to be inspected or an indication that the inspection area or part thereof is beyond the jurisdiction or control of any State;

(c) The location and boundaries of the inspection area specified on a map, taking into account all information on which the request was based and all other available technical information, in consultation with the requesting State Party;

(d) The planned types of activity of the inspection team in the inspection area;

(e) The point of entry to be used by the inspection team;

(f) Any transit or basing points, as appropriate;

(g) The name of the head of the inspection team;

(h) The names of members of the inspection team;

(i) The name of the proposed observer, if any; and

(j) The list of equipment to be used in the inspection area.

If a decision by the Executive Council pursuant to Article IV, paragraphs 46 to 49, necessitates a modification of the inspection mandate, the Director-General may update the mandate with respect to sub-paragraphs (d), (h) and (j), as appropriate. The Director-General shall immediately notify the inspected State Party of any such modification.

Notification of Inspection

43. The notification made by the Director-General pursuant to Article IV, paragraph 55 shall include the following information:

(a) The inspection mandate;

(b) The date and estimated time of arrival of the inspection team at the point of entry;

(c) The means of arrival at the point of entry;

(d) If appropriate, the standing diplomatic clearance number for non-scheduled aircraft; and

(e) A list of any equipment which the Director-General requests the inspected State Party to make available to the inspection team for use in the inspection area.

44. The inspected State Party shall acknowledge receipt of the notification by the Director-General no later than 12 hours after having received the notification.

D. PRE-INSPECTION ACTIVITIES

Entry into the Territory of the Inspected State Party, Activities at the Point of Entry and Transfer to the Inspection Area

45. The inspected State Party that has been notified of the arrival of the inspection team shall ensure the immediate entry of the inspection team into its territory.

46. When a non-scheduled aircraft is used for travel to the point of entry, the Technical Secretariat shall provide the inspected State Party with a flight plan, through the National Authority,

for the flight of the aircraft from the last airfield prior to entering the airspace of that State Party to the point of entry, no less than six hours before the scheduled departure time from that airfield. Such a plan shall be filed in accordance with the procedures of the International Civil Aviation Organization applicable to civil aircraft. The Technical Secretariat shall include in the remarks section of the flight plan the standing diplomatic clearance number and the appropriate notation identifying the aircraft as an inspection aircraft. If a military aircraft is used, the Technical Secretariat shall request prior authorization from the inspected State Party to enter its airspace.

47. No less than three hours before the scheduled departure of the inspection team from the last airfield prior to entering the airspace of the inspected State Party, the inspected State Party shall ensure that the flight plan filed in accordance with paragraph 46 is approved, so that the inspection team may arrive at the point of entry by the estimated arrival time.

48. Where necessary, the head of the inspection team and the representative of the inspected State Party shall agree on a basing point and a flight plan from the point of entry to the basing point and, if necessary, to the inspection area.

49. The inspected State Party shall provide for or arrange parking, security protection, servicing and fuel as required by the Technical Secretariat for the aircraft of the inspection team at the point of entry and, where necessary, at the basing point and at the inspection area. Such aircraft shall not be liable for landing fees, departure tax, and similar charges. This paragraph shall also apply to aircraft used for overflight during the on-site inspection.

50. Subject to paragraph 51, there shall be no restriction by the inspected State Party on the inspection team bringing approved equipment that is in conformity with the inspection mandate into the territory of that State Party, or on its use in accordance with the provisions of the Treaty and this Protocol.

51. The inspected State Party shall have the right, without prejudice to the time-frame specified in paragraph 54, to check

in the presence of inspection team members at the point of entry that the equipment has been approved and certified in accordance with paragraph 38. The inspected State Party may exclude equipment that is not in conformity with the inspection mandate or that has not been approved and certified in accordance with paragraph 38.

52. Immediately upon arrival at the point of entry and without prejudice to the time-frame specified in paragraph 54, the head of the inspection team shall present to the representative of the inspected State Party the inspection mandate and an initial inspection plan prepared by the inspection team specifying the activities to be carried out by it. The inspection team shall be briefed by representatives of the inspected State Party with the aid of maps and other documentation as appropriate. The briefing shall include relevant natural terrain features, safety and confidentiality issues, and logistical arrangements for the inspection. The inspected State Party may indicate locations within the inspection area that, in its view, are not related to the purpose of the inspection.

53. After the pre-inspection briefing, the inspection team shall, as appropriate, modify the initial inspection plan, taking into account any comments by the inspected State Party. The modified inspection plan shall be made available to the representative of the inspected State Party.

54. The inspected State Party shall do everything in its power to provide assistance and to ensure the safe conduct of the inspection team, the approved equipment specified in paragraphs 50 and 51 and baggage from the point of entry to the inspection area no later than 36 hours after arrival at the point of entry, if no other timing has been agreed upon within the time-frame specified in paragraph 57.

55. To confirm that the area to which the inspection team has been transported corresponds to the inspection area specified in the inspection mandate, the inspection team shall have the right to use approved location-finding equipment. The inspected State Party shall assist the inspection team in this task.

E. CONDUCT OF INSPECTIONS

General Rules

56. The inspection team shall discharge its functions in accordance with the provisions of the Treaty and this Protocol.

57. The inspection team shall begin its inspection activities in the inspection area as soon as possible, but in no case later than 72 hours after arrival at the point of entry.

58. The activities of the inspection team shall be so arranged as to ensure the timely and effective discharge of its functions and the least possible inconvenience to the inspected State Party and disturbance to the inspection area.

59. In cases where the inspected State Party has been requested, pursuant to paragraph 43 (e) or in the course of the inspection, to make available any equipment for use by the inspection team in the inspection area, the inspected State Party shall comply with the request to the extent it can.

60. During the on-site inspection the inspection team shall have, inter alia:

(a) The right to determine how the inspection will proceed, consistent with the inspection mandate and taking into account any steps taken by the inspected State Party consistent with the provisions on managed access;

(b) The right to modify the inspection plan, as necessary, to ensure the effective execution of the inspection;

(c) The obligation to take into account the recommendations and suggested modifications by the inspected State Party to the inspection plan;

(d) The right to request clarifications in connection with ambiguities that may arise during the inspection;

(e) The obligation to use only those techniques specified in paragraph 69 and to refrain from activities that are not relevant to the purpose of the inspection. The team shall collect and document such facts as are related to the purpose of the inspection, but shall neither seek nor document information that is clearly unrelated thereto. Any material collected and subsequently found not to be relevant shall be returned to the inspected State Party;

(f) The obligation to take into account and include in its report data and explanations on the nature of the event that triggered the request, provided by the inspected State Party from the national monitoring networks of the inspected State Party and from other sources;

(g) The obligation to provide the inspected State Party, at its request, with copies of the information and data collected in the inspection area; and

(h) The obligation to respect the confidentiality and the safety and health regulations of the inspected State Party.

61. During the on-site inspection the inspected State Party shall have, inter alia:

(a) The right to make recommendations at any time to the inspection team regarding possible modification of the inspection plan;

(b) The right and the obligation to provide a representative to liaise with the inspection team;

(c) The right to have representatives accompany the inspection team during the performance of its duties and observe all inspection activities carried out by the inspection team. This shall not delay or otherwise hinder the inspection team in the exercise of its functions;

(d) The right to provide additional information and to request the collection and documentation of additional facts it believes are relevant to the inspection;

(e) The right to examine all photographic and measurement products as well as samples and to retain any photographs or parts thereof showing sensitive sites not related to the purpose of the inspection. The inspected State Party shall have the right to receive duplicate copies of all photographic and measurement products. The inspected State Party shall have the right to retain photographic originals and first-generation photographic products and to put photographs or parts thereof under joint seal within its territory. The inspected State Party shall have the right to provide its own camera operator to take still/video photographs as requested by the inspection team. Otherwise, these functions shall be performed by members of the inspection team;

(f) The right to provide the inspection team, from its national monitoring networks and from other sources, with data and explanations on the nature of the event that triggered the request; and

(g) The obligation to provide the inspection team with such clarification as may be necessary to resolve any ambiguities that arise during the inspection.

Communications

62. The members of the inspection team shall have the right at all times during the on-site inspection to communicate with each other and with the Technical Secretariat. For this purpose they may use their own duly approved and certified equipment with the consent of the inspected State Party, to the extent that the inspected State Party does not provide them with access to other telecommunications.

Observer

63. In accordance with Article IV, paragraph 61, the requesting State Party shall liaise with the Technical Secretariat to co-ordinate the arrival of the observer at the same point of entry or basing point as the inspection team within a reasonable period of the arrival of the inspection team.

64. The observer shall have the right throughout the inspection to be in communication with the embassy of the requesting State Party located in the inspected State Party or, in the case of absence of an embassy, with the requesting State Party itself.

65. The observer shall have the right to arrive at the inspection area and to have access to and within the inspection area as granted by the inspected State Party.

66. The observer shall have the right to make recommendations to the inspection team throughout the inspection.

67. Throughout the inspection, the inspection team shall keep the observer informed about the conduct of the inspection and the findings.

68. Throughout the inspection, the inspected State Party shall provide or arrange for the amenities necessary for the observer similar to those enjoyed by the inspection team as described in paragraph 11. All costs in connection with the stay of the observer on the territory of the inspected State Party shall be borne by the requesting State Party.

Inspection Activities and Techniques

69. The following inspection activities may be conducted and techniques used, in accordance with the provisions on managed access, on collection, handling and analysis of samples, and on overflights:

(a) Position finding from the air and at the surface to confirm the boundaries of the inspection area and establish co-ordinates of locations therein, in support of the inspection activities;

(b) Visual observation, video and still photography and multi-spectral imaging, including infrared measurements, at and below the surface, and from the air, to search for anomalies or artifacts;

(c) Measurement of levels of radioactivity above, at and below the surface, using gamma radiation monitoring and energy resolution analysis from the air, and at or under the surface, to search for and identify radiation anomalies;

(d) Environmental sampling and analysis of solids, liquids and gases from above, at and below the surface to detect anomalies;

(e) Passive seismological monitoring for aftershocks to localize the search area and facilitate determination of the nature of an event;

(f) Resonance seismometry and active seismic surveys to search for and locate underground anomalies, including cavities and rubble zones;

(g) Magnetic and gravitational field mapping, ground penetrating radar and electrical conductivity measurements at the surface and from the air, as appropriate, to detect anomalies or artifacts; and

(h) Drilling to obtain radioactive samples.

70. Up to 25 days after the approval of the on-site inspection in accordance with Article IV, paragraph 46, the inspection team shall have the right to conduct any of the activities and use any of the techniques listed in paragraph 69 (a) to (e). Following the approval of the continuation of the inspection in accordance with Article IV, paragraph 47, the inspection team shall have the right to conduct any of the activities and use any of the techniques listed in paragraph 69 (a) to (g). The inspection team shall only conduct drilling after the approval of the Executive Council in accordance with Article IV, paragraph 48. If the inspection team requests an extension of the inspection duration in accordance with Article IV, paragraph 49, it shall indicate in its request which of the activities and techniques listed in paragraph 69 it intends to carry out in order to be able to fulfil its mandate.

Overflights

71. The inspection team shall have the right to conduct an overflight over the inspection area during the on-site inspection for the purposes of providing the inspection team with a general orientation of the inspection area, narrowing down and optimizing the locations for ground-based inspection and facilitating the collection of factual evidence, using equipment specified in paragraph 79.

72. The overflight shall be conducted as soon as practically possible. The total duration of the overflight over the inspection area shall be no more than 12 hours.

73. Additional overflights using equipment specified in paragraphs 79 and 80 may be conducted subject to the agreement of the inspected State Party.

74. The area to be covered by overflights shall not extend beyond the inspection area.

75. The inspected State Party shall have the right to impose restrictions or, in exceptional cases and with reasonable justification, prohibitions on the overflight of sensitive sites not related to the purpose of the inspection. Restrictions may relate to the flight altitude, the number of passes and circling, the duration of hovering, the type of aircraft, the number of inspectors on board, and the type of measurements or observations. If the inspection team considers that the restrictions or prohibitions on the overflight of sensitive sites may impede the fulfilment of its mandate, the inspected State Party shall make every reasonable effort to provide alternative means of inspection.

76. Overflights shall be conducted according to a flight plan duly filed and approved in accordance with aviation rules and regulations of the inspected State Party. Flight safety regulations of the inspected State Party shall be strictly observed throughout all flying operations.

77. During overflights landing should normally be authorized only for purposes of staging or refuelling.

78. Overflights shall be conducted at altitudes as requested by the inspection team consistent with the activities to be conducted, visibility conditions, as well as the aviation and the safety regulations of the inspected State Party and its right to protect sensitive information not related to the purposes of the inspection. Overflights shall be conducted up to a maximum altitude of 1,500 metres above the surface.

79. For the overflight conducted pursuant to paragraphs 71 and 72, the following equipment may be used on board the aircraft:

(a) Field glasses;

(b) Passive location-finding equipment;

(c) Video cameras; and

(d) Hand-held still cameras.

80. For any additional overflights conducted pursuant to paragraph 73, inspectors on board the aircraft may also use portable, easily installed equipment for:

(a) Multi-spectral (including infrared) imagery;

(b) Gamma spectroscopy; and

(c) Magnetic field mapping.

81. Overflights shall be conducted with a relatively slow fixed or rotary wing aircraft. The aircraft shall afford a broad, unobstructed view of the surface below.

82. The inspected State Party shall have the right to provide its own aircraft, pre-equipped as appropriate in accordance with the technical requirements of the relevant operational manual, and crew. Otherwise, the aircraft shall be provided or rented by the Technical Secretariat.

83. If the aircraft is provided or rented by the Technical Secretariat, the inspected State Party shall have the right to check the aircraft to ensure that it is equipped with approved inspection equipment. Such checking shall be completed within the time-frame specified in paragraph 57.

84. Personnel on board the aircraft shall consist of:

(a) The minimum number of flight crew consistent with the safe operation of the aircraft;

(b) Up to four members of the inspection team;

(c) Up to two representatives of the inspected State Party;

(d) An observer, if any, subject to the agreement of the inspected State Party; and

(e) An interpreter, if necessary.

85. Procedures for the implementation of overflights shall be detailed in the Operational Manual for On-Site Inspections.

Managed Access

86. The inspection team shall have the right to access the inspection area in accordance with the provisions of the Treaty and this Protocol.

87. The inspected State Party shall provide access within the inspection area in accordance with the time-frame specified in paragraph 57.

88. Pursuant to Article IV, paragraph 57 and paragraph 86 above, the rights and obligations of the inspected State Party shall include:

(a) The right to take measures to protect sensitive installations and locations in accordance with this Protocol;

(b) The obligation, when access is restricted within the inspection area, to make every reasonable effort to satisfy the requirements of the inspection mandate through alternative means. Resolving any questions regarding one or more aspects of the inspection shall not delay or interfere with the conduct of the inspection team of other aspects of the inspection; and

(c) The right to make the final decision regarding any access of the inspection team, taking into account its obligations under this Treaty and the provisions on managed access.

89. Pursuant to Article IV, paragraph 57 (b) and paragraph 88 (a) above, the inspected State Party shall have the right throughout the inspection area to take measures to protect sensitive installations and locations and to prevent disclosure of confidential information not related to the purpose of the inspection. Such measures may include, inter alia:

(a) Shrouding of sensitive displays, stores, and equipment;

(b) Restricting measurements of radionuclide activity and nuclear radiation to determining the presence or absence of those types and energies of radiation relevant to the purpose of the inspection;

(c) Restricting the taking of or analysing of samples to determining the presence or absence of radioactive or other products relevant to the purpose of the inspection;

(d) Managing access to buildings and other structures in accordance with paragraphs 90 and 91; and

(e) Declaring restricted-access sites in accordance with paragraphs 92 to 96.

90. Access to buildings and other structures shall be deferred until after the approval of the continuation of the on-site inspection in accordance with Article IV, paragraph 47, except for access to buildings and other structures housing the entrance

to a mine, other excavations, or caverns of large volume not otherwise accessible. For such buildings and structures, the inspection team shall have the right only of transit, as directed by the inspected State Party, in order to enter such mines, caverns or other excavations.

91. If, following the approval of the continuation of the inspection in accordance with Article IV, paragraph 47, the inspection team demonstrates credibly to the inspected State Party that access to buildings and other structures is necessary to fulfil the inspection mandate and that the necessary activities authorized in the mandate could not be carried out from the outside, the inspection team shall have the right to gain access to such buildings or other structures. The head of the inspection team shall request access to a specific building or structure indicating the purpose of such access, the specific number of inspectors, as well as the intended activities. The modalities for access shall be subject to negotiation between the inspection team and the inspected State Party. The inspected State Party shall have the right to impose restrictions or, in exceptional cases and with reasonable justification, prohibitions, on the access to buildings and other structures.

92. When restricted-access sites are declared pursuant to paragraph 89 (e), each such site shall be no larger than 4 square kilometres. The inspected State Party has the right to declare up to 50 square kilometres of restricted-access sites. If more than one restricted-access site is declared, each such site shall be separated from any other such site by a minimum distance of 20 metres. Each restricted-access site shall have clearly defined and accessible boundaries.

93. The size, location, and boundaries of restricted access sites shall be presented to the head of the inspection team no later than the time that the inspection team seeks access to a location that contains all or part of such a site.

94. The inspection team shall have the right to place equipment and take other steps necessary to conduct its inspection up to the boundary of a restricted-access site.

95. The inspection team shall be permitted to observe visually all open places within the restricted-access site from the boundary of the site.

96. The inspection team shall make every reasonable effort to fulfil the inspection mandate outside the declared restricted-access sites prior to requesting access to such sites. If at any time the inspection team demonstrates credibly to the inspected State Party that the necessary activities authorized in the mandate could not be carried out from the outside and that access to a restricted-access site is necessary to fulfil the mandate, some members of the inspection team shall be granted access to accomplish specific tasks within the site. The inspected State Party shall have the right to shroud or otherwise protect sensitive equipment, objects and materials not related to the purpose of the inspection. The number of inspectors shall be kept to the minimum necessary to complete the tasks related to the inspection. The modalities for such access shall be subject to negotiation between the inspection team and the inspected State Party.

Collection, Handling and Analysis of Samples

97. Subject to paragraphs 86 to 96 and 98 to 100, the inspection team shall have the right to collect and remove relevant samples from the inspection area.

98. Whenever possible, the inspection team shall analyse samples on-site. Representatives of the inspected State Party shall have the right to be present when samples are analysed on-site. At the request of the inspection team, the inspected State Party shall, in accordance with agreed procedures, provide assistance for the analysis of samples on-site. The inspection team shall have the right to transfer samples for off-site analysis at laboratories designated by the Organization only if it demonstrates that the necessary sample analysis cannot be performed on-site.

99. The inspected State Party shall have the right to retain portions of all samples collected when these samples are analysed and may take duplicate samples.

100. The inspected State Party shall have the right to request that any unused samples or portions thereof be returned.

101. The designated laboratories shall conduct chemical and physical analysis of the samples transferred for off-site analysis. Details of such analysis shall be elaborated in the Operational Manual for On-Site Inspections.

102. The Director-General shall have the primary responsibility for the security, integrity and preservation of samples and for ensuring that the confidentiality of samples transferred for off-site analysis is protected. The Director-General shall do so in accordance with procedures contained in the Operational Manual for On-Site Inspections. The Director-General shall, in any case:

(a) Establish a stringent regime governing the collection, handling, transport and analysis of samples;

(b) Certify the laboratories designated to perform different types of analysis;

(c) Oversee the standardization of equipment and procedures at these designated laboratories and of mobile analytical equipment and procedures;

(d) Monitor quality control and overall standards in relation to the certification of these laboratories and in relation to mobile equipment and procedures; and

(e) Select from among the designated laboratories those which shall perform analytical or other functions in relation to specific investigations.

103. When off-site analysis is to be performed, samples shall be analysed in at least two designated laboratories. The Technical Secretariat shall ensure the expeditious processing of the analysis. The samples shall be accounted for by the Technical Secretariat and any unused samples or portions thereof shall be returned to the Technical Secretariat.

104. The Technical Secretariat shall compile the results of the laboratory analysis of samples relevant to the purpose of the inspection. Pursuant to Article IV, paragraph 63, the Director-General shall transmit any such results promptly to the inspected

State Party for comments and thereafter to the Executive Council and to all other States Parties and shall include detailed information concerning the equipment and methodology employed by the designated laboratories.

Conduct of Inspections in Areas beyond the Jurisdiction or Control of Any State

105. In case of an on-site inspection in an area beyond the jurisdiction or control of any State, the Director-General shall consult with the appropriate States Parties and agree on any transit or basing points to facilitate a speedy arrival of the inspection team in the inspection area.

106. The States Parties on whose territory transit or basing points are located shall, as far as possible, assist in facilitating the inspection, including transporting the inspection team, its baggage and equipment to the inspection area, as well as providing the relevant amenities specified in paragraph 11. The Organization shall reimburse assisting States Parties for all costs incurred.

107. Subject to the approval of the Executive Council, the Director-General may negotiate standing arrangements with States Parties to facilitate assistance in the event of an onsite inspection in an area beyond the jurisdiction or control of any State.

108. In cases where one or more States Parties have conducted an investigation of an ambiguous event in an area beyond the jurisdiction or control of any State before a request is made for an on-site inspection in that area, any results of such investigation may be taken into account by the Executive Council in its deliberations pursuant to Article IV.

Post-Inspection Procedures

109. Upon conclusion of the inspection, the inspection team shall meet with the representative of the inspected State Party to review the preliminary findings of the inspection team and to clarify any ambiguities. The inspection team shall provide the representative of the inspected State Party with its preliminary findings in written form according to a standardized format, together with a list of any samples and other material taken from the inspection area pursuant to paragraph 98. The document

shall be signed by the head of the inspection team. In order to indicate that he or she has taken notice of the contents of the document, the representative of the inspected State Party shall countersign the document. The meeting shall be completed no later than 24 hours after the conclusion of the inspection.

Departure

110. Upon completion of the post-inspection procedures, the inspection team and the observer shall leave, as soon as possible, the territory of the inspected State Party. The inspected State Party shall do everything in its power to provide assistance and to ensure the safe conduct of the inspection team, equipment and baggage to the point of exit. Unless agreed otherwise by the inspected State Party and the inspection team, the point of exit used shall be the same as the point of entry.

PART III—CONFIDENCE-BUILDING MEASURES

1. Pursuant to Article IV, paragraph 68, each State Party shall, on a voluntary basis, provide the Technical Secretariat with notification of any chemical explosion using 300 tonnes or greater of TNT-equivalent blasting material detonated as a single explosion anywhere on its territory, or at any place under its jurisdiction or control. If possible, such notification shall be provided in advance. Such notification shall include details on location, time, quantity and type of explosive used, as well as on the configuration and intended purpose of the blast.

2. Each State Party shall, on a voluntary basis, as soon as possible after the entry into force of this Treaty provide to the Technical Secretariat, and at annual intervals thereafter update, information related to its national use of all other chemical explosions greater than 300 tonnes TNT-equivalent. In particular, the State Party shall seek to advise:

(a) The geographic locations of sites where the explosions originate;

(b) The nature of activities producing them and the general profile and frequency of such explosions;

(c) Any other relevant detail, if available; and to assist the Technical Secretariat in clarifying the origins of any such event detected by the International Monitoring System.

3. A State Party may, on a voluntary and mutually acceptable basis, invite representatives of the Technical Secretariat or of other States Parties to visit sites within its territory referred to in paragraphs 1 and 2.

4. For the purpose of calibrating the International Monitoring System, States Parties may liaise with the Technical Secretariat to carry out chemical calibration explosions or to provide relevant information on chemical explosions planned for other purposes.

ANNEX 1 TO THE PROTOCOL

Table 1-A

List of Seismological Stations Comprising the Primary Network

#	State Responsible for Station	Location	Latitude	Longitude	Type
1	Argentina	PLCA Paso Flores	40.7 S	70.6 W	3-C
2	Australia	WRA Warramunga, NT	19.9 S	134.3 E	array
3	Australia	ASAR Alice Springs, NT	23.7 S	133.9 E	array
4	Australia	STKA Stephens Creek, SA	31.9 S	141.6 E	3-C
5	Australia	MAW Mawson, Antarctica	67.6 S	62.9 E	3-C
6	Bolivia	LPAZ La Paz	16.3 S	68.1 W	3-C
7	Brazil	BDFB Brasilia	15.6 S	48.0 W	3-C
8	Canada	ULMC Lac du Bonnet, Man.	50.2 N	95.9 W	3-C
9	Canada	YKAC Yellowknife, N.W.T.	62.5 N	114.6 W	array
10	Canada	SCH Schefferville, Quebec	54.8 N	66.8 W	3-C
11	Central African Republic	BGCA Bangui	05.2 N	18.4 E	3-C
12	China	HAI Hailar	49.3 N	119.7 E	3-C > array
13	China	LZH Lanzhou	36.1 N	103.8 E	3-C > array
14	Colombia	XSA El Rosal	04.9 N	74.3 W	3-C
15	Côte d'Ivoire	DBIC Dimbroko	06.7 N	04.9 W	3-C
16	Egypt	LXEG Luxor	26.0 N	33.0 E	array
17	Finland	FINES Lahti	61.4 N	26.1 E	array
18	France	PPT Tahiti	17.6 S	149.6 W	3-C
19	Germany	GEC2 Freyung	48.9 N	13.7 E	array

20	To be determined	To be determined	To be determined	To be determined	To be determined
21	Iran (Islamic Republic of)	THR Tehran	35.8 N	51.4 E	3-C
22	Japan	MJAR Matsushiro	36.5 N	138.2 E	array
23	Kazakstan	MAK Makanchi	46.8 N	82.0 E	array
24	Kenya	KMBO Kilimambogo	01.1 S	37.2 E	3-C
25	Mongolia	JAVM Javhlant	48.0 N	106.8 E	3-C > array
26	Niger	New Site	to be determined	to be determined	3-C > array
27	Norway	NAO Hamar	60.8 N	10.8 E	array
28	Norway	ARAO Karasjok	69.5 N	25.5 E	array
29	Pakistan	PRPK Pari	33.7 N	73.3 E	array
30	Paraguay	CPUP Villa Florida	26.3 S	57.3 W	3-C
31	Republic of Korea	KSRS Wonju	37.5 N	127.9 E	array
32	Russian Federation	KBZ Khabaz	43.7 N	42.9 E	3-C
33	Russian Federation	ZAL Zalesovo	53.9 N	84.8 E	3-C > array
34	Russian Federation	NRI Norilsk	69.0 N	88.0 E	3-C
35	Russian Federation	PDY Peleduy	59.6 N	112.6 E	3-C > array
36	Russian Federation	PET Petropavlovsk-Kamchatskiy	53.1 N	157.8 E	3-C > array
37	Russian Federation	USK Ussuriysk	44.2 N	132.0 E	3-C > array
38	Saudi Arabia	New Site	to be determined	to be determined	array
39	South Africa	BOSA Boshof	28.6 S	25.6 E	3-C
40	Spain	ESDC Sonseca	39.7 N	04.0 W	array
41	Thailand	CMTO Chiang Mai	18.8 N	99.0 E	array
42	Tunisia	THA Thala	35.6 N	08.7 E	3-C
43	Turkey	BRTR Belbashi The array is subject to relocation at Keskin	39.9 N	32.8 E	array
44	Turkmenistan	GEYT Alibeck	37.9 N	58.1 E	array
45	Ukraine	AKASG Malin	50.4 N	29.1 E	array
46	United States of America	LJTX Lajitas, TX	29.3 N	103.7 W	array
47	United States of America	MNV Mina, NV	38.4 N	118.2 W	array
48	United States of America	PIWY Pinedale, WY	42.8 N	109.6 W	array
49	United States of America	ELAK Eielson, AK	64.8 N	146.9 W	array
50	United States of America	VNDA Vanda, Antarctica	77.5 S	161.9	E 3-C

Key: 3-C > array: Indicates that the site could start operations in the International Monitoring System as a three-component station and be upgraded to an array at a later time.

Table 1-B
List of Seismological Stations Comprising the Auxiliary Network

#	State Responsible for Station	Location	Latitude	Longitude	Type
1	Argentina	CFA Coronel Fontana	31.6 S	68.2 W	3-C
2	Argentina	USHA Ushuaia	55.0 S	68.0 W	3-C
3	Armenia	GNI Garni	40.1 N	44.7 E	3-C
4	Australia	CTA Charters Towers, QLD	20.1 S	146.3 E	3-C
5	Australia	FITZ Fitzroy Crossing, WA	18.1 S	125.6 E	3-C
6	Australia	NWAO Narrogin, WA	32.9 S	117.2 E	3-C
7	Bangladesh	CHT Chittagong	22.4 N	91.8 E	3-C
8	Bolivia	SIV San Ignacio	16.0 S	61.1 W	3-C
9	Botswana	LBTB Lobatse	25.0 S	25.6 E	3-C
10	Brazil	PTGA Pitinga	0.7 S	60.0 W	3-C
11	Brazil	RGNB Rio Grande do Norte	6.9 S	37.0 W	3-C
12	Canada	FRB Iqaluit, N.W.T.	63.7 N	68.5 W	3-C
13	Canada	DLBC Dease Lake, B.C.	58.4 N	130.0 W	3-C
14	Canada	SADO Sadowa, Ont.	44.8 N	79.1 W	3-C
15	Canada	BBB Bella Bella, B.C.	52.2 N	128.1 W	3-C
16	Canada	MBC Mould Bay, N.W.T.	76.2 N	119.4 W	3-C
17	Canada	INK Inuvik, N.W.T.	68.3 N	133.5 W	3-C
18	Chile	RPN Easter Island	27.2 S	109.4 W	3-C
19	Chile	LVC Limon Verde	22.6 S	68.9 W	3-C
20	China	BJT Baijiatuan	40.0 N	116.2	E 3-C

21 China	KMI Kunming	25.2 N	102.8	E 3-C
22 China	SSE Sheshan	31.1 N	121.2 E	3-C
23 China	XAN Xi'an	34.0 N	108.9 E	3-C
24 Cook Islands	RAR Rarotonga	21.2 S	159.8 W	3-C
25 Costa Rica	JTS Las Juntas de Abangares	10.3 N	85.0 W	3-C
26 Czech Republic	VRAC Vranov	49.3 N	16.6 E	3-C
27 Denmark	SFJ Søndre Strømfjord, Greenland	67.0 N	50.6 W	3-C
28 Djibouti	ATD Arta Tunnel	11.5 N	42.9 E	3-C
29 Egypt	KEG Kottamya	29.9 N	31.8 E	3-C
30 Ethiopia	FURI Furi	8.9 N	38.7 E	3-C
31 Fiji	MSVF Monasavu, Viti Levu	17.8 S	178.1	E 3-C
32 France	NOUC Port Laguerre, New Caledonia	22.1 S	166.3 E	3-C
33 France	KOG Kourou, French Guiana	5.2 N	52.7 W	3-C
34 Gabon	BAMB Bambay	1.7 S	13.6 E	3-C
35 Germany/South	— Africa SANAE Station, Antarctica	71.7 S	2.9 W	3-C
36 Greece	IDI Anogia, Crete	35.3 N	24.9 E	3-C
37 Guatemala	RDG Rabir	15.0 N	90.5 W	3-C
38 Iceland	BORG Borgarnes	64.8 N	21.3 W	3-C
39 To be determined	To be determined	To be determined	To be determined	To be determined

40 Indonesia	PACI Cibinong, Jawa Barat	6.5 S	107.0 E	3-C
41 Indonesia	JAY Jayapura, Irian Jaya	2.5 S	140.7 E	3-C
42 Indonesia	SWI Sorong, Irian Jaya	0.9 S	131.3 E	3-C
43 Indonesia	PSI Parapat, Sumatera	2.7 N	98.9 E	3-C
44 Indonesia	KAPI Kappang, Sulawesi Selatan	5.0 S	119.8 E	3-C
45 Indonesia	KUG Kupang, Nusatenggara Timur	10.2 S	123.6 E	3-C
46 Iran (Islamic Republic of)	KRM Kerman	30.3 N	57.1 E	3-C
47 Iran (Islamic Republic of)	MSN Masjed-e-Soleyman	31.9 N	49.3 E	3-C
48 Israel	MBH Eilath	29.8 N	34.9 E	3-C
49 Israel	PARD Parod	32.6 N	35.3 E	array
50 Italy	ENAS Enna, Sicily	37.5 N	14.3 E	3-C
51 Japan	JNU Ohita, Kyushu	33.1 N	130.9 E	3-C
52 Japan	JOW Kunigami, Okinawa	26.8 N	128.3 E	3-C
53 Japan	JHJ Hachijojima, Izu Islands	33.1 N	139.8 E	3-C
54 Japan	JKA Kamikawa-asahi, Hokkaido	44.1 N	142.6 E	3-C
55 Japan	JCJ Chichijima, Ogasawara	27.1 N	142.2 E	3-C
56 Jordan	— Ashqof	32.5 N	37.6 E	3-C
57 Kazakstan	BRVK Borovoye	53.1 N	70.3 E	array
58 Kazakstan	KURK Kurchatov	50.7 N	78.6 E	array

59 Kazakstan	AKTO Aktyubinsk	50.4 N	58.0 E	3-C
60 Kyrgyzstan	AAK Ala-Archa	42.6 N	74.5 E	3-C
61 Madagascar	TAN Antananarivo	18.9 S	47.6 E	3-C
62 Mali	KOWA Kowa	14.5 N	4.0 W	3-C
63 Mexico	TEYM Tepich, Yucatan	20.2 N	88.3 W	3-C
64 Mexico	TUVM Tuzandepeti, Veracruz	18.0 N	94.4 W	3-C
65 Mexico	LPBM La Paz, Baja California Sur	24.2 N	110.2 W	3-C
66 Morocco	MDT Midelt	32.8 N	4.6 W	3-C
67 Namibia	TSUM Tsumeb	19.1 S	17.4 E	3-C
68 Nepal	EVN Everest	28.0 N	86.8 E	3-C
69 New Zealand	EWZ Erewhon, South Island	43.5 S	170.9 E	3-C
70 New Zealand	RAO Raoul Island	29.2 S	177.9 W	3-C
71 New Zealand	URZ Urewera, North Island	38.3 S	177.1 E	3-C
72 Norway	SPITS Spitsbergen	78.2 N	16.4 E	array
73 Norway	JMI Jan Mayen	70.9 N	8.7 W	3-C
74 Oman	WSAR Wadi Sarin	23.0 N	58.0 E	3-C
75 Papua New Guinea	PMG Port Moresby	9.4 S	147.2 E	3-C
76 Papua New Guinea	BIAL Bialla	5.3 S	151.1 E	3-C
77 Peru	CAJP Cajamarca	7.0 S	78.0 W	3-C
78 Peru	NNA Nana	12.0 S	76.8 W	3-C

79 Philippines	DAV Davao, Mindanao	7.1 N	125.6 E	3-C
80 Philippines	TGY Tagaytay, Luzon	14.1 N	120.9 E	3-C
81 Romania Muntele Rosu	MLR	45.5 N	25.9 E	3-C
82 Russian Federation	KIRV Kirov	58.6 N	49.4 E	3-C
83 Russian Federation	KIVO Kislovodsk	44.0 N	42.7 E	array
84 Russian Federation	OBN Obninsk	55.1 N	36.6 E	3-C
85 Russian Federation	ARU Arti	56.4 N	58.6 E	3-C
86 Russian Federation	SEY Seymchan	62.9 N	152.4 E	3-C
87 Russian Federation	TLY Talaya	51.7 N	103.6 E	3-C
88 Russian Federation	YAK Yakutsk	62.0N	129.7 E	3-C
89 Russian Federation	URG Urgal	51.1N	132.3 E	3-C
90 Russian Federation	BIL Bilibino	68.0 N	166.4 E	3-C
91 Russian Federation	TIXI Tiksi	71.6 N	128.9 E	3-C
92 Russian Federation	YSS Yuzhno-Sakhalinsk	47.0 N	142.8 E	3-C
93 Russian Federation	MA2 Magadan	59.6 N	150.8 E	3-C
94 Russian Federation	ZIL Zilim	53.9 N	57.0 E	3-C
95 Samoa	AFI Afiamalu	13.9 S	171.8 W	3-C
96 Saudi Arabia	RAYN Ar Rayn	23.6 N	45.6 E	3-C
97 Senegal	MBO Mbour	14.4 N	17.0 W	3-C
98 Solomon Islands	HNR Honiara, Guadalcanal	9.4 S	160.0 E	3-C
99 South Africa	SUR Sutherland	32.4 S	20.8 E	3-C
100 Sri Lanka	COC Colombo	6.9 N	79.9 E	3-C

101 Sweden	HFS Hagfors	60.1 N	13.7 E	array
102 Switzerland	DAVOS Davos	46.8 N	9.8 E	3-C
103 Uganda	MBRU Mbarara	0.4 S	30.4 E	3-C
104 United Kingdom	EKA Eskdalemuir	55.3 N	3.2 W	array
105 United States of America	GUMO Guam, Marianas Islands	13.6 N	144.9 E	3-C
106 United States of America	PMSA Palmer Station, Antarctica	64.8 S	64.1 W	3-C
107 United States of America	TKL Tuckaleechee Caverns, TN	35.7 N	83.8 W	3-C
108 United States of America	PFCA Piñon Flat, CA	33.6 N	116.5 W	3-C
109 United States of America	YBH Yreka, CA	41.7 N	122.7 W	3-C
110 United States of America	KDC Kodiak Island, AK	57.8 N	152.5 W	3-C
111 United States of America	ALQ Albuquerque, NM	35.0 N	106.5 W	3-C
112 United States of America	ATTU Attu Island, AK	52.8 N	172.7 E	3-C
113 United States of America	ELK Elko, NV	40.7 N	115.2 W	3-C
114 United States of America	SPA South Pole, Antarctica	90.0 S	—	3-C
115 United States of America	NEW Newport, WA	48.3 N	117.1 W	3-C
116 United States of America	SJG San Juan, PR	18.1 N	66.2 W	3-C
117 Venezuela	SDV Santo Domingo	8.9 N	70.6 W	3-C
118 Venezuela	PCRV Puerto la Cruz	10.2 N	64.6 W	3-C
119 Zambia	LSZ Lusaka	15.3 S	28.2 E	3-C
120 Zimbabwe	BUL Bulawayo	to be advised	to be advised	3-C

Table 2
A List of Radionuclide Stations

#	State Responsible for Station	Location	Latitude	Longitude
1	Argentina	Buenos Aires	34.0 S	58.0 W
2	Argentina	Salta	24.0 S	65.0 W
3	Argentina	Bariloche	41.1 S	71.3 W
4	Australia	Melbourne, VIC	37.5 S	144.6 E
5	Australia	Mawson, Antarctica	67.6 S	62.5 E
6	Australia	Townsville, QLD	19.2 S	146.8 E
7	Australia	Macquarie Island	54.0 S	159.0 E
8	Australia	Cocos Islands	12.0 S	97.0 E
9	Australia	Darwin, NT	12.4 S	130.7 E
10	Australia	Perth, WA	31.9 S	116.0 E
11	Brazil	Rio de Janeiro	22.5 S	43.1 W
12	Brazil	Recife	8.0 S	35.0 W
13	Cameroon	Douala	4.2 N	9.9 E
14	Canada	Vancouver, B.C.	49.3 N	123.2 W
15	Canada	Resolute, N.W.T.	74.7 N	94.9 W
16	Canada	Yellowknife, N.W.T.	62.5 N	114.5 W
17	Canada	St. John's, N.L.	47.0 N	53.0 W
18	Chile	Punta Arenas	53.1 S	70.6 W
19	Chile	Hanga Roa, Easter Island	27.1 S	108.4 W
20	China	Beijing	39.8 N	116.2 E
21	China	Lanzhou	35.8 N	103.3 E
22	China	Guangzhou	23.0 N	113.3 E
23	Cook Islands	Rarotonga	21.2 S	159.8 W
24	Ecuador	Isla San Cristóbal, Galápagos Islands	1.0 S	89.2 W
25	Ethiopia	Filtu	5.5 N	42.7 E
26	Fiji	Nadi	18.0 S	177.5 E
27	France	Papeete, Tahiti	17.0 S	150.0 W
28	France	Pointe-à-Pitre, Guadeloupe	17.0 N	62.0 W
29	France	Réunion	21.1 S	55.6 E
30	France	Port-aux-Français, Kerguelen	49.0 S	70.0 E
31	France	Cayenne, French Guiana	5.0 N	52.0 W
32	France	Dumont d'Urville, Antarctica	66.0 S	140.0 E
33	Germany	Schauinsland/Freiburg	47.9 N	7.9 E
34	Iceland	Reykjavik	64.4 N	21.9 W
35	To be determined	To be determined	To be determined	To be determined
36	Iran (Islamic Republic of)	Tehran	35.0 N	52.0 E
37	Japan	Okinawa	26.5 N	127.9 E
38	Japan	Takasaki, Gunma	36.3 N	139.0 E

39	Kiribati	Kiritimati	2.0 N	157.0 W
40	Kuwait	Kuwait City	29.0 N	48.0 E
41	Libya	Misratah	32.5 N	15.0 E
42	Malaysia	Kuala Lumpur	2.6 N	101.5 E
43	Mauritania	Nouakchott	18.0 N	17.0 W
44	Mexico	Baja California	28.0 N	113.0 W
45	Mongolia	Ulaanbaatar	47.5 N	107.0 E
46	New Zealand	Chatham Island	44.0 S	176.5 W
47	New Zealand	Kaitaia	35.1 S	173.3 E
48	Niger	Bilma	18.0 N	13.0 E
49	Norway	Spitsbergen	78.2 N	16.4 E
50	Panama	Panama City	8.9 N	79.6 W
51	Papua New Guinea	New Hanover	3.0 S	150.0 E
52	Philippines	Quezon City	14.5 N	121.0 E
53	Portugal	Ponta Delgada, São Miguel, Azores	37.4 N	25.4 W
54	Russian Federation	Kirov	58.6 N	49.4 E
55	Russian Federation	Norilsk	69.0 N	88.0E
56	Russian Federation	Peleduy	59.6 N	112.6 E
57	Russian Federation	Bilibino	68.0 N	166.4 E
58	Russian Federation	Ussuriysk	43.7 N	131.9 E
59	Russian Federation	Zalesovo	53.9 N	84.8 E
60	Russian Federation	Petropavlovsk-Kamchatskiy	53.1 N	158.8 E
61	Russian Federation	Dubna	56.7 N	37.3 E
62	South Africa	Marion Island	46.5 S	37.0 E
63	Sweden	Stockholm	59.4 N	18.0 E
64	Tanzania	Dar es Salaam	6.0 S	39.0 E
65	Thailand	Bangkok	13.8 N	100.5 E
66	United Kingdom	BIOT/Chagos Archipelago	7.0 S	72.0 E
67	United Kingdom	St. Helena	16.0 S	6.0 W
68	United Kingdom	Tristan da Cunha	37.0 S	12.3 W
69	United Kingdom	Halley, Antarctica	76.0 S	28.0 W
70	United States of America	Sacramento, CA	38.7 N	121.4 W
71	United States of America	Sand Point, AK	55.0 N	160.0 W
72	United States of America	Melbourne, FL	28.3 N	80.6 W
73	United States of America	Palmer Station, Antarctica	64.5 S	64.0 W
74	United States of America	Ashland, KS	37.2 N	99.8 W
75	United States of America	Charlottesville, VA	38.0 N	78.0 W
76	United States of America	Salchaket, AK	64.4 N	147.1 W
77	United States of America	Wake Island	19.3 N	166.6 E
78	United States of America	Midway Islands	28.0 N	177.0 W
79	United States of America	Oahu, HI	21.5 N	158.0 W
80	United States of America	Upi, Guam	13.7 N	144.9 E

Table 2-B
List of Radionuclide Laboratories

#	State Responsible for Laboratory	Name and Place of Laboratory
1	Argentina	National Board of Nuclear Regulation Buenos Aires
2	Australia	Australian Radiation Laboratory Melbourne, VIC
3	Austria	Austrian Research Center Seibersdorf
4	Brazil	Institute of Radiation Protection and Dosimetry Rio de Janeiro
5	Canada	Health Canada Ottawa, Ont.
6	China	Beijing
7	Finland	Centre for Radiation and Nuclear Safety Helsinki
8	France	Atomic Energy Commission Montlhéry
9	Israel	Soreq Nuclear Research Centre Yavne
10	Italy	Laboratory of the National Agency for the Protection of the Environment Rome
11	Japan	Japan Atomic Energy Research Institute Tokai, Ibaraki
12	New Zealand	National Radiation Laboratory Christchurch
13	Russian Federation	Central Radiation Control Laboratory, Ministry of Defence Special Verification Service Moscow
14	South Africa	Atomic Energy Corporation Pelindaba
15	United Kingdom	AWE Blacknest Chilton
16	United States of America	McClellan Central Laboratories Sacramento, CA

Table 3

List of Hydroacoustic Stations

#	State Responsible for Station	Location	Latitude	Longitude	Type
1	Australia	Cape Leeuwin, WA	34.4 S	115.1 E	Hydrophone
2	Canada	Queen Charlotte Islands, B.C.	53.3 N	132.5 W	T-phase
3	Chile	Juan Fernández Island	33.7 S	78.8 W	Hydrophone
4	France	Crozet Islands	46.5 S	52.2 E	Hydrophone
5	France	Guadeloupe	16.3 N	61.1 W	T-phase
6	Mexico	Clarión Island	18.2 N	114.6 W	T-phase
7	Portugal	Flores	39.3 N	31.3 W	T-phase
8	United Kingdom	BIOT/Chagos Archipelago	7.3 S	72.4 E	Hydrophone
9	United Kingdom	Tristan da Cunha	37.2 S	12.5 W	T-phase
10	United Kingdom	Ascension	8.0 S	14.4 W	Hydrophone
11	United States of America	Wake Island	19.3 N	166.6 E	Hydrophone

Table 4

List of Infrasound Stations

#	State Responsible for Station	Location	Latitude	Longitude
1	Argentina	Paso Flores	40.7 S	70.6 W
2	Argentina	Ushuaia	55.0 S	68.0 W
3	Australia	Davis Base, Antarctica	68.4 S	77.6 E
4	Australia	Narrogin, WA	32.9 S	117.2 E
5	Australia	Hobart, TAS	42.1 S	147.2 E
6	Australia	Cocos Islands	12.3 S	97.0 E
7	Australia	Warramunga, NT	19.9 S	134.3 E
8	Bolivia	La Paz	16.3 S	68.1 W
9	Brazil	Brasilia	15.6 S	48.0 W
10	Canada	Lac du Bonnet, Man.	50.2 N	95.9 W
11	Cape Verde	Cape Verde Islands	16.0 N	24.0 W
12	Central African Republic	Bangui	5.2 N	18.4 E
13	Chile	Easter Island	27.0 S	109.2 W
14	Chile Juan	Fernández Island	33.8 S	80.7 W
15	China	Beijing	40.0 N	116.0 E
16	China	Kunming	25.0 N	102.8 E
17	Côte d'Ivoire	Dimbokro	6.7 N	4.9 W
18	Denmark	Dundas, Greenland	76.5 N	68.7 W
19	Djibouti	Djibouti	11.3 N	43.5 E
20	Ecuador	Galápagos Islands	0.0 N	91.7 W

21 France	Marquesas Islands	10.0 S	140.0 W
22 France	Port LaGuerre, New Caledonia	22.1 S	166.3 E
23 France	Kerguelen	49.2 S	69.1 E
24 France	Tahiti	17.6 S	149.6 W
25 France	Kourou, French Guiana	5.2 N	52.7 W
26 Germany	Freyung	48.9 N	13.7 E
27 Germany	Georg von Neumayer, Antarctica	70.6 S	8.4 W
28 To be determined	To be determined	To be determined	To be determined
29 Iran (Islamic Republic of)	Tehran	35.7 N	51.4 E
30 Japan	Tsukuba	36.0 N	140.1 E
31 Kazakstan	Aktyubinsk	50.4 N	58.0 E
32 Kenya	Kilimanbogo	1.3 S	36.8 E
33 Madagascar	Antananarivo	18.8 S	47.5 E
34 Mongolia	Javhlant	48.0 N	106.8 E
35 Namibia	Tsumeb	19.1 S	17.4 E
36 New Zealand	Chatham Island	44.0 S	176.5 W
37 Norway	Karasjok	69.5 N	25.5 E
38 Pakistan	Rahimyar Khan	28.2 N	70.3 E
39 Palau	Palau	7.5 N	134.5 E
40 Papua New Guinea	Rabaul	4.1 S	152.1 E
41 Paraguay	Villa Florida	26.3 S	57.3 W
42 Portugal	Azores	37.8	N 25.5 W
43 Russian Federation	Dubna	56.7 N	37.3 E
44 Russian Federation	Petropavlovsk-Kamchatskiy	53.1 N	158.8 E
45 Russian Federation	Ussuriysk	43.7 N	131.9 E
46 Russian Federation	Zalesovo	53.9 N	84.8 E
47 South Africa	Boshof	28.6 S	25.4 E
48 Tunisia	Thala	35.6 N	8.7 E
49 United Kingdom	Tristan da Cunha	37.0 S	12.3 W
50 United Kingdom	Ascension	8.0 S	14.3 W
51 United Kingdom	Bermuda	32.0 N	64.5 W
52 United Kingdom	BIOT/Chagos Archipelago	5.0 S	72.0 E
53 United States of America	Eielson, AK	64.8 N	146.9 W
54 United States of America	Siple Station, Antarctica	75.5 S	83.6 W
55 United States of America	Windless Bight, Antarctica	77.5 S	161.8 E
56 United States of America	Newport, WA	48.3 N	117.1 W
57 United States of America	Piñon Flat, CA	33.6 N	116.5 W
58 United States of America	Midway Islands	28.1N	177.2 W
59 United States of America	Hawaii, HI	19.6 N	155.3 W
60 United States of America	Wake Island	19.3 N	166.6 E

ANNEX 2 TO THE PROTOCOL

List of Characterization Parameters for International Data Centre Standard Event Screening

1. The International Data Centre standard event screening criteria shall be based on the standard event characterization parameters determined during the combined processing of data from all the monitoring technologies in the International Monitoring System. Standard event screening shall make use of both global and supplementary screening criteria to take account of regional variations where applicable.

2. For events detected by the International Monitoring System seismic component, the following parameters, inter alia, may be used:

- location of the event;
- depth of the event;
- ratio of the magnitude of surface waves to body waves;
- signal frequency content;
- spectral ratios of phases;
- spectral scalloping;
- first motion of the P-wave;
- focal mechanism;
- relative excitation of seismic phases;
- comparative measures to other events and groups of events; and
- regional discriminants where applicable.

3. For events detected by the International Monitoring System hydroacoustic component, the following parameters, inter alia, may be used:

- signal frequency content including corner frequency, wide-band energy, and mean centre frequency and bandwidth;
- frequency-dependent duration of signals;
- spectral ratio; and

- indications of bubble-pulse signals and bubble-pulse delay.

4. For events detected by the International Monitoring System infrasound component, the following parameters, inter alia, may be used:

- signal frequency content and dispersion;
- signal duration; and
- peak amplitude.

5. For events detected by the International Monitoring System radionuclide component, the following parameters, inter alia, may be used:

- concentration of background natural and man-made radionuclides;
- concentration of specific fission and activation products outside normal observations; and
- ratios of one specific fission and activation product to another.

2

Treaty on the Prevention of the Placement of Weapons in Outer Space, the Threat or Use of Force against Outer Space Objects

12 February 2008

The States Parties to this Treaty,

Reaffirming that outer space plays an ever-increasing role in the future development of humankind,

Emphasizing the rights to explore and use outer space freely for peaceful purposes,

Interested in keeping outer space from turning into an arena for military confrontation, in assuring security in outer space and safe functioning of space objects,

Recognizing that prevention of the placement of weapons and of an arms race in outer space would avert a grave danger for international peace and security,

Designing to keep outer space as a sphere where no weapon of any kind is placed,

Noting that the existing agreements on arms control and disarmament relevant to outer space, including the bilateral ones, and the existing legal regimes concerning the use of outer space play a positive role in exploration of outer space and in regulating outer space activities, and should be strictly complied with; although they are unable to effectively prevent the placement of weapons and an arms race in outer space,

Recalling the resolution of the General Assembly of the United Nations "Prevention of an arms race in outer space", where, inter alia, a conviction was expressed in the need for examination of further measures in the search for effective and verifiable bilateral and multilateral agreements in order to prevent an arms race in outer space,

Have agreed on the following:

Article I

For the purpose of this Treaty:

(a) the term "outer space" means space beyond the elevation of 100 km above ocean level of the Earth;

(b) the term "outer space object" means any device, designed for functioning in outer space, being launched into an orbit around any celestial body, or being in the orbit around any celestial body, or on any celestial body except the Earth, or leaving the orbit around any celestial body towards this celestial body, or moving from any celestial body towards another celestial body, or placed in outer space by any other means;

(c) the term "weapons in outer space" means any device placed in outer space, based on any physical principle, specially produced or converted to eliminate, damage or disrupt normal function of objects in outer space, on the Earth or in its air, as well as to eliminate population, components of biosphere critical to human existence or inflict damage to them;

(d) a weapon will be considered as "placed" in outer space if it orbits the Earth at least once, or follows a section of such an orbit before leaving this orbit, or is stationed on a permanent basis somewhere in outer space;

(e) the "use of force" or "threat of force" mean any hostile actions against outer space objects including, inter alia, those aimed at their destruction, damage, temporarily or permanently injuring normal functioning, deliberate alteration of the parameters of their orbit, or the threat of these actions.

Article II

States Parties undertake not to place in orbit around the Earth any objects carrying any kind of weapons, not to install such weapons on celestial bodies, and not to station such weapons in outer space in any other manner; not to resort to the threat or use of force against outer space objects; not to assist or encourage other states, groups of states or international organizations to participate in activities prohibited by the Treaty.

Article III

Each State Party shall take all necessary measures to prevent any activity prohibited by the Treaty on its territory or in any other place under its jurisdiction or control.

Article IV

Nothing in this Treaty can be interpreted as impeding the rights of the States Parties to explore and use outer space for peaceful purposes in accordance with international law, which include but are not limited to the Charter of the United Nations and the Outer Space Treaty.

Article V

Nothing in this Treaty can be construed as impeding the realization by the States Parties of the sovereign right for self-defense in accordance with Article 51 of the Charter of the United Nations.

Article VI

With a view to facilitate assurance of compliance with the Treaty provisions and to promote transparency and confidence-building in outer space activities, the States Parties shall practice on a voluntary basis, unless agreed otherwise, agreed confidence-building measures.

Measures of verification of compliance with the Treaty may be the subject of an additional protocol.

Article VII

When a dispute arises between States Parties concerning the application or the interpretation of this Treaty, the parties concerned shall first consult together with a view to settling the dispute by negotiation and cooperation.

When the parties concerned do not come to an agreement after consultation, the disputed situation that has arisen may be referred to the Executive organization of the Treaty along with provision of the relevant argumentation.

Each State Party shall undertake to cooperate in the settlement of the disputed situation that has arisen with the Executive organization of the Treaty.

Article VIII

To promote the implementation of the objectives and the provisions of the Treaty, States Parties shall establish the Executive organization of the Treaty which shall:

(a) receive for consideration inquiries by any State Party or a group of States Parties related to the grounds that have arisen to believe that the violation of the Treaty by any State Party is taking place;

(b) consider matters concerning the compliance with the obligations taken by States Parties;

(c) organize and conduct consultations with the State Parties with the view to settle down the situation that has arisen in connection with the violation of a State Party of the Treaty;

(d) take measures to put an end to the violation of the Treaty by any State Party.

The title, status, specific functions and forms of work of the Executive organization of the Treaty shall be the subject of an additional protocol to the Treaty.

Article IX

International intergovernmental organizations may take part in the Treaty. Provisions defining variants and modalities of their participation in the Treaty shall be the subject of an additional protocol to the Treaty.

Article X

Any State Party may propose amendments to the Treaty. The text of any proposed amendment shall be submitted to the Depository who shall promptly circulate it to all States Parties. Upon the request of at least one third of the States Parties shall be invited to consider the proposed amendment.

Any amendment to the Treaty shall be approved by a majority of the votes of the States Parties. The amendment shall enter into force for all the States Parties in accordance with the procedures of the entry into force of the Treaty.

Article XI

The Treaty shall be of unlimited duration.

Each State Party shall in exercising its national sovereignty have the right to withdraw from the Treaty if it decides that extraordinary events, related to the subject matter of this Treaty, have jeopardized the supreme interests of its country. It shall notify the Depository in written form of the decision taken six months in advance of the withdrawal from the Treaty.

Article XII

The Treaty shall be opened for signature by all States at the United Nations headquarters in New York. Any State which did not sign the Treaty before its entry into force may accede to it at any time.

The Treaty shall be subject to ratification by signatory States in accordance with their constitutional norms. Instruments of ratification or accession shall be deposited with the Secretary-General of the United Nations, who is hereby designated the Depository of the Treaty.

Article XIII

The Treaty shall enter into force upon the deposit of instruments of ratification by twenty States, including all Permanent Member States of the United Nations Security Council.

For States whose instruments of ratification or accession are deposited after the entry into force of the Treaty, it shall enter into force on the date of the deposit of their instruments of ratification or accession.

Article XIV

The Treaty, of which the Arabic, Chinese, English, French, Russian and Spanish texts are equally authentic, shall be deposited with the Secretary-General of the United Nations, who shall send duly certified copies thereof to all signatory and acceding States.

3

Text of Strategic Offensive Reductions Treaty

24 May 2002

The United States of America and the Russian Federation, hereinafter referred to as the Parties,

Embarking upon the path of new relations for a new century and committed to the goal of strengthening their relationship through cooperation and friendship,

Believing that new global challenges and threats require the building of a qualitatively new foundation for strategic relations between the Parties,

Desiring to establish a genuine partnership based on the principles of mutual security, cooperation, trust, openness, and predictability,

Committed to implementing significant reductions in strategic offensive arms,

Proceeding from the Joint Statements by the President of the United States of America and the President of the Russian Federation on Strategic Issues of July 22, 2001 in Genoa and on a New Relationship between the United States and Russia of November 13, 2001 in Washington,

Mindful of their obligations under the Treaty Between the United States of America and the Union of Soviet Socialist

Republics on the Reduction and Limitation of Strategic Offensive Arms of July 31, 1991, hereinafter referred to as the START Treaty,

Mindful of their obligations under Article VI of the Treaty on the Non-Proliferation of Nuclear Weapons of July 1, 1968, and

Convinced that this Treaty will help to establish more favorable conditions for actively promoting security and cooperation, and enhancing international stability,

Have agreed as follows:

ARTICLE I

Each Party shall reduce and limit strategic nuclear warheads, as stated by the President of the United States of America on November 13, 2001 and as stated by the President of the Russian Federation on November 13, 2001 and December 13, 2001 respectively, so that by December 31, 2012 the aggregate number of such warheads does not exceed 1700-2200 for each Party. Each Party shall determine for itself the composition and structure of its strategic offensive arms, based on the established aggregate limit for the number of such warheads.

ARTICLE II

The Parties agree that the START Treaty remains in force in accordance with its terms.

ARTICLE III

For purposes of implementing this Treaty, the Parties shall hold meetings at least twice a year of a Bilateral Implementation Commission.

ARTICLE IV

1. This Treaty shall be subject to ratification in accordance with the constitutional procedures of each Party. This Treaty shall enter into force on the date of the exchange of instruments of ratification.

2. This Treaty shall remain in force until December 31, 2012 and may be extended by agreement of the Parties or superseded earlier by a subsequent agreement.

3. Each Party, in exercising its national sovereignty, may withdraw from this Treaty upon three months written notice to the other Party.

ARTICLE V

This Treaty shall be registered pursuant to Article 102 of the Charter of the United Nations.

Done at Moscow on May 24, 2002, in two copies, each in the English and Russian languages, both texts being equally authentic.

FOR THE UNITED STATES OF AMERICA:

FOR THE RUSSIAN FEDERATION:

4

Chemical Weapons Convention (CWC)

Preamble

The States Parties to this Convention,

Determined to act with a view to achieving effective progress towards general and complete disarmament under strict and effective international control, including the prohibition and elimination of all types of weapons of mass destruction,

Desiring to contribute to the realization of the purposes and principles of the Charter of the United Nations,

Recalling that the General Assembly of the United Nations has repeatedly condemned all actions contrary to the principles and objectives of the Protocol for the Prohibition of the Use in War of Asphyxiating, Poisonous or Other Gases, and of Bacteriological Methods of Warfare, signed at Geneva on 17 June 1925 (the Geneva Protocol of 1925),

Recognizing that this Convention reaffirms principles and objectives of and obligations assumed under the Geneva Protocol of 1925, and the Convention on the Prohibition of the Development, Production and Stockpiling of Bacteriological (Biological) and Toxin Weapons and on their Destruction signed at London, Moscow and Washington on 10 April 1972,

Bearing in mind the objective contained in Article IX of the Convention on the Prohibition of the Development, Production and Stockpiling of Bacteriological (Biological) and Toxin Weapons and on their Destruction,

Determined for the sake of all mankind, to exclude completely the possibility of the use of chemical weapons, through the implementation of the provisions of this Convention, thereby complementing the obligations assumed under the Geneva Protocol of 1925,

Recognizing the prohibition, embodied in the pertinent agreements and relevant principles of international law, of the use of herbicides as a method of warfare,

Considering that achievements in the field of chemistry should be used exclusively for the benefit of mankind,

Desiring to promote free trade in chemicals as well as international cooperation and exchange of scientific and technical information in the field of chemical activities for purposes not prohibited under this Convention in order to enhance the economic and technological development of all States Parties,

Convinced that the complete and effective prohibition of the development, production, acquisition, stockpiling, retention, transfer and use of chemical weapons, and their destruction, represent a necessary step towards the achievement of these common objectives,

Have agreed as follows:

ARTICLE I: GENERAL OBLIGATIONS

1. Each State Party to this Convention undertakes never under any circumstances:

(a) To develop, produce, otherwise acquire, stockpile or retain chemical weapons, or transfer, directly or indirectly, chemical weapons to anyone;

(b) To use chemical weapons;

(c) To engage in any military preparations to use chemical weapons;

(d) To assist, encourage or induce, in any way, anyone to engage in any activity prohibited to a State Party under this Convention.

2. Each State Party undertakes to destroy chemical weapons it owns or possesses, or that are located in any place under its jurisdiction or control, in accordance with the provisions of this Convention.

3. Each State Party undertakes to destroy all chemical weapons it abandoned on the territory of another State Party, in accordance with the provisions of this Convention.

4. Each State Party undertakes to destroy any chemical weapons production facilities it owns or possesses, or that are located in any place under its jurisdiction or control, in accordance with the provisions of this Convention.

5. Each State Party undertakes not to use riot control agents as a method of warfare.

ARTICLE II: DEFINITIONS AND CRITERIA

For the purposes of this Convention:

1. "Chemical Weapons" means the following, together or separately:

(a) Toxic chemicals and their precursors, except where intended for purposes not prohibited under this Convention, as long as the types and quantities are consistent with such purposes;

(b) Munitions and devices, specifically designed to cause death or other harm through the toxic properties of those toxic chemicals specified in subparagraph (a), which would be released as a result of the employment of such munitions and devices;

(c) Any equipment specifically designed for use directly in connection with the employment of munitions and devices specified in subparagraph (b).

2. "Toxic Chemical" means:

Any chemical which through its chemical action on life processes can cause death, temporary incapacitation or permanent harm to humans or animals. This includes all such chemicals, regardless of their origin or of their method of production, and regardless of whether they are produced in facilities, in munitions or elsewhere.

(For the purpose of implementing this Convention, toxic chemicals which have been identified for the application of verification measures are listed in Schedules contained in the Annex on Chemicals.)

3. "Precursor" means:

Any chemical reactant which takes part at any stage in the production by whatever method of a toxic chemical. This includes any key component of a binary or multicomponent chemical system.

(For the purpose of implementing this Convention, precursors which have been identified for the application of verification measures are listed in Schedules contained in the Annex on Chemicals.)

4. "Key Component of Binary or Multicomponent Chemical Systems" (hereinafter referred to as "key component") means:

The precursor which plays the most important role in determining the toxic properties of the final product and reacts rapidly with other chemicals in the binary or multicomponent system.

5. "Old Chemical Weapons" means:

(a) Chemical weapons which were produced before 1925; or

(b) Chemical weapons produced in the period between 1925 and 1946 that have deteriorated to such extent that they can no longer be used as chemical weapons.

6. "Abandoned Chemical Weapons" means:

Chemical weapons, including old chemical weapons, abandoned by a State after 1 January 1925 on the territory of another State without the consent of the latter.

7. "Riot Control Agent" means:

Any chemical not listed in a Schedule, which can produce rapidly in humans sensory irritation or disabling physical effects which disappear within a short time following termination of exposure.

8. "Chemical Weapons Production Facility":

(a) Means any equipment, as well as any building housing such equipment, that was designed, constructed or used at any time since 1 January 1946:

(i) As part of the stage in the production of chemicals ("final technological stage") where the material flows would contain, when the equipment is in operation:

(1) Any chemical listed in Schedule 1 in the Annex on Chemicals; or

(2) Any other chemical that has no use, above 1 tonne per year on the territory of a State Party or in any other place under the jurisdiction or control of a State Party, for purposes not prohibited under this Convention, but can be used for chemical weapons purposes;

or

(ii) For filling chemical weapons, including, inter alia, the filling of chemicals listed in Schedule 1 into munitions, devices or bulk storage containers the filling of chemicals into Containers that form part of assembled binary munitions and devices or into chemical submunitions that form part of assembled unitary munitions and devices, and the loading of the containers and chemical submunitions into the respective munitions and devices;

(b) Does not mean:

(i) Any facility having a production capacity for synthesis of chemicals specified in subparagraph (a) (i) that is less than 1 tonne;

(ii) Any facility in which a chemical specified in subparagraph (a) (i) is or was produced as an unavoidable byproduct of activities for purposes not prohibited under this Convention, provided that the chemical does not exceed 3 per cent of the total product and that the facility is subject to declaration and inspection under the Annex on Implementation and Verification (hereinafter referred to as "Verification Annex"); or

(iii) The single smallscale facility for production of chemicals listed in Schedule 1 for purposes not prohibited under this Convention as referred to in Part VI of the Verification Annex.

9. "Purposes Not Prohibited Under this Convention" means:

(a) Industrial, agricultural, research, medical, pharmaceutical or other peaceful purposes:

(b) Protective purposes, namely those purposes directly related to protection against toxic chemicals and to protection against chemical weapons;

(c) Military purposes not connected with the use of chemical weapons and not dependent on the use of the toxic properties of chemicals as a method of warfare;

(d) Law enforcement including domestic riot control purposes.

10. "Production Capacity" means:

The annual quantitative potential for manufacturing a specific chemical based on the technological process actually used or, if the process is not yet operational, planned to be used at the relevant facility. It shall be deemed to be equal to the nameplate capacity or, if the nameplate capacity is not available, to the design capacity. The nameplate capacity is the product output under conditions optimized for maximum quantity for the production facility, as demonstrated by one or more testruns. The design capacity is the corresponding theoretically calculated product output.

11. "Organization" means the Organization for the Prohibition of Chemical Weapons established pursuant to Article VIII of this Convention.

12. For the purposes of Article VI:

(a) "Production" of a chemical means its formation through chemical reaction;

(b) "Processing" of a chemical means a physical process, such as formulation, extraction and purification, in which a chemical is not converted into another chemical;

(c) "Consumption" of a chemical means its conversion into another chemical via a chemical reaction.

ARTICLE III: DECLARATIONS

1. Each State Party shall submit to the Organization, not later than 30 days after this Convention enters into force for it, the following declarations, in which it shall:

(a) With respect to chemical weapons:

(i) Declare whether it owns or possesses any chemical weapons, or whether there are any chemical weapons located in any place under its jurisdiction or control;

(ii) Specify the precise location, aggregate quantity and detailed inventory of chemical weapons it owns or possesses, or that are located in any place under its jurisdiction or control, in accordance with Part IV (A), paragraphs 1 to 3, of the Verification Annex, except for those chemical weapons referred to in sub-paragraph (iii);

(iii) Report any chemical weapons on its territory that are owned and possessed by another State and located in any place under the jurisdiction or control of another State, in accordance with Part IV (A), paragraph 4, of the Verification Annex;

(iv) Declare whether it has transferred or received, directly or indirectly, any chemical weapons since 1 January 1946 and specify the transfer or receipt of such weapons, in accordance with Part IV (A), paragraph 5, of the Verification Annex:

(v) Provide its general plan for destruction of chemical weapons that it owns or possesses, or that are located in any place under its jurisdiction or control, in accordance with Part IV (A), paragraph 6, of the Verification Annex;

(b) With respect to old chemical weapons and abandoned chemical weapons:

(i) Declare whether it has on its territory old chemical weapons and provide all available information in accordance with Part IV (B), paragraph 3, of the Verification Annex;

(ii) Declare whether there are abandoned chemical weapons on its territory and provide all available information in accordance with Part IV (B), paragraph 8, of the Verification Annex;

(iii) Declare whether it has abandoned chemical weapons on the territory of other States and provide all available information in accordance with Part IV (B), paragraph 10, of the Verification Annex;

(c) With respect to chemical weapons production facilities:

(i) Declare whether it has or has had any chemical weapons production facility under its ownership or possession, or that is or has been located in any place under its jurisdiction or control at any time since 1 January 1946;

(ii) Specify any chemical weapons production facility it has or has had under its ownership or possession or that is or has been located in any place under its jurisdiction or control at any time since 1 January 1946, in accordance with Part V, paragraph 1, of the Verification Annex, except for those facilities referred to in sub-paragraph (iii);

(iii) Report any chemical weapons production facility on its territory that another State has or has had under its ownership and possession and that is or has been located in any place under the jurisdiction or control of another State at any time since 1 January 1946, in accordance with Part V, paragraph 2, of the Verification Annex;

(iv) Declare whether it has transferred or received, directly or indirectly, any equipment for the production of chemical weapons since 1 January 1946 and specify the transfer or receipt of such equipment, in accordance with Part V, paragraphs 3 to 5, of the Verification Annex;

(v) Provide its general plan for destruction of any chemical weapons production facility it owns or possesses, or that is located in any place under its jurisdiction or control, in accordance with Part V, paragraph 6, of the Verification Annex;

(vi) Specify actions to be taken for closure of any chemical weapons production facility it owns or possesses, or that is located in any place under its jurisdiction or control, in accordance with Part V, paragraph 1 (i), of the Verification Annex;

(vii) Provide its general plan for any temporary conversion of any chemical weapons production facility it owns or possesses, or that is located in any place under its jurisdiction or control, into a chemical weapons destruction facility, in accordance with Part V, paragraph 7, of the Verification Annex;

(d) With respect to other facilities:

Specify the precise location, nature and general scope of activities of any facility or establishment under its ownership or possession, or located in any place under its jurisdiction or control, and that has been designed, constructed or used since 1 January 1946 primarily for development of chemical weapons. Such declaration shall include, inter alia, laboratories and test and evaluation sites;

(e) With respect to riot control agents:

Specify the chemical name, structural formula and Chemical Abstracts Service (CAS) registry number, if assigned, of each chemical it holds for riot control purposes. This declaration shall be updated not later than 30 days after any change becomes effective.

2. The provisions of this Article and the relevant provisions of Part IV of the Verification Annex shall not, at the discretion of a State Party, apply to chemical weapons buried on its territory before 1 January 1977 and which remain buried, or which had been dumped at sea before 1 January 1985.

ARTICLE IV: CHEMICAL WEAPONS

1. The provisions of this Article and the detailed procedures for its implementation shall apply to all chemical weapons owned or possessed by a State Party, or that are located in any place under its jurisdiction or control, except old chemical weapons and abandoned chemical weapons to which Part IV (B) of the Verification Annex applies.

2. Detailed procedures for the implementation of this Article are set forth in the Verification Annex.

3. All locations at which chemical weapons specified in paragraph 1 are stored or destroyed shall be subject to systematic verification through onsite inspection and monitoring with onsite instruments, in accordance with Part IV (A) of the Verification Annex.

4. Each State Party shall, immediately after the declaration under Article III, paragraph 1, has been submitted, provide access to chemical weapons specified in paragraph 1 for the purpose of systematic verification of the declaration through onsite inspection. Thereafter, each State Party shall not remove any of these chemical weapons, except to a chemical weapons destruction facility. It shall provide access to such chemical weapons, for the purpose of systematic onsite verification.

5. Each State Party shall provide access to any chemical weapons destruction facilities and their storage areas, that it owns or possesses, or that are located in any place under its jurisdiction or control, for the purpose of systematic verification through onsite inspection and monitoring with onsite instruments.

6. Each State Party shall destroy all chemical weapons specified in paragraph 1 pursuant to the Verification Annex and in accordance with the agreed rate and sequence of destruction (hereinafter referred to as "order of destruction"). Such destruction shall begin not later than two years after this Convention enters into force for it and shall finish not later than 10 years after entry into force of this Convention. A State Party is not precluded from destroying such chemical weapons at a faster rate.

7. Each State Party shall:

(a) Submit detailed plans for the destruction of chemical weapons specified in paragraph 1 not later than 60 days before each annual destruction period begins, in accordance with Part IV (A), paragraph 29, of the Verification Annex; the detailed plans shall encompass all stocks to be destroyed during the next annual destruction period:

(b) Submit declarations annually regarding the implementation of its plans for destruction of chemical weapons specified in paragraph 1, not later than 60 days after the end of each annual destruction period; and

(c) Certify, not later than 30 days after the destruction process has been completed, that all chemical weapons specified in paragraph 1 have been destroyed.

8. If a State ratifies or accedes to this Convention after the 10 year period for destruction set forth in paragraph 6, it shall destroy chemical weapons specified in paragraph 1 as soon as possible. The order of destruction and procedures for stringent verification for such a State Party shall be determined by the Executive Council.

9. Any chemical weapons discovered by a State Party after the initial declaration of chemical weapons shall be reported, secured and destroyed in accordance with Part IV (A) of the Verification Annex.

10. Each State Party, during transportation, sampling, storage and destruction of chemical weapons, shall assign the highest priority to ensuring the safety of people and to protecting the environment. Each State Party shall transport, sample, store and destroy chemical weapons in accordance with its national standards for safety and emissions.

11. Any State Party which has on its territory chemical weapons that are owned or possessed by another State, or that are located in any place under the jurisdiction or control of another State, shall make the fullest efforts to ensure that these

chemical weapons are removed from its territory not later than one year after this Convention enters into force for it. If they are not removed within one year, the State Party may request the Organization and other States Parties to provide assistance in the destruction of these chemical weapons.

12. Each State Party undertakes to cooperate with other States Parties that request information or assistance on a bilateral basis or through the Technical Secretariat regarding methods and technologies for the safe and efficient destruction of chemical weapons.

13. In carrying out verification activities pursuant to this Article and Part IV (A) of the Verification Annex, the Organization shall consider measures to avoid unnecessary duplication of bilateral or multilateral agreements on verification of chemical weapons storage and their destruction among States Parties.

To this end, the Executive Council shall decide to limit verification to measures complementary to those undertaken pursuant to such a bilateral or multilateral agreement, if it considers that:

(a) Verification provisions of such an agreement are consistent with the verification provisions of this Article and Part IV (A) of the Verification Annex;

(b) Implementation of such an agreement provides for sufficient assurance of compliance with the relevant provisions of this Convention; and

(c) Parties to the bilateral or multilateral agreement keep the Organization fully informed about their verification activities.

14. If the Executive Council takes a decision pursuant to paragraph 13, the Organization shall have the right to monitor the implementation of the bilateral or multilateral agreement.

15. Nothing in paragraphs 13 and 14 shall affect the obligation of a State Party to provide declarations pursuant to Article III, this Article and Part IV (A) of the Verification Annex.

16. Each State Party shall meet the costs of destruction of chemical weapons it is obliged to destroy. It shall also meet the

costs of verification of storage and destruction of these chemical weapons unless the Executive Council decides otherwise. If the Executive Council decides to limit verification measures of the Organization pursuant to paragraph 13, the costs of complementary verification and monitoring by the Organization shall be paid in accordance with the United Nations scale of assessment, as specified in Article VIII, paragraph 7.

17. The provisions of this Article and the relevant provisions of Part IV of the Verification Annex shall not, at the discretion of a State Party, apply to chemical weapons buried on its territory before 1 January 1977 and which remain buried, or which had been dumped at sea before 1 January 1985.

ARTICLE V: CHEMICAL WEAPONS PRODUCTION FACILITIES

1. The provisions of this Article and the detailed procedures for its implementation shall apply to any and all chemical weapons production facilities owned or possessed by a State Party, or that are located in any place under its jurisdiction or control.

2. Detailed procedures for the implementation of this Article are set forth in the Verification Annex.

3. All chemical weapons production facilities specified in paragraph 1 shall be subject to systematic verification through onsite inspection and monitoring with onsite instruments in accordance with Part V of the Verification Annex.

4. Each State Party shall cease immediately all activity at chemical weapons production facilities specified in paragraph 1, except activity required for closure.

5. No State Party shall construct any new chemical weapons production facilities or modify any existing facilities for the purpose of chemical weapons production or for any other activity prohibited under this Convention.

6. Each State Party shall, immediately after the declaration under Article III, paragraph 1 (c), has been submitted, provide access to chemical weapons production facilities specified in paragraph 1, for the purpose of systematic verification of the declaration through onsite inspection.

7. Each State Party shall:

(a) Close, not later than 90 days after this Convention enters into force for it, all chemical weapons production facilities specified in paragraph 1, in accordance with Part V of the Verification Annex, and give notice thereof; and

(b) Provide access to chemical weapons production facilities specified in paragraph 1, subsequent to closure, for the purpose of systematic verification through onsite inspection and monitoring with onsite instruments in order to ensure that the facility remains closed and is subsequently destroyed.

8. Each State Party shall destroy all chemical weapons production facilities specified in paragraph 1 and related facilities and equipment, pursuant to the Verification Annex and in accordance with an agreed rate and sequence of destruction (hereinafter referred to as "order of destruction"). Such destruction shall begin not later than one year after this Convention enters into force for it, and shall finish not later than 10 years after entry into force of this Convention. A State Party is not precluded from destroying such facilities at a faster rate.

9. Each State Party shall:

(a) Submit detailed plans for destruction of chemical weapons production facilities specified in paragraph 1, not later than 180 days before the destruction of each facility begins;

(b) Submit declarations annually regarding the implementation of its plans for the destruction of all chemical weapons production facilities specified in paragraph 1, not later than 90 days after the end of each annual destruction period; and

(c) Certify, not later than 30 days after the destruction process has been completed, that all chemical weapons production facilities specified in paragraph 1 have been destroyed.

10. If a State ratifies or accedes to this Convention after the 10-year period for destruction set forth in paragraph 8, it shall

destroy chemical weapons production facilities specified in paragraph 1 as soon as possible. The order of destruction and procedures for stringent verification for such a State Party shall be determined by the Executive Council.

11. Each State Party, during the destruction of chemical weapons production facilities, shall assign the highest priority to ensuring the safety of people and to protecting the environment. Each State Party shall destroy these chemical weapons production facilities in accordance with its national standards for safety and emissions.

12. Chemical weapons production facilities specified in paragraph 1 may be temporarily converted for destruction of chemical weapons in accordance with Part V, paragraphs 18 to 25, of the Verification Annex. Such a converted facility must be destroyed as soon as it is no longer in use for destruction of chemical weapons but, in any case, not later than 10 years after entry into force of this Convention.

13. A State Party may request, in exceptional cases of compelling need, permission to use a chemical weapons production facility specified in paragraph 1 for purposes not prohibited under this Convention. Upon the recommendation of the Executive Council, the Conference of the States Parties shall decide whether or not to approve the request and shall establish the conditions upon which approval is contingent in accordance with Part V, Section D, of the Verification Annex.

14. The chemical weapons production facility shall be converted in such a manner that the converted facility is not more capable of being reconverted into a chemical weapons production facility than any other facility used for industrial, agricultural, research, medical, pharmaceutical or other peaceful purposes not involving chemicals listed in Schedule 1.

15. All converted facilities shall be subject to systematic verification through onsite inspection and monitoring with on site instruments in accordance with Part V, Section D, of the Verification Annex.

16. In carrying out verification activities pursuant to this Article and Part V of the Verification Annex, the Organization

shall consider measures to avoid unnecessary duplication of bilateral or multilateral agreements on verification of chemical weapons production facilities and their destruction among States Parties.

To this end, the Executive Council shall decide to limit the verification to measures complementary to those undertaken pursuant to such a bilateral or multilateral agreement, if it considers that:

(a) Verification provisions of such an agreement are consistent with the verification provisions of this Article and Part V of the Verification Annex;

(b) Implementation of the agreement provides for sufficient assurance of compliance with the relevant provisions of this Convention; and

(c) Parties to the bilateral or multilateral agreement keep the Organization fully informed about their verification activities.

17. If the Executive Council takes a decision pursuant to paragraph 16, the Organization shall have the right to monitor the implementation of the bilateral or multilateral agreement.

18. Nothing in paragraphs 16 and 17 shall affect the obligation of a State Party to make declarations pursuant to Article III, this Article and Part V of the Verification Annex.

19. Each State Party shall meet the costs of destruction of chemical weapons production facilities it is obliged to destroy. It shall also meet the costs of verification under this Article unless the Executive Council decides otherwise. If the Executive Council decides to limit verification measures of the Organization pursuant to paragraph 16, the costs of complementary verification and monitoring by the Organization shall be paid in accordance with the United Nations scale of assessment, as specified in Article VIII, paragraph 7.

ARTICLE VI: ACTIVITIES NOT PROHIBITED UNDER THIS CONVENTION

1. Each State Party has the right, subject to the provisions of this Convention, to develop, produce, otherwise acquire, retain,

transfer and use toxic chemicals and their precursors for purposes not prohibited under this Convention.

2. Each State Party shall adopt the necessary measures to ensure that toxic chemicals and their precursors are only developed, produced, otherwise acquired, retained, transferred, or used within its territory or in any other place under its jurisdiction or control for purposes not prohibited under this Convention. To this end, and in order to verify that activities are in accordance with obligations under this Convention, each State Party shall subject toxic chemicals and their precursors listed in Schedules 1, 2 and 3 of the Annex on Chemicals, facilities related to such chemicals, and other facilities as specified in the Verification Annex, that are located on its territory or in any other place under its jurisdiction or control, to verification measures as provided in the Verification Annex.

3. Each State Party shall subject chemicals listed in Schedule 1 (hereinafter referred to as "Schedule 1 chemicals") to the prohibitions on production, acquisition, retention, transfer and use as specified in Part VI of the Verification Annex. It shall subject Schedule 1 chemicals and facilities specified in Part VI of the Verification Annex to systematic verification through onsite inspection and monitoring with onsite instruments in accordance with that Part of the Verification Annex.

4. Each State Party shall subject chemicals listed in Schedule 2 (hereinafter referred to as "Schedule 2 chemicals") and facilities specified in Part VII of the Verification Annex to data monitoring and onsite verification in accordance with that Part of the Verification Annex.

5. Each State Party shall subject chemicals listed in Schedule 3 (hereinafter referred to as "Schedule 3 chemicals") and facilities specified in Part VIII of the Verification Annex to data monitoring and onsite verification in accordance with that Part of the Verification Annex.

6. Each State Party shall subject facilities specified in Part IX of the Verification Annex to data monitoring and eventual onsite verification in accordance with that Part of the Verification Annex unless decided otherwise by the Conference of the States

Parties pursuant to Part IX, paragraph 22, of the Verification Annex.

7. Not later than 30 days after this Convention enters into force for it, each State Party shall make an initial declaration on relevant chemicals and facilities in accordance with the Verification Annex.

8. Each State Party shall make annual declarations regarding the relevant chemicals and facilities in accordance with the Verification Annex.

9. For the purpose of onsite verification, each State Party shall grant to the inspectors access to facilities as required in the Verification Annex.

10. In conducting verification activities, the Technical Secretariat shall avoid undue intrusion into the State Party's chemical activities for purposes not prohibited under this Convention and, in particular, abide by the provisions set forth in the Annex on the Protection of Confidential Information (hereinafter referred to as "Confidentiality Annex").

11. The provisions of this Article shall be implemented in a manner which avoids hampering the economic or technological development of States Parties and international cooperation in the field of chemical activities for purposes not prohibited under this Convention, including the international exchange of scientific and technical information and chemicals and equipment for the production, processing or use of chemicals for purposes not prohibited under this Convention.

ARTICLE VII: NATIONAL IMPLEMENTATION MEASURES

General undertakings

1. Each State Party shall, in accordance with its constitutional processes, adopt the necessary measures to implement its obligations under this Convention. In particular, it shall:

(a) Prohibit natural and legal persons anywhere on its territory or in any other place under its jurisdiction as recognized by international law from undertaking any activity prohibited to a State Party under this

Convention, including enacting penal legislation with respect to such activity;

(b) Not permit in any place under its control any activity prohibited to a State Party under this Convention; and

(c) Extend its penal legislation enacted under subparagraph (a) to any activity prohibited to a State Party under this Convention undertaken anywhere by natural persons, possessing its nationality, in conformity with international law.

2. Each State Party shall cooperate with other States Parties and afford the appropriate form of legal assistance to facilitate the implementation of the obligations under paragraph 1.

3. Each State Party, during the implementation of its obligations under this Convention, shall assign the highest priority to ensuring the safety of people and to protecting the environment, and shall cooperate as appropriate with other States Parties in this regard.

Relations between the State Party and the Organization

4. In order to fulfill its obligations under this Convention, each State Party shall designate or establish a National Authority to serve as the national focal point for effective liaison with the Organization and other States Parties. Each State Party shall notify the Organization of its National Authority at the time that this Convention enters into force for it.

5. Each State Party shall inform the Organization of the legislative and administrative measures taken to implement this Convention.

6. Each State Party shall treat as confidential and afford special handling to information and data that it receives in confidence from the Organization in connection with the implementation of this Convention. It shall treat such information and data exclusively in connection with its rights and obligations under this Convention and in accordance with the provisions set forth in the Confidentiality Annex.

7. Each State Party undertakes to cooperate with the Organization in the exercise of all its functions and in particular to provide assistance to the Technical Secretariat.

ARTICLE VIII: THE ORGANIZATION

A. General Provisions

1. The States Parties to this Convention hereby establish the Organization for the Prohibition of Chemical Weapons to achieve the object and purpose of this Convention, to ensure the implementation of its provisions, including those for international verification of compliance with it, and to provide a forum for consultation and cooperation among States Parties.

2. All States Parties to this Convention shall be members of the Organization. A State Party shall not be deprived of its membership in the Organization.

3. The seat of the Headquarters of the Organization shall be The Hague, Kingdom of the Netherlands.

4. There are hereby established as the organs of the Organization: the Conference of the States Parties, the Executive Council, and the Technical Secretariat.

5. The Organization shall conduct its verification activities provided for under this Convention in the least intrusive manner possible consistent with the timely and efficient accomplishment of their objectives. It shall request only the information and data necessary to fulfill its responsibilities under this Convention. It shall take every precaution to protect the confidentiality of information on civil and military activities and facilities coming to its knowledge in the implementation of this Convention and, in particular, shall abide by the provisions set forth in the Confidentiality Annex.

6. In undertaking its verification activities the Organization shall consider measures to make use of advances in science and technology.

7. The costs of the Organization's activities shall be paid by States Parties in accordance with the United Nations scale of assessment adjusted to take into account differences in membership between the United Nations and this Organization, and subject to the provisions of Articles IV and V. Financial contributions of States Parties to the Preparatory Commission shall be deducted in an appropriate way from their contributions

to the regular budget. The budget of the Organization shall comprise two separate chapters, one relating to administrative and other costs, and one relating to verification costs.

8. A member of the Organization which is in arrears in the payment of its financial contribution to the Organization shall have no vote in the Organization if the amount of its arrears equals or exceeds the amount of the contribution due from it for the preceding two full years. The Conference of States Parties may, nevertheless, permit such a member to vote if it is satisfied that the failure to pay is due to conditions beyond the control of the member.

B. The Conference of the States Parties

Composition, procedures and decision-making

9. The Conference of the States Parties (hereinafter referred to as "the Conference") shall be composed of all members of this Organization. Each member shall have one representative in the Conference, who may be accompanied by alternates and advisers.

10. The first session of the Conference shall be convened by the depositary not later than 30 days after the entry into force of this Convention.

11. The Conference shall meet in regular sessions which shall be held annually unless it decides otherwise.

12. Special sessions of the Conference shall be convened:

(a) When decided by the Conference;

(b) When requested by the Executive Council;

(c) When requested by any member and supported by one third of the members; or

(d) In accordance with paragraph 22 to undertake reviews of the operation of this Convention.

Except in the case of subparagraph (d), the special session shall be convened not later than 30 days after receipt of the request by the Director-General of the Technical Secretariat, unless specified otherwise in the request.

13. The Conference shall also be convened in the form of an Amendment Conference in accordance with Article XV, paragraph 2.

14. Sessions of the Conference shall take place at the seat of the Organization unless the Conference decides otherwise.

15. The Conference shall adopt its rules of procedure. At the beginning of each regular session, it shall elect its Chairman and such other officers as may be required. They shall hold office until a new Chairman and other officers are elected at the next regular session.

16. A majority of the members of the Organization shall constitute a quorum for the Conference.

17. Each member of the Organization shall have one vote in the Conference.

18. The Conference shall take decisions on questions of procedure by a simple majority of the members present and voting. Decisions on matters of substance should be taken as far as possible by consensus. If consensus is not attainable when an issue comes up for decision, the Chairman shall defer any vote for 24 hours and during this period of deferment shall make every effort to facilitate achievement of consensus, and shall report to the Conference before the end of this period. If consensus is not possible at the end of 24 hours, the Conference shall take the decision by a two-thirds majority of members present and voting unless specified otherwise in this Convention. When the issue arises as to whether the question is one of substance or not, that question shall be treated as a matter of substance unless otherwise decided by the Conference by the majority required for decisions on matters of substance.

Powers and Functions

19. The Conference shall be the principal organ of the Organization. It shall consider any questions, matters or issues within the scope of this Convention, including those relating to the powers and functions of the Executive Council and the Technical Secretariat. It may make recommendations and take decisions on any questions, matters or issues related to this Convention raised by a State Party or brought to its attention by the Executive Council.

20. The Conference shall oversee the implementation of this Convention, and act in order to promote its object and purpose.

The Conference shall review compliance with this Convention. It shall also oversee the activities of the Executive Council and the Technical Secretariat and may issue guidelines in accordance with this Convention to either of them in the exercise of their functions.

The Conference shall:

(a) Consider and adopt at its regular sessions the report, programme and budget of the Organization, submitted by the Executive Council, as well as consider other reports;

(b) Decide on the scale of financial contributions to be paid by States Parties in accordance with paragraph 7;

(c) Elect the members of the Executive Council;

(d) Appoint the Director-General of the Technical Secretariat (hereinafter referred to as "the Director-General");

(e) Approve the rules of procedure of the Executive Council submitted by the latter;

(f) Establish such subsidiary organs as it finds necessary for the exercise of its functions in accordance with this Convention;

(g) Foster international cooperation for peaceful purposes in the field of chemical activities;

(h) Review scientific and technological developments that could affect the operation of this Convention and, in this context, direct the Director-General to establish a Scientific Advisory Board to enable him, in the performance of his functions, to render specialized advice in areas of science and technology relevant to this Convention, to the Conference, the Executive Council or States Parties. The Scientific Advisory Board shall be composed of independent experts appointed in accordance with terms of reference adopted by the Conference;

(i) Consider and approve at its first session any draft agreements, provisions and guidelines developed by the Preparatory Commission;

(j) Establish at its first session the voluntary fund for assistance in accordance with Article X;

(k) Take the necessary measures to ensure compliance with this Convention and to redress and remedy any situation which contravenes the provisions of this Convention, in accordance with Article XII.

22. The Conference shall not later than one year after the expiry of the fifth and the tenth year after the entry into force of this Convention, and at such other times within that time period as may be decided upon, convene in special sessions to undertake reviews of the operation of this Convention. Such reviews shall take into account any relevant scientific and technological developments. At intervals of five years thereafter, unless otherwise decided upon, further sessions of the Conference shall be convened with the same objective.

C. The Executive Council

Composition, procedure and decision-making

23. The Executive Council shall consist of 41 members. Each State Party shall have the right, in accordance with the principle of rotation, to serve on the Executive Council. The members of the Executive Council shall be elected by the Conference for a term of two years. In order to ensure the effective functioning of this Convention, due regard being specially paid to equitable geographical distribution, to the importance of chemical industry, as well as to political and security interests, the Executive Council shall be composed as follows:

(a) Nine States Parties from Africa to be designated by States Parties located in this region. As a basis for this designation it is understood that, out of these nine States Parties, three members shall, as a rule, be the States Parties with the most significant national chemical industry in the region as determined by internationally reported and published data; in addition, the regional group shall agree also to take into account other regional factors in designating these three members;

(b) Nine States Parties from Asia to be designated by States Parties located in this region. As a basis for this designation it is understood that, out of these nine States Parties, four members shall, as a rule, be the States Parties with the most significant national chemical industry in the region as determined by internationally reported and published data: in addition, the regional group shall agree also to take into account other regional factors in designating these four members;

(c) Five States Parties from Eastern Europe to be designated by States Parties located in this region. As a basis for this designation it is understood that, out of these five States Parties, one member shall, as a rule, be the State Party with the most significant national chemical industry in the region as determined by internationally reported and published data; in addition, the regional group shall agree also to take into account other regional factors in designating this one member;

(d) Seven States Parties from Latin America and the Caribbean to be designated by States Parties located in this region. As a basis for this designation it is understood that, out of these seven States Parties, three members shall, as a rule, be the States Parties with the most significant national chemical industry in the region as determined by internationally reported and published data; in addition, the regional group shall agree also to take into account other regional factors in designating these three members;

(e) Ten States Parties from among Western European and Other States to be designated by States Parties located in this region. As a basis for this designation it is understood that, out of these ten States Parties, five members shall, as a rule, be the States Parties with the most significant national chemical industry in the region as determined by internationally reported and published data; in addition, the regional group shall agree also to take into account other regional factors in designating these five members;

(f) One further State Party to be designated consecutively by States Parties located in the regions of Asia and

Latin America and the Caribbean. As a basis for this designation it is understood that this State Party shall be a rotating member from these regions.

24. For the first election of the Executive Council 20 members shall be elected for a term of one year, due regard being paid to the established numerical proportions as described in paragraph 23.

25. After the full implementation of Articles IV and V the Conference may, upon the request of a majority of the members of the Executive Council, review the composition of the Executive Council taking into account developments related to the principles specified in paragraph 23 that are governing its composition.

26. The Executive Council shall elaborate its rules of procedure and submit them to the Conference for approval.

27. The Executive Council shall elect its Chairman from among its members.

28. The Executive Council shall meet for regular sessions. Between regular sessions it shall meet as often as may be required for the fulfillment of its powers and functions.

29. Each member of the Executive Council shall have one vote. Unless otherwise specified in this Convention, the Executive Council shall take decisions on matters of substance by a two-thirds majority of all its members. The Executive Council shall take decisions on questions of procedure by a simple majority of all its members. When the issue arises as to whether the question is one of substance or not, that question shall be treated as a matter of substance unless otherwise decided by the Executive Council by the majority required for decisions on matters of substance.

Powers and functions

30. The Executive Council shall be the executive organ of the Organization. It shall be responsible to the Conference. The Executive Council shall carry out the powers and functions entrusted to it under this Convention, as well as those functions delegated to it by the Conference. In so doing, it shall act in conformity with the recommendations, decisions and guidelines

of the Conference and assure their proper and continuous implementation.

31. The Executive Council shall promote the effective implementation of, and compliance with, this Convention. It shall supervise the activities of the Technical Secretariat, cooperate with the National Authority of each State Party and facilitate consultations and cooperation among States Parties at their request.

32. The Executive Council shall:

(a) Consider and submit to the Conference the draft programme and budget of the Organization;

(b) Consider and submit to the Conference the draft report of the Organization on the implementation of this Convention, the report on the performance of its own activities and such special reports as it deems necessary or which the Conference may request;

(c) Make arrangements for the sessions of the Conference including the preparation of the draft agenda.

33. The Executive Council may request the convening of a special session of the Conference.

34. The Executive Council shall:

(a) Conclude agreements or arrangements with States and international organizations on behalf of the Organization, subject to prior approval by the Conference;

(b) Conclude agreements with States Parties on behalf of the Organization in connection with Article X and supervise the voluntary fund referred to in Article X;

(c) Approve agreements or arrangements relating to the implementation of verification activities, negotiated by the Technical Secretariat with States Parties.

35. The Executive Council shall consider any issue or matter within its competence affecting this Convention and its implementation, including concerns regarding compliance, and cases of non-compliance, and, as appropriate, inform States

Parties and bring the issue or matter to the attention of the Conference.

36. In its consideration of doubts or concerns regarding compliance and cases of noncompliance, including, inter alia, abuse of the rights provided for under this Convention, the Executive Council shall consult with the States Parties involved and, as appropriate, request the State Party to take measures to redress the situation within a specified time. To the extent that the Executive Council considers further action to be necessary, it shall take, inter alia, one or more of the following measures:

(a) Inform all States Parties of the issue or matter;

(b) Bring the issue or matter to the attention of the Conference;

(c) Make recommendations to the Conference regarding measures to redress the situation and to ensure compliance.

The Executive Council shall, in cases of particular gravity and urgency, bring the issue or matter, including relevant information and conclusions, directly to the attention of the United Nations General Assembly and the United Nations Security Council. It shall at the same time inform all States Parties of this step.

D. The Technical Secretariat

37. The Technical Secretariat shall assist the Conference and the Executive Council in the performance of their functions. The Technical Secretariat shall carry out the verification measures provided for in this Convention. It shall carry out the other functions entrusted to it under this Convention as well as those functions delegated to it by the Conference and the Executive Council.

38. The Technical Secretariat shall:

(a) Prepare and submit to the Executive Council the draft programme and budget of the Organization;

(b) Prepare and submit to the Executive Council the draft report of the Organization on the implementation of this Convention and such other reports as the Conference or the Executive Council may request;

(c) Provide administrative and technical support to the Conference, the Executive Council and subsidiary organs;

(d) Address and receive communications on behalf of the Organization to and from States Parties on matters pertaining to the implementation of this Convention;

(e) Provide technical assistance and technical evaluation to States Parties in the implementation of the provisions of this Convention, including evaluation of scheduled and unscheduled chemicals.

39. The Technical Secretariat shall:

(a) Negotiate agreements or arrangements relating to the implementation of verification activities with States Parties, subject to approval by the Executive Council;

(b) Not later than 180 days after entry into force of this Convention, coordinate the establishment and maintenance of permanent stockpiles of emergency and humanitarian assistance by States Parties in accordance with Article X, paragraphs 7 (b) and (c). The Technical Secretariat may inspect the items maintained for serviceability. Lists of items to be stockpiled shall be considered and approved by the Conference pursuant to paragraph 21 (i) above;

(c) Administer the voluntary fund referred to in Article X, compile declarations made by the States Parties and register, when requested, bilateral agreements concluded between States Parties or between a State Party and the Organization for the purposes of Article X.

40. The Technical Secretariat shall inform the Executive Council of any problem that has arisen with regard to the discharge of its functions, including doubts, ambiguities or uncertainties about compliance with this Convention that have come to its notice in the performance of its verification activities and that it has been unable to resolve or clarify through its consultations with the State Party concerned.

41. The Technical Secretariat shall comprise a Director-General, who shall be its head and chief administrative officer, inspectors and such scientific, technical and other personnel as may be required.

42. The Inspectorate shall be a unit of the Technical Secretariat and shall act under the supervision of the Director-General.

43. The Director-General shall be appointed by the Conference upon the recommendation of the Executive Council for a term of four years, renewable for one further term, but not thereafter.

44. The Director-General shall be responsible to the Conference and the Executive Council for the appointment of the staff and the organization and functioning of the Technical Secretariat. The paramount consideration in the employment of the staff and in the determination of the conditions of service shall be the necessity of securing the highest standards of efficiency, competence and integrity. Only citizens of States Parties shall serve as the Director-General, as inspectors or as other members of the professional and clerical staff. Due regard shall be paid to the importance of recruiting the staff on as wide a geographical basis as possible. Recruitment shall be guided by the principle that the staff shall be kept to a minimum necessary for the proper discharge of the responsibilities of the Technical Secretariat.

45. The Director-General shall be responsible for the organization and functioning of the Scientific Advisory Board referred to in paragraph 21 (h). The Director-General shall, in consultation with States Parties, appoint members of the Scientific Advisory Board, who shall serve in their individual capacity. The members of the Board shall be appointed on the basis of their expertise in the particular scientific fields relevant to the implementation of this Convention. The Director-General may also, as appropriate, in consultation with members of the Board, establish temporary working groups of scientific experts to provide recommendations on specific issues. In regard to the

above, States Parties may submit lists of experts to the Director-General.

46. In the performance of their duties, the Director-General, the inspectors and the other members of the staff shall not see or receive instructions from any Government or from any other source external to the Organization. They shall refrain from any action that might reflect on their positions as international officers responsible only to the Conference and the Executive Council.

47. Each State Party shall respect the exclusively international character of the responsibilities of the Director-General, the inspectors and the other members of the staff and not seek to influence them in the discharge of their responsibilities.

E. Privileges and Immunities

48. The Organization shall enjoy on the territory and in any other place under the jurisdiction or control of a State Party such legal capacity and such privileges and immunities as are necessary for the exercise of its functions.

49. Delegates of States Parties, together with their alternates and advisers, representatives appointed to the Executive Council together with their alternates and advisers, the Director-General and the staff of the Organization shall enjoy such privileges and immunities as are necessary in the independent exercise of their functions in connection with the Organization.

50. The legal capacity, privileges, and immunities referred to in this Article shall be defined in agreements between the Organization and the States Parties as well as in an agreement between the Organization and the State in which the headquarters of the Organization is seated. These agreements shall be considered and approved by the Conference pursuant to paragraph 21 (i).

51. Notwithstanding paragraphs 48 and 49, the privileges and immunities enjoyed by the Director-General and the staff of the Technical Secretariat during the conduct of verification activities shall be those set forth in Part II, Section B, of the Verification Annex.

ARTICLE IX: CONSULTATIONS, COOPERATION AND FACT-FINDING

1. States Parties shall consult and cooperate, directly among themselves, or through the Organization or other appropriate international procedures, including procedures within the framework of the United Nations and in accordance with its Charter, on any matter which may be raised relating to the object and purpose, or the implementation of the provisions, of this Convention.

2. Without prejudice to the right of any State Party to request a challenge inspection, States Parties should, whenever possible, first make every effort to clarify and resolve, through exchange of information and consultations among themselves, any matter which may cause doubt about compliance with this Convention, or which gives rise to concerns about a related matter which may be considered ambiguous. A State Party which receives a request from another State Party for clarification of any matter which the requesting State Party believes causes such a doubt or concern shall provide the requesting State Party as soon as possible, but in any case not later than 10 days after the request, with information sufficient to answer the doubt or concern raised along with an explanation of how the information provided resolves the matter. Nothing in this Convention shall affect the right of any two or more States Parties to arrange by mutual consent for inspections or any other procedures among themselves to clarify and resolve any matter which may cause doubt about compliance or gives rise to a concern about a related matter which may be considered ambiguous. Such arrangements shall not affect the rights and obligations of any State Party under other provisions of this Convention.

Procedure for requesting clarification

3. A State Party shall have the right to request the Executive Council to assist in clarifying any situation which may be considered ambiguous or which gives rise to a concern about the possible non-compliance of another State Party with this Convention. The Executive Council shall provide appropriate information in its possession relevant to such a concern.

4. A State Party shall have the right to request the Executive Council to obtain clarification from another State Party on any situation which may be considered ambiguous or which gives rise to a concern about its possible non-compliance with this Convention. In such a case, the following shall apply:

(a) The Executive Council shall forward the request for clarification to the State Party concerned through the Director-General not later than 24 hours after its receipt;

(b) The requested State Party shall provide the clarification to the Executive Council as soon as possible, but in any case not later than 10 days after the receipt of the request;

(c) The Executive Council shall take note of the clarification and forward it to the requesting State Party not later than 24 hours after its receipt;

(d) If the requesting State Party deems the clarification to be inadequate, it shall have the right to request the Executive Council to obtain from the requested State Party further clarification;

(e) For the purpose of obtaining further clarification requested under subparagraph (d), the Executive Council may call on the Director-General to establish a group of experts from the Technical Secretariat, or if appropriate staff are not available in the Technical Secretariat, from elsewhere, to examine all available information and data relevant to the situation causing the concern. The group of experts shall submit a factual report to the Executive Council on its findings;

(f) If the requesting State Party considers the clarification obtained under subparagraphs (d) and (e) to be unsatisfactory, it shall have the right to request a special session of the Executive Council in which States Parties involved that are not members of the Executive Council shall be entitled to take part. In such a special session, the Executive Council shall consider the matter and may recommend any measure it deems appropriate to resolve the situation.

5. A State Party shall also have the right to request the Executive Council to clarify any situation which has been considered ambiguous or has given rise to a concern about its possible non-compliance with this Convention. The Executive Council shall respond by providing such assistance as appropriate.

6. The Executive Council shall inform the States Parties about any request for clarification provided in this Article.

7. If the doubt or concern of a State Party about a possible non-compliance has not been resolved within 60 days after the submission of the request for clarification to the Executive Council, or it believes its doubts warrant urgent consideration, notwithstanding its right to request a challenge inspection, it may request a special session of the Conference in accordance with Article VIII, paragraph 12 (c). At such a special session, the Conference shall consider the matter and may recommend any measure it deems appropriate to resolve the situation.

Procedures for Challenge Inspections

8. Each State Party has the right to request an onsite challenge inspection of any facility or location in the territory or in any other place under the jurisdiction or control of any other State Party for the sole purpose of clarifying and resolving any questions concerning possible non-compliance with the provisions of this Convention, and to have this inspection conducted anywhere without delay by an inspection team designated by the Director-General and in accordance with the Verification Annex.

9. Each State Party is under the obligation to keep the inspection request within the scope of this Convention and to provide in the inspection request all appropriate information on the basis of which a concern has arisen regarding possible non-compliance with this Convention as specified in the Verification Annex. Each State Party shall refrain from unfounded inspection requests, care being taken to avoid abuse. The challenge inspection shall be carried out for the sole purpose of determining facts relating to the possible non-compliance.

10. For the purpose of verifying compliance with the provisions of this Convention, each State Party shall permit the

Technical Secretariat to conduct the onsite challenge inspection pursuant to paragraph 8.

11. Pursuant to a request for a challenge inspection of a facility or location, and in accordance with the procedures provided for in the Verification Annex, the inspected State Party shall have:

(a) The right and the obligation to make every reasonable effort to demonstrate its compliance with this Convention and, to this end, to enable the inspection team to fulfill its mandate;

(b) The obligation to provide access within the requested site for the sole purpose of establishing facts relevant to the concern regarding possible non-compliance; and

(c) The right to take measures to protect sensitive installations, and to prevent disclosure of confidential information and data, not related to this Convention.

12. With regard to an observer, the following shall apply:

(a) The requesting State Party may, subject to the agreement of the inspected State Party, send a representative who may be a national either of the requesting State Party or of a third State Party, to observe the conduct of the challenge inspection.

(b) The inspected State Party shall then grant access to the observer in accordance with the Verification Annex.

(c) The inspected State Party shall, as a rule, accept the proposed observer, but if the inspected State Party exercises a refusal, that fact shall be recorded in the final report.

13. The requesting State Party shall present an inspection request for an onsite challenge inspection to the Executive Council and at the same time to the Director-General for immediate processing.

14. The Director-General shall immediately ascertain that the inspection request meets the requirements specified in Part X, paragraph 4, of the Verification Annex, and, if necessary, assist the requesting State Party in filing the inspection request

accordingly. When the inspection request fulfills the requirements, preparations for the challenge inspection shall begin.

15. The Director-General shall transmit the inspection request to the inspected State Party not less than 12 hours before the planned arrival of the inspection team at the point of entry.

16. After having received the inspection request, the Executive Council shall take cognizance of the Director-General's actions on the request and shall keep the case under its consideration throughout the inspection procedure. However, its deliberations shall not delay the inspection process.

17. The Executive Council may, not later than 12 hours after having received the inspection request, decide by a three-quarter majority of all its members against carrying out the challenge inspection, if it considers the inspection request to be frivolous, abusive or clearly beyond the scope of this Convention as described in paragraph 8. Neither the requesting nor the inspected State Party shall participate in such a decision. If the Executive Council decides against the challenge inspection, preparations shall be stopped, no further action on the inspection request shall be taken, and the States Parties concerned shall be informed accordingly.

18. The Director-General shall issue an inspection mandate for the conduct of the challenge inspection. The inspection mandate shall be the inspection request referred to in paragraphs 8 and 9 put into operational terms, and shall conform with the inspection request.

19. The challenge inspection shall be conducted in accordance with Part X or, in the case of alleged use, in accordance with Part XI of the Verification Annex. The inspection team shall be guided by the principle of conducting the challenge inspection in the least intrusive manner possible, consistent with the effective and timely accomplishment of its mission.

20. The inspected State Party shall assist the inspection team throughout the challenge inspection and facilitate its task. If the inspected State Party proposes, pursuant to Part X, Section C, of the Verification Annex, arrangements to demonstrate compliance with this Convention, alternative to full and comprehensive

access, it shall make every reasonable effort, through consultations with the inspection team, to reach agreement on the modalities for establishing the facts with the aim of demonstrating its compliance.

21. The final report shall contain the factual findings as well as an assessment by the inspection team of the degree and nature of access and cooperation granted for the satisfactory implementation of the challenge inspection. The Director-General shall promptly transmit the final report of the inspection team to the requesting State Party, to the inspected State Party, to the Executive Council and to all other States Parties. The Director-General shall further transmit promptly to the Executive Council the assessments of the requesting and of the inspected States Parties, as well as the views of other States Parties which may be conveyed to the Director-General for that purpose, and then provide them to all States Parties.

22. The Executive Council shall, in accordance with its powers and functions, review the final report of the inspection team as soon as it is presented, and address any concerns as to:

(a) Whether any non-compliance has occurred;

(b) Whether the request had been within the scope of this Convention; and

(c) Whether the right to request a challenge inspection had been abused.

23. If the Executive Council reaches the conclusion, in keeping with its powers and functions, that further action may be necessary with regard to paragraph 22, it shall take the appropriate measures to redress the situation and to ensure compliance with this Convention, including specific recommendations to the Conference. In the case of abuse, the Executive Council shall examine whether the requesting State Party should bear any of the financial implications of the challenge inspection.

24. The requesting State Party and the inspected State Party shall have the right to participate in the review process. The Executive Council shall inform the States Parties and the next session of the Conference of the outcome of the process.

25. If the Executive Council has made specific recommendations to the Conference, the Conference shall consider action in accordance with Article XII.

ARTICLE X: ASSISTANCE AND PROTECTION AGAINST CHEMICAL WEAPONS

1. For the purposes of this Article, "Assistance" means the coordination and delivery to States Parties of protection against chemical weapons, including, inter alia, the following: detection equipment and alarm systems; protective equipment; decontamination equipment and decontaminants; medical antidotes and treatments; and advice on any of these protective measures.

2. Nothing in this Convention shall be interpreted as impeding the right of any State Party to conduct research into, develop, produce, acquire, transfer or use means of protection against chemical weapons, for purposes not prohibited under this Convention.

3. Each State Party undertakes to facilitate, and shall have the right to participate in, the fullest possible exchange of equipment, material and scientific and technological information concerning means of protection against chemical weapons.

4. For the purposes of increasing the transparency of national programmes related to protective purposes, each State Party shall provide annually to the Technical Secretariat information on its programme, in accordance with procedures to be considered and approved by the Conference pursuant to Article VIII, paragraph 21 (i).

5. The Technical Secretariat shall establish, not later than 180 days after entry into force of this Convention and maintain, for the use of any requesting State Party, a data bank containing freely available information concerning various means of protection against chemical weapons as well as such information as may be provided by States Parties.

The Technical Secretariat shall also, within the resources available to it, and at the request of a State Party, provide expert advice and assist the State Party in identifying how its programmes for the development and improvement of a protective capacity against chemical weapons could be implemented.

6. Nothing in this Convention shall be interpreted as impeding the right of States Parties to request and provide assistance bilaterally and to conclude individual agreements with other States Parties concerning the emergency procurement of assistance.

7. Each State Party undertakes to provide assistance through the Organization and to this end to elect to take one or more of the following measures:

(a) To contribute to the voluntary fund for assistance to be established by the Conference at its first session;

(b) To conclude, if possible not later than 180 days after this Convention enters into force for it, agreements with the Organization concerning the procurement, upon demand, of assistance;

(c) To declare, not later than 180 days after this Convention enters into force for it, the kind of assistance it might provide in response to an appeal by the Organization. If, however, a State Party subsequently is unable to provide the assistance envisaged in its declaration, it is still under the obligation to provide assistance in accordance with this paragraph.

8. Each State Party has the right to request and, subject to the procedures set forth in paragraphs 9, 10 and 11, to receive assistance and protection against the use or threat of use of chemical weapons if it considers that:

(a) Chemical weapons have been used against it;

(b) Riot control agents have been used against it as a method of warfare; or

(c) It is threatened by actions or activities of any State that are prohibited for States Parties by Article I.

9. The request, substantiated by relevant information, shall be submitted to the Director-General, who shall transmit it immediately to the Executive Council and to all States Parties. The Director-General shall immediately forward the request to

States Parties which have volunteered, in accordance with paragraphs 7 (b) and (c), to dispatch emergency assistance in case of use of chemical weapons or use of riot control agents as a method of warfare, or humanitarian assistance in case of serious threat of use of chemical weapons or serious threat of use of riot control agents as a method of warfare to the State Party concerned not later than 12 hours after receipt of the request. The Director-General shall initiate, not later than 24 hours after receipt of the request, an investigation in order to provide foundation for further action. He shall complete the investigation within 72 hours and forward a report to the Executive Council. If additional time is required for completion of the investigation, an interim report shall be submitted within the same time frame. The additional time required for investigation shall not exceed 72 hours. It may, however, be further extended by similar periods. Reports at the end of each additional period shall be submitted to the Executive Council. The investigation shall, as appropriate and in conformity with the request and the information accompanying the request, establish relevant facts related to the request as well as the type and scope of supplementary assistance and protection needed.

10. The Executive Council shall meet not later than 24 hours after receiving an investigation report to consider the situation and shall take a decision by simple majority within the following 24 hours on whether to instruct the Technical Secretariat to provide supplementary assistance. The Technical Secretariat shall immediately transmit to all States Parties and relevant international organizations the investigation report and the decision taken by the Executive Council. When so decided by the Executive Council, the Director-General shall provide assistance immediately. For this purpose, the Director-General may cooperate with the requesting State Party, other States Parties and relevant international organizations. The States Parties shall make the fullest possible efforts to provide assistance.

11. If the information available from the ongoing investigation or other reliable sources would give sufficient proof that there are victims of use of chemical weapons and immediate action is indispensable, the Director-General shall notify all States Parties

and shall take emergency measures of assistance, using the resources the Conference has placed at his disposal for such contingencies. The Director-General shall keep the Executive Council informed of actions undertaken pursuant to this paragraph.

ARTICLE XI: ECONOMIC AND TECHNOLOGICAL DEVELOPMENT

1. The provisions of this Convention shall be implemented in a manner which avoids hampering the economic or technological development of States Parties, and international cooperation in the field of chemical activities for purposes not prohibited under this Convention including the international exchange of scientific and technical information and chemicals and equipment for the production, processing or use of chemicals for purposes not prohibited under this Convention.

2. Subject to the provisions of this Convention and without prejudice to the principles and applicable rules of international law, the States Parties shall:

(a) Have the right, individually or collectively, to conduct research with, to develop, produce, acquire, retain, transfer, and use chemicals;

(b) Undertake to facilitate, and have the right to participate in, the fullest possible exchange of chemicals, equipment and scientific and technical information relating to the development and application of chemistry for purposes not prohibited under this Convention;

(c) Not maintain among themselves any restrictions, including those in any international agreements, incompatible with the obligations undertaken under this Convention, which would restrict or impede trade and the development and promotion of scientific and technological knowledge in the field of chemistry for industrial, agricultural, research, medical, pharmaceutical or other peaceful purposes;

(d) Not use this Convention as grounds for applying any measures other than those provided for, or permitted, under this Convention nor use any other international agreement for pursuing an objective inconsistent with this Convention;

(e) Undertake to review their existing national regulations in the field of trade in chemicals in order to render them consistent with the object and purpose of this Convention.

ARTICLE XII: MEASURES TO REDRESS A SITUATION AND TO ENSURE COMPLIANCE, INCLUDING SANCTIONS

1. The Conference shall take the necessary measures, as set forth in paragraphs 2, 3 and 4, to ensure compliance with this Convention and to redress and remedy any situation which contravenes the provisions of this Convention. In considering action pursuant to this paragraph, the Conference shall take into account all information and recommendations on the issues submitted by the Executive Council.

2. In cases where a State Party has been requested by the Executive Council to take measures to redress a situation raising problems with regard to its compliance, and where the State Party fails to fulfill the request within the specified time, the Conference may, inter alia, upon the recommendation of the Executive Council, restrict or suspend the State Party's rights and privileges under this Convention until it undertakes the necessary action to conform with its obligations under this Convention.

3. In cases where serious damage to the object and purpose of this Convention may result from activities prohibited under this Convention, in particular by Article I, the Conference may recommend collective measures to States Parties in conformity with international law.

4. The Conference shall, in cases of particular gravity, bring the issue, including relevant information and conclusions, to the attention of the United Nations General Assembly and the United Nations Security Council.

ARTICLE XIII: RELATION TO OTHER INTERNATIONAL AGREEMENTS

Nothing in this Convention shall be interpreted as in any way limiting or detracting from the obligations assumed by any

State under the Protocol for the Prohibition of the Use in War of Asphyxiating, Poisonous or Other Gases, and of Bacteriological Methods of Warfare, signed at Geneva on 17 June 1925, and under the Convention on the Prohibition of the Development, Production and Stockpiling of Bacteriological (Biological) and Toxin Weapons and on Their Destruction, signed at London, Moscow and Washington on 10 April 1972.

ARTICLE XIV: SETTLEMENT OF DISPUTES

1. Disputes that may arise concerning the application or the interpretation of this Convention shall be settled in accordance with the relevant provisions of this Convention and in conformity with the provisions of the Charter of the United Nations.

2. When a dispute arises between two or more States Parties, or between one or more States Parties and the Organization, relating to the interpretation or application of this Convention, the parties concerned shall consult together with a view to the expeditious settlement of the dispute by negotiation or by other peaceful means of the parties' choice, including recourse to appropriate organs of this Convention and, by mutual consent, referral to the International Court of Justice in conformity with the Statute of the Court. The States Parties involved shall keep the Executive Council informed of actions being taken.

3. The Executive Council may contribute to the settlement of a dispute by whatever means it deems appropriate, including offering its good offices, calling upon the States Parties to a dispute to start the settlement process of their choice and recommending a timelimit for any agreed procedure.

4. The Conference shall consider questions related to disputes raised by States Parties or brought to its attention by the Executive Council. The Conference shall, as it finds necessary, establish or entrust organs with tasks related to the settlement of these disputes in conformity with Article VIII, paragraph 21(f).

5. The Conference and the Executive Council are separately empowered, subject to authorization from the General Assembly of the United Nations, to request the International Court of Justice to give an advisory opinion on any legal question arising within the scope of the activities of the Organization. An

agreement between the Organization and the United Nations shall be concluded for this purpose in accordance with Article VIII, paragraph 34 (a).

6. This Article is without prejudice to Article IX or to the provisions on measures to redress a situation and to ensure compliance, including sanctions.

ARTICLE XV: AMENDMENTS

1. Any State Party may propose amendments to this Convention. Any State Party may also propose changes, as specified in paragraph 4, to the Annexes of this Convention. Proposals for amendments shall be subject to the procedures in paragraphs 2 and 3. Proposals for changes, as specified in paragraph 4, shall be subject to the procedures in paragraph 5.

2. The text of a proposed amendment shall be submitted to the Director-General for circulation to all States Parties and to the Depositary. The proposed amendment shall be considered only by an Amendment Conference. Such an Amendment Conference shall be convened if one third or more of the States Parties notify the Director-General not later than 30 days after its circulation that they support further consideration of the proposal. The Amendment Conference shall be held immediately following a regular session of the Conference unless the requesting States Parties ask for an earlier meeting. In no case shall an Amendment Conference be held less than 60 days after the circulation of the proposed amendment.

3. Amendments shall enter into force for all States Parties 30 days after deposit of the instruments of ratification or acceptance by all the States Parties referred to under subparagraph (b) below:

(a) When adopted by the Amendment Conference by a positive vote of a majority of all States Parties with no State Party casting a negative vote; and

(b) Ratified or accepted by all those States Parties casting a positive vote at the Amendment Conference.

4. In order to ensure the viability and the effectiveness of this Convention, provisions in the Annexes shall be subject to changes

in accordance with paragraph 5, if proposed changes are related only to matters of an administrative or technical nature. All changes to the Annex on Chemicals shall be made in accordance with paragraph 5. Sections A and C of the Confidentiality Annex, Part X of the Verification Annex, and those definitions in Part I of the Verification Annex which relate exclusively to challenge inspections, shall not be subject to changes in accordance with paragraph 5.

5. Proposed changes referred to in paragraph 4 shall be made in accordance with the following procedures:

(a) The test of the proposed changes shall be transmitted together with the necessary information to the Director-General. Additional information for the evaluation of the proposal may be provided by any State Party and the Director-General. The Director-General shall promptly communicate any such proposals and information to all States Parties, the Executive Council and the Depositary;

(b) Not later than 60 days after its receipt, the Director-General shall evaluate the proposal to determine all its possible consequences for the provisions of this Convention and its implementation and shall communicate any such information to all States Parties and the Executive Council;

(c) The Executive Council shall examine the proposal in the light of all information available to it, including whether the proposal fulfills the requirements of paragraph 4. Not later than 90 days after its receipt, the Executive Council shall notify its recommendation, with appropriate explanations, to all States Parties for consideration. States Parties shall acknowledge receipt within 10 days;

(d) If the Executive Council recommends to all States Parties that the proposal be adopted, it shall be considered approved if no State Party objects to it within 90 days after receipt of the recommendation. If the Executive Council recommends that the proposal be rejected, it shall be considered rejected if no State Party objects to the rejection within 90 days after receipt of the recommendation;

(e) If a recommendation of the Executive Council does not meet with the acceptance required under subparagraph (d), a decision on the proposal, including whether it fulfills the requirements of paragraph 4, shall be taken as a matter of substance by the Conference at its next session;

(f) The Director-General shall notify all States Parties and the Depositary of any decision under this paragraph;

(g) Changes approved under this procedure shall enter into force for all States Parties 180 days after the date of notification by the Director-General of their approval unless another time period is recommended by the Executive Council or decided by the Conference.

ARTICLE XVI: DURATION AND WITHDRAWAL

1. This Convention shall be of unlimited duration.

2. Each State Party shall, in exercising its national sovereignty, have the right to withdraw from this Convention if it decides that extraordinary events, related to the subject matter of this Convention, have jeopardized the supreme interests of its country. It shall give notice of such withdrawal 90 days in advance to all other States Parties, the Executive Council, the Depositary and the United Nations Security Council. Such notice shall include a statement of the extraordinary events it regards as having jeopardized its supreme interests.

3. The withdrawal of a State Party from this Convention shall not in any way affect the duty of States to continue fulfilling the obligations assumed under any relevant rules of international law, particularly the Geneva Protocol of 1925.

ARTICLE XVII: STATUS OF THE ANNEXES

The Annexes form an integral part of this Convention. Any reference to this Convention includes the Annexes.

ARTICLE XVIII: SIGNATURE

This Convention shall be open for signature for all States before its entry into force.

ARTICLE XIX: RATIFICATION

This Convention shall be subject to ratification by States Signatories according to their respective constitutional processes.

ARTICLE XX: ACCESSION

Any State which does not sign this Convention before its entry into force may accede to it at any time thereafter.

ARTICLE XXI: ENTRY INTO FORCE

1. This Convention shall enter into force 180 days after the date of the deposit of the 65th instrument of ratification, but in no case earlier than two years after its opening for signature.

2. For States whose instruments of ratification or accession are deposited subsequent to the entry into force of this Convention, it shall enter into force on the 30th day following the date of deposit of their instrument of ratification or accession.

ARTICLE XXII: RESERVATIONS

The Articles of this Convention shall not be subject to reservations. The Annexes of this Convention shall not be subject to reservations incompatible with its object and purpose.

ARTICLE XXIII: DEPOSITARY

The Secretary-General of the United Nations is hereby designated as the Depositary of this Convention and shall, inter alia:

(a) Promptly inform all signatory and acceding States of the date of each signature, the date of deposit of each instrument of ratification or accession and the date of the entry into force of this Convention, and of the receipt of other notices;

(b) Transmit duly certified copies of this Convention to the Governments of all signatory and acceding States; and

(c) Register this Convention pursuant to Article 102 of the Charter of the United Nations.

ARTICLE XXIV: AUTHENTIC TEXTS

This Convention, of which the Arabic, Chinese, English, French, Russian and Spanish texts are equally authentic, shall be deposited with the Secretary-General of the United Nations.

IN WITNESS WHEREOF the undersigned, being duly authorized to that effect, have signed this Convention.

DONE at Paris on the thirteenth day of January, One Thousand and Nine Hundred Ninety Three.

5

Draft Convention on the Prohibition of the Use of Nuclear Weapons

The States Parties to the present Convention,

Alarmed by the threat to the very survival of mankind posed by the existence of nuclear weapons,

Convinced that any use of nuclear weapons constitutes a violation of the Charter of the United Nations and a crime against humanity,

Desiring to achieve a multilateral, universal and binding agreement prohibiting the use or threat of use of nuclear weapons,

Bearing in mind the advisory opinion of the International Court of Justice that there exists an obligation of all States to pursue in good faith and bring to a conclusion negotiations leading to nuclear disarmament in all its aspects under strict and effective international control,

Determined, therefore, to achieve a universal nuclear weapons convention prohibiting the development, production, stockpiling and use of nuclear weapons, leading to their ultimate destruction,

Convinced that the present Convention would be an important step in a phased programme towards the complete elimination of nuclear weapons within a time-bound framework,

Determined to continue negotiations for the achievement of this goal,

Have agreed as follows:

ARTICLE 1

The States Parties to the present Convention solemnly undertake not to use or threaten to use nuclear weapons under any circumstances.

ARTICLE 2

The present Convention shall be of unlimited duration.

ARTICLE 3

1. The present Convention shall be open to all States for signature. Any State that does not sign the Convention before its entry into force in accordance with paragraph 3 of the present article may accede to it at any time.

2. The present Convention shall be subject to ratification by signatory States. Instruments of ratification or accession shall be deposited with the Secretary-General of the United Nations.

3. The present Convention shall enter into force on the deposit of instruments of ratification by twenty-five Governments, including the Governments of the five nuclear-weapon States, in accordance with paragraph 2 of the present article.

4. For States whose instruments of ratification or accession are deposited after the entry into force of the Convention, it shall enter into force on the date of the deposit of their instruments of ratification or accession.

5. The depositary shall promptly inform all signatory and acceding States of the date of each signature, the date of deposit of each instrument of ratification or accession and the date of entry into force of the present Convention, as well as of the receipt of other notices.

6. The present Convention shall be registered by the depositary in accordance with Article 102 of the Charter of the United Nations.

ARTICLE 4

The present Convention, of which the Arabic, Chinese, English, French, Russian and Spanish texts are equally authentic, shall be deposited with the Secretary-General of the United Nations, who shall send duly certified copies thereof to the Governments of the signatory and acceding States.

IN WITNESS WHEREOF, the undersigned, being duly authorized thereto by their respective Governments, have signed the present Convention, opened for signature at on the day of one thousand nine hundred and

6

Bilateral Destruction Agreement (BDA)

1 June 1990

Agreement between the United States of America and the Union of Soviet Socialist Republics on destruction and non-production of chemical weapons and on measures to facilitate the multilateral convention on banning chemical weapons U.S. arms control and disarmament agency, Washington, D.C. 20451 office of public affairs (202) 647-8677

The United States of America and the Union of Soviet Socialist Republics, hereinafter referred to as "the Parties,"

Determined to make every effort to conclude and to bring into force at the earliest date a convention providing for a global ban on the development, production, stockpiling and use of chemical weapons and on their destruction, hereinafter referred to as "the multilateral convention,"

Aware of their special responsibility in the area of chemical weapons disarmament,

Desiring to halt the production of chemical weapons and to begin the destruction of the preponderance of their chemical weapons stockpiles, without waiting for the mulitateral convention to enter into force,

Recalling the Memorandum of Understanding between the Government of the United States of America and the Government of the Union of Soviet Socialist Republics Regarding a Bilateral Verification Experiment and Data Exchange Related to Prohibition of Chemical Weapons, signed at Jackson Hole, Wyoming on September 23, 1989, hereinafter referred to as "the Memorandum,"

Recalling the bilateral commitment to cooperate with respect to the destruction of chemical weapons, contained in the joint statement on chemical weapons issued at Jackson Hole, Wyoming on September 23, 1989, and mindful of the efforts of each Party aimed at the destruction of chemical weapons and desiring to cooperate in this area,

Have agreed as follows

ARTICLE I—GENERAL PROVISIONS AND AREAS OF COOPERATION

1. In accordance with provisions of this Agreement, the Parties undertake:

1. to cooperate regarding methods and technologies for the safe and efficient destruction of chemical weapons;
2. not to produce chemical weapons;
3. to reduce their chemical weapons stockpiles to equal, low levels;
4. to cooperate in developing, testing, and carrying out appropriate inspection procedures; and
5. to adopt practical measures to encourage all chemical weapons-capable states to become parties to the multilateral convention.

2. Each Party, during its destruction of chemical weapons, shall assign the highest priority to ensuring the safety of people and to protecting the environment. Each Party shall destroy its chemical weapons in accordance with stringent national standards for safety and emissions.

ARTICLE II—COOPERATION REGARDING METHODS AND TECHNOLOGIES OF DESTRUCTION

1. To implement their undertaking to cooperate regarding the destruction of chemical weapons, the Parties shall negotiate a specific program of cooperation. For this purpose, the Parties

may create special groups of experts, as appropriate. The program may include matters related to: methods and specific technologies for the destruction of chemical weapons; measures to ensure safety and protection of people and the environment; construction and operation of destruction facilities; the appropriate equipment for destruction, past, current and planned destruction activities; monitoring of destruction of chemical weapons; or such other topics as the Parties may agree. Activities to implement this program may include: exchanges of visits to relevant facilities; exchanges of documents; meetings and discussions among experts; or such other activities as the Parties may agree.

2. Each Party shall, as appropriate, cooperate with other states that request information or assistance regarding the destruction of chemical weapons. The Parties may respond jointly to such requests.

ARTICLE III—CESSATION OF THE PRODUCTION OF CHEMICAL WEAPONS

Upon entry into force of this Agreement and thereafter, each Party shall not produce chemical weapons.

ARTICLE IV—DESTRUCTION OF CHEMICAL WEAPONS

1. Each Party shall reduce and limit its chemical weapons so that, by no later than December 31, 2002, and thereafter, its aggregate quantity of chemical weapons does not exceed 5000 agent tons. In this Agreement, "tons" means metric tons.

2. Each Party shall begin its destruction of chemical weapons by no later than December 31, 1992.

3. By no later than December 31, 1999, each Party shall have destroyed at least 50 percent of its aggregate quantity of chemical weapons. The aggregate quantity of chemical weapons of a Party shall be the amount of chemical weapons declared in the data exchange carried out on December 29, 1989, or declared thereafter, pursuant to the Memorandum, as updated in accordance with paragraph 6(b) of this Article.

4. In the event that a Party determines that it cannot achieve an annual rate of destruction of chemical weapons of at least 1000 agent tons during 1995, or that it cannot destroy at least 1000 agent tons during each year after 1995, that Party shall, at

the earliest possible time, notify the other Party, in accordance with Paragraph 10 of this Article.

5. Each Party, in its destruction of chemical weapons, shall also destroy the munitions, devices and containers from which the chemicals have been removed. Each Party shall reduce and limit its other empty munitions and devices for chemical weapons purposes so that, by no later than December 31, 2002, and thereafter, the aggregate capacity of such munitions and devices does not exceed the volume of the remaining bulk agent of that Party.

6. Thirty days after the entry into force of this Agreement, each Party shall inform the other Party of the following:

1. its current general plan for the destruction of chemical weapons pursuant to this Agreement and its detailed plan for the destruction of chemical weapons during the calendar year following the year in which this Agreement enters into force. The detailed plan shall encompass all of the chemical weapons to be destroyed during the calendar year, and shall include their locations, types and quantities, the methods of their destruction, and the locations of the destruction facilities that are to be used; and
2. any changes, as of the entry into force of this Agreement, in the data contained in the data exchange carried out on December 29, 1989, or provided thereafter, pursuant to the Memorandum.

7. Beginning in the calendar year following the year in which this Agreement enters into force, each Party shall inform the other Party annually, by no later than November 30, of its detailed plan for the destruction of chemical weapons during the following calendar year.

8. Beginning in the calendar year following the year in which this Agreement enters into force, each Party shall inform the other Party annually, by no later than April 15, of the following:

1. any further changes, as of December 31 of the previous year, to the data contained in the data exchange carried out on December 29, 1989, or provided thereafter, pursuant to the Memorandum;

2. the implementation during the previous calendar year of its detailed plan for the destruction of chemical weapons; and
3. any update to the general and detailed plans provided pursuant to paragraphs 6(a) or 7 of this Article.

9. Each Party shall limit its chemical weapons storage facilities so that, by no later than December 31, 2002, and thereafter, the number of such facilities does not exceed eight. Each Party plans to have all such facilities located on its national territory. This is without prejudice to its rights and obligations, including those under the Protocol for the Prohibition of the Use in War of Asphyxiating, Poisonous or Other Gases, and of Bacteriological Methods of Warfare, signed at Geneva on June 17, 1925.

10. If a Party experiences problems that will prevent it from destroying its chemical weapons at a rate sufficient to meet the levels specified in this Article, that Party shall immediately notify the other Party and provide a full explanation. The Parties shall promptly consult on measures necessary to resolve the problems. Under no circumstances shall the Party not experiencing problems in its destruction of chemical weapons be required to destroy its chemical weapons at a more rapid rate than the Party that has experienced such problems.

ARTICLE V—INSPECTION ACTIVITIES

1. Each Party shall provide access to each of its chemical weapons production facilities for systematic on-site inspection to confirm that production of chemical weapons is not occurring at those facilities.

2. Each Party shall identify and provide access to each of its chemical weapons destruction facilities and the chemical weapons holding areas within these destruction facilities for systematic on-site inspection of the destruction of chemical weapons. Such inspection shall be accomplished through the continuous presence of inspectors and continuous monitoring with on-site instruments.

3. When a Party has removed all of its chemical weapons from a particular chemical weapons storage facility, it shall promptly notify the other Party. The Party receiving the notification shall have the right to conduct, promptly after its

receipt of the notification, an on-site inspection to confirm that no chemical weapons are present at that facility. Each Party shall also have the right to inspect, not more than once each calendar year, subsequent to the year of the notification and until such time as the multilateral convention enters into force, each chemical weapons storage facility for which it has received a notification pursuant to this paragraph, to determine that chemical weapons are not being stored there.

4. When a Party has completed its destruction of chemical weapons pursuant to this Agreement, it shall promptly notify the other Party. In its notification, the Party shall specify the chemical weapons storage facilities where its remaining chemical weapons are located and provide a detailed inventory of the chemical weapons at each of these storage facilities. Each Party, promptly after it has received such a notification, shall have the right to inspect each of the chemical weapons storage facilities specified in the notification, to determine the quantities and types of chemical weapons at each facility.

5. Each Party shall also have the right to inspect, not more than once each calendar year, subsequent to the year in which destruction begins and until such time as the multilateral convention enters into force, each chemical weapons storage facility of the other Party that is not already subject to annual inspection pursuant to paragraph 3 of this Article, to determine the quantities and types of chemical weapons that are being stored there.

6. On the basis of the reports of its inspectors and other information available to it, each Party shall determine whether the provisions of this Agreement are being satisfactorily fulfilled and shall communicate its conclusions to the other Party.

7. Detailed provisions for the implementation of the inspection measures provided for in this Article shall be set forth in the document on inspection procedures. The Parties shall work to complete this document by December 31, 1990.

ARTICLE VI—MEASURES TO FACILITATE THE MULTILATERAL CONVENTION

The Parties shall cooperate in making every effort to conclude the multilateral convention at the earliest date and to implement it effectively. Toward those ends, the Parties agree, in addition to their other obligations in this Agreement, to the following:

1. Each Party shall reduce and limit its chemical weapons so that, by no later than the end of the eighth year after entry into force of the multilateral convention, its aggregate quantity of chemical weapons does not exceed 500 agent tons.
2. Upon signature of this Agreement, the Parties shall enter into consultations with other participants in the multilateral negotiations and shall propose that a special conference of states parties to the multilateral convention be held at the end of the eighth year after its entry into force. This special conference would, inter alia, determine, in accordance with agreed procedures, whether the participation in the multilateral convention is sufficient for proceeding to the total elimination of all remaining chemical weapons stocks over the subsequent two years.
3. The Parties shall intensify their cooperation with each other and with other states to ensure that all chemical weapons-capable states become parties to the multilateral convention.
4. The Parties declare their intention to be among the original parties to the multilateral convention.
5. To gain experience and thereby facilitate the elaboration and implementation of the multilateral convention, the Parties agree to conduct bilateral verification experiments involving trial challenge inspections at facilities not declared under the Memorandum or subsequently. The detailed modalities for such experiments, including the number and location of the facilities to be inspected, as well as the procedures to be used, shall be agreed between the Parties no later than six months after the signing of this Agreement.

ARTICLE VII—CONSULTATIONS

The Parties, in order to resolve questions related to this Agreement that may arise, shall use normal diplomatic channels, specifically-designated representatives, or such other means as they may agree.

ARTICLE VIII—RELATIONSHIP TO OTHER DOCUMENTS

1. After the multilateral convention enters into force, the provisions of the multilateral convention shall take precedence over the provisions of this Agreement in cases of incompatible obligations therein. Otherwise, the provisions of this Agreement shall supplement the provisions of the multilateral convention in its operation between the Parties. After the multilateral convention is signed, the Parties to this Agreement shall consult with each other in order to resolve any questions concerning the relationship of this Agreement to the multilateral convention.

2. The chemical weapons, chemical weapons storage facilities, and chemical weapons production facilities subject to this Agreement are those that are subject to declaration under the Memorandum.

ARTICLE IX—AMENDMENTS

Each Party may propose amendments to this Agreement. Agreed amendments shall enter into force in accordance with the procedures governing the entry into force of this Agreement

ARTICLE X—ENTRY INTO FORCE; DURATION; WITHDRAWAL

1. This Agreement shall enter into force upon an exchange of instruments stating acceptance of the Agreement by each Party.
2. This Agreement shall be of unlimited duration, unless the Parties agree to terminate it after the entry into force of the multilateral convention.
3. Each Party shall, in exercising its national sovereignty, have the right to withdraw from this Agreement if it decides that extraordinary events related to the subject matter of this Agreement have jeopardized its supreme interests. It shall give notice of its decision to the other Party six months prior to withdrawal from the Agreement. Such notice shall include a statement of the extraordinary events the notifying Party regards as having jeopardized its supreme interests.

DONE at Washington, in duplicate, this 1st day of June, 1990, in the English and Russian languages, each text being equally authentic

FOR THE UNITED STATES OF AMERICA

FOR THE UNION OF SOVIET SOCIALIST REPUBLICS

Agreed statement in connection with the agreement between the United States of America and the Union of Soviet Socialist Republics on destruction and non-production of chemical weapons and on measures to facilitate the multilateral convention on banning Chemical Weapons

Paragraph 2 of Artide VI of the Agreement stipulates that, "Upon signature of this Agreement, the Parties shall enter into consultations with other participants in the multilateral negotiations and shall propose that a special conference of states parties to the multilateral convention be held at the end of the eighth year after its entry into force. This special conference would, inter alia, determine, in accordance with agreed procedures, whether the participation in the multilateral convention is sufficient for proceeding to the total elimination of all remaining chemical weapons stocks over the subsequent two years."

In this connection, the Parties agree that an affirmative decision would require the agreement of a majority of the states parties that attend the special conference, with such majority including those states parties attending the special conference that had taken the following three steps:

1. presented officially and publicly, before December 31, 1991, before the Conference on Disarmament, a written declaration that they were at the time of that declaration in possession of chemical weapons;
2. signed the multilateral convention within thirty days after it was opened for signature; and
3. became a party to the multilateral convention by no later than one year after its entry into force.

7

Treaty between the United States of America and the Union of Soviet Socialist Republics on the Elimination of their Intermediate-range and Shorter-range Missiles

Signed at Washington December 8, 1987
Ratification advised by U.S. Senate May 27, 1988
Instruments of ratification exchanged June 1, 1988
Entered into force June 1, 1988
Proclaimed by U.S. President December 27, 1988

The United States of America and the Union of Soviet Socialist Republics, hereinafter referred to as the Parties,

Conscious that nuclear war would have devastating consequences for all mankind,

Guided by the objective of strengthening strategic stability,

Convinced that the measures set forth in this Treaty will help to reduce the risk of outbreak of war and strengthen international peace and security, and

Mindful of their obligations under Article VI of the Treaty on the Non-Proliferation of Nuclear Weapons,

Have agreed as follows:

ARTICLE I

In accordance with the provisions of this Treaty which includes the Memorandum of Understanding and Protocols which form an integral part thereof, each Party shall eliminate its intermediate-range and shorter-range missiles, not have such systems thereafter, and carry out the other obligations set forth in this Treaty.

ARTICLE II

For the purposes of this Treaty:

1. The term "ballistic missile" means a missile that has a ballistic trajectory over most of its flight path. The term "ground-launched ballistic missile (GLBM)" means a ground-launched ballistic missile that is a weapon-delivery vehicle.

2. The term "cruise missile" means an unmanned, self-propelled vehicle that sustains flight through the use of aerodynamic lift over most of its flight path. The term "ground-launched cruise missile (GLCM)" means a ground-launched cruise missile that is a weapon-delivery vehicle.

3. The term "GLBM launcher" means a fixed launcher or a mobile land-based transporter-erector-launcher mechanism for launching a GLBM.

4. The term "GLCM launcher" means a fixed launcher or a mobile land-based transporter-erector-launcher mechanism for launching a GLCM.

5. The term "intermediate-range missile" means a GLBM or a GLCM having a range capability in excess of 1000 kilometers but not in excess of 5500 kilometers.

6. The term "shorter-range missile" means a GLBM or a GLCM having a range capability equal to or in excess of 500 kilometers but not in excess of 1000 kilometers.

7. The term "deployment area" means a designated area within which intermediate-range missiles and launchers of such missiles may operate and within which one or more missile operating bases are located.

8. The term "missile operating base" means:

(a) in the case of intermediate-range missiles, a complex of facilities, located within a deployment area, at which intermediate-range missiles and launchers of such missiles normally operate, in which support structures associated with such missiles and launchers are also located and in which support equipment associated with such missiles and launchers is normally located; and

(b) in the case of shorter-range missiles, a complex of facilities, located any place, at which shorter-range missiles and launchers of such missiles normally operate and in which support equipment associated with such missiles and launchers is normally located.

9. The term "missile support facility," as regards intermediate-range or shorter-range missiles and launchers of such missiles, means a missile production facility or a launcher production facility, a missile repair facility or a launcher repair facility, a training facility, a missile storage facility or a launcher storage facility, a test range, or an elimination facility as those terms are defined in the Memorandum of Understanding.

10. The term "transit" means movement, notified in accordance with paragraph 5(f) of Article IX of this Treaty, of an intermediate-range missile or a launcher of such a missile between missile support facilities, between such a facility and a deployment area or between deployment areas, or of a shorter-range missile or a launcher of such a missile from a missile support facility or a missile operating base to an elimination facility.

11. The term "deployed missile" means an intermediate-range missile located within a deployment area or a shorter-range missile located at a missile operating base.

12. The term "non-deployed missile" means an intermediate-range missile located outside a deployment area or a shorter-range missile located outside a missile operating base.

13. The term "deployed launcher" means a launcher of an intermediate-range missile located within a deployment area or a launcher of a shorter-range missile located at a missile operating base.

14. The term "non-deployed launcher" means a launcher of an intermediate-range missile located outside a deployment area or a launcher of a shorter-range missile located outside a missile operating base.

15. The term "basing country" means a country other than the United States of America or the Union of Soviet Socialist Republics on whose territory intermediate-range or shorter-range missiles of the Parties, launchers of such missiles or support structures associated with such missiles and launchers were located at any time after November 1, 1987. Missiles or launchers in transit are not considered to be "located."

ARTICLE III

1. For the purposes of this Treaty, existing types of intermediate-range missiles are:

(a) for the United States of America, missiles of the types designated by the United States of America as the Pershing II and the BGM-109G, which are known to the Union of Soviet Socialist Republics by the same designations; and

(b) for the Union of Soviet Socialist Republics, missiles of the types designated by the Union of Soviet Socialist Republics as the RSD-10, the R-12 and the R-14, which are known to the United States of America as the SS-20, the SS-4 and the SS-5, respectively.

2. For the purposes of this Treaty, existing types of shorter-range missiles are:

(a) for the United States of America, missiles of the type designated by the United States of America as the Pershing IA, which is known to the Union of Soviet Socialist Republics by the same designation; and

(b) for the Union of Soviet Socialist Republics, missiles of the types designated by the Union of Soviet Socialist Republics as the OTR-22 and the OTR-23, which are known to the United States of America as the SS-12 and the SS-23, respectively.

ARTICLE IV

1. Each Party shall eliminate all its intermediate-range missiles and launchers of such missiles, and all support structures and support equipment of the categories listed in the Memorandum of Understanding associated with such missiles and launchers,

so that no later than three years after entry into force of this Treaty and thereafter no such missiles, launchers, support structures or support equipment shall be possessed by either Party.

2. To implement paragraph 1 of this Article, upon entry into force of this Treaty, both Parties shall begin and continue throughout the duration of each phase, the reduction of all types of their deployed and non-deployed intermediate-range missiles and deployed and non-deployed launchers of such missiles and support structures and support equipment associated with such missiles and launchers in accordance with the provisions of this Treaty. These reductions shall be implemented in two phases so that:

(a) by the end of the first phase, that is, no later than 29 months after entry into force of this Treaty:

(i) the number of deployed launchers of intermediate-range missiles for each Party shall not exceed the number of launchers that are capable of carrying or containing at one time missiles considered by the Parties to carry 171 warheads;

(ii) the number of deployed intermediate-range missiles for each Party shall not exceed the number of such missiles considered by the Parties to carry 180 warheads;

(iii) the aggregate number of deployed and non-deployed launchers of intermediate-range missiles for each Party shall not exceed the number of launchers that are capable of carrying or containing at one time missiles considered by the Parties to carry 200 warheads;

(iv) the aggregate number of deployed and non-deployed intermediate-range missiles for each Party shall not exceed the number of such missiles considered by the Parties to carry 200 warheads; and

(v) the ratio of the aggregate number of deployed and non-deployed intermediate-range GLBMs of existing types for each Party to the aggregate number of deployed and non-deployed intermediate-range missiles of existing types possessed by that Party shall not exceed the ratio of such intermediate-range GLBMs to such intermediate-range missiles for that Party as of November 1, 1987, as set forth in the Memorandum of Understanding; and

(b) by the end of the second phase, that is, no later than three years after entry into force of this Treaty, all intermediate-range missiles of each Party, launchers of such missiles and all support structures and support equipment of the categories listed in the Memorandum of Understanding associated with such missiles and launchers, shall be eliminated.

ARTICLE V

1. Each Party shall eliminate all its shorter-range missiles and launchers of such missiles, and all support equipment of the categories listed in the Memorandum of Understanding associated with such missiles and launchers, so that no later than 18 months after entry into force of this Treaty and thereafter no such missiles, launchers or support equipment shall be possessed by either Party.

2. No later than 90 days after entry into force of this Treaty, each Party shall complete the removal of all its deployed shorter-range missiles and deployed and non-deployed launchers of such missiles to elimination facilities and shall retain them at those locations until they are eliminated in accordance with the procedures set forth in the Protocol on Elimination. No later than 12 months after entry into force of this Treaty, each Party shall complete the removal of all its non-deployed shorter-range missiles to elimination facilities and shall retain them at those locations until they are eliminated in accordance with the procedures set forth in the Protocol on Elimination.

3. Shorter-range missiles and launchers of such missiles shall not be located at the same elimination facility. Such facilities shall be separated by no less than 1000 kilometers.

ARTICLE VI

1. Upon entry into force of this Treaty and thereafter, neither Party shall:

(a) produce or flight-test any intermediate-range missiles or produce any stages of such missiles or any launchers of such missiles; or

(b) produce, flight-test or launch any shorter-range missiles or produce any stages of such missiles or any launchers of such missiles.

2. Notwithstanding paragraph 1 of this Article, each Party shall have the right to produce a type of GLBM not limited by this Treaty which uses a stage which is outwardly similar to, but not interchangeable with, a stage of an existing type of intermediate-range GLBM having more than one stage, providing that that Party does not produce any other stage which is outwardly similar to, but not interchangeable with, any other stage of an existing type of intermediate-range GLBM.

ARTICLE VII

For the purposes of this Treaty:

1. If a ballistic missile or a cruise missile has been flight-tested or deployed for weapon delivery, all missiles of that type shall be considered to be weapon-delivery vehicles.

2. If a GLBM or GLCM is an intermediate-range missile, all GLBMs or GLCMs of that type shall be considered to be intermediate-range missiles. If a GLBM or GLCM is a shorter-range missile, all GLBMs or GLCMs of that type shall be considered to be shorter-range missiles.

3. If a GLBM is of a type developed and tested solely to intercept and counter objects not located on the surface of the earth, it shall not be considered to be a missile to which the limitations of this Treaty apply.

4. The range capability of a GLBM not listed in Article III of this Treaty shall be considered to be the maximum range to which it has been tested. The range capability of a GLCM not listed in Article III of this Treaty shall be considered to be the maximum distance which can be covered by the missile in its

standard design mode flying until fuel exhaustion, determined by projecting its flight path onto the earths sphere from the point of launch to the point of impact. GLBMs or GLCMs that have a range capability equal to or in excess of 500 kilometers but not in excess of 1000 kilometers shall be considered to be shorter-range missiles. GLBMs or GLCMs that have a range capability in excess of 1000 kilometers but not in excess of 5500 kilometers shall be considered to be intermediate-range missiles.

5. The maximum number of warheads an existing type of intermediate-range missile or shorter-range missile carries shall be considered to be the number listed for missiles of that type in the Memorandum of Understanding.

6. Each GLBM or GLCM shall be considered to carry the maximum number of warheads listed for a GLBM or GLCM of the type in the Memorandum of Understanding.

7. If a launcher has been tested for launching a GLBM or a GLCM, all launchers of that type shall be considered to have been tested for launching GLBMs or GLCMs.

8. If a launcher has contained or launched a particular type of GLBM or GLCM, all launchers of that type shall be considered to be launchers of that type of GLBM or GLCM.

9. The number of missiles each launcher of an existing type of intermediate-range missile or shorter-range missile shall be considered to be capable of carrying or containing at one time is the number listed for launchers of missiles of that type in the Memorandum of Understanding.

10. Except in the case of elimination in accordance with the procedures set forth in the Protocol on Elimination, the following shall apply:

(a) for GLBMs which are stored or moved in separate stages, the longest stage of an intermediate-range or shorter-range GLBM shall be counted as a complete missile;

(b) for GLBMs which are not stored or moved in separate stages, a canister of the type used in the launch of an intermediate-range GLBM, unless a Party proves to the satisfaction of the other Party that it does not contain such a missile, or an assembled intermediate-range or shorter-range GLBM, shall be counted as a complete missile; and

(c) for GLCMs, the airframe of an intermediate-range or shorter-range GLCM shall be counted as a complete missile.

11. A ballistic missile which is not a missile to be used in a ground-based mode shall not be considered to be a GLBM if it is test-launched at a test site from a fixed land-based launcher which is used solely for test purposes and which is distinguishable from GLBM launchers. A cruise missile which is not a missile to be used in a ground-based mode shall not be considered to be a GLCM if it is test-launched at a test site from a fixed land-based launcher which is used solely for test purposes and which is distinguishable from GLCM launchers.

12. Each Party shall have the right to produce and use for booster systems, which might otherwise be considered to be intermediate-range or shorter-range missiles, only existing types of booster stages for such booster systems. Launches of such booster systems shall not be considered to be flight-testing of intermediate-range or shorter-range missiles provided that:

(a) stages used in such booster systems are different from stages used in those missiles listed as existing types of intermediate-range or shorter-range missiles in Article III of this Treaty;

(b) such booster systems are used only for research and development purposes to test objects other than the booster systems themselves;

(c) the aggregate number of launchers for such booster systems shall not exceed 35 for each Party at any one time; and

(d) the launchers for such booster systems are fixed, emplaced above ground and located only at research and development launch sites which are specified in the Memorandum of Understanding.

Research and development launch sites shall not be subject to inspection pursuant to Article XI of this Treaty.

ARTICLE VIII

1. All intermediate-range missiles and launchers of such missiles shall be located in deployment areas, at missile support facilities or shall be in transit. Intermediate-range missiles or launchers of such missiles shall not be located elsewhere.

2. Stages of intermediate-range missiles shall be located in deployment areas, at missile support facilities or moving between deployment areas, between missile support facilities or between missile support facilities and deployment areas.

3. Until their removal to elimination facilities as required by paragraph 2 of Article V of this Treaty, all shorter-range missiles and launchers of such missiles shall be located at missile operating bases, at missile support facilities or shall be in transit. Shorter-range missiles or launchers of such missiles shall not be located elsewhere.

4. Transit of a missile or launcher subject to the provisions of this Treaty shall be completed within 25 days.

5. All deployment areas, missile operating bases and missile support facilities are specified in the Memorandum of Understanding or in subsequent updates of data pursuant to paragraphs 3, 5(a) or 5(b) of Article IX of this Treaty. Neither Party shall increase the number of, or change the location or boundaries of, deployment areas, missile operating bases or missile support facilities, except for elimination facilities, from those set forth in the Memorandum of Understanding. A missile support facility shall not be considered to be part of a deployment area even though it may be located within the geographic boundaries of a deployment area.

6. Beginning 30 days after entry into force of this Treaty, neither Party shall locate intermediate-range or shorter-range missiles, including stages of such missiles, or launchers of such missiles at missile production facilities, launcher production facilities or test ranges listed in the Memorandum of Understanding.

7. Neither Party shall locate any intermediate-range or shorter-range missiles at training facilities.

8. A non-deployed intermediate-range or shorter-range missile shall not be carried on or contained within a launcher of such a type of missile, except as required for maintenance conducted at repair facilities or for elimination by means of launching conducted at elimination facilities.

9. Training missiles and training launchers for intermediate-range or shorter-range missiles shall be subject to the same locational restrictions as are set forth for intermediate-range and shorter-range missiles and launchers of such missiles in paragraphs 1 and 3 of this Article.

ARTICLE IX

1. The Memorandum of Understanding contains categories of data relevant to obligations undertaken with regard to this Treaty and lists all intermediate-range and shorter-range missiles, launchers of such missiles, and support structures and support equipment associated with such missiles and launchers, possessed by the Parties as of November 1, 1987. Updates of that data and notifications required by this Article shall be provided according to the categories of data contained in the Memorandum of Understanding.

2. The Parties shall update that data and provide the notifications required by this Treaty through the Nuclear Risk Reduction Centers, established pursuant to the Agreement Between the United States of America and the Union of Soviet Socialist Republics on the Establishment of Nuclear Risk Reduction Centers of September 15, 1987.

3. No later than 30 days after entry into force of this Treaty, each Party shall provide the other Party with updated data, as of the date of entry into force of this Treaty, for all categories of data contained in the Memorandum of Understanding.

4. No later than 30 days after the end of each six-month interval following the entry into force of this Treaty, each Party shall provide updated data for all categories of data contained in the Memorandum of Understanding by informing the other Party of all changes, completed and in process, in that data, which have occurred during the six-month interval since the preceding data exchange, and the net effect of those changes.

5. Upon entry into force of this Treaty and thereafter, each Party shall provide the following notifications to the other Party:

(a) notification, no less than 30 days in advance, of the scheduled date of the elimination of a specific deployment area, missile operating base or missile support facility;

(b) notification, no less than 30 days in advance, of changes in the number or location of elimination facilities, including the location and scheduled date of each change;

(c) notification, except with respect to launches of intermediate-range missiles for the purpose of their elimination, no less than 30 days in advance, of the scheduled date of the initiation of the elimination of intermediate-range and shorter-range missiles, and stages of such missiles, and launchers of such missiles and support structures and support equipment associated with such missiles and launchers, including:

(i) the number and type of items of missile systems to be eliminated;

(ii) the elimination site;

(iii) for intermediate-range missiles, the location from which such missiles, launchers of such missiles and support equipment associated with such missiles and launchers are moved to the elimination facility; and

(iv) except in the case of support structures, the point of entry to be used by an inspection team conducting an inspection pursuant to paragraph 7 of Article XI of this Treaty and the estimated time of departure of an inspection team from the point of entry to the elimination facility;

(d) notification, no less than ten days in advance, of the scheduled date of the launch, or the scheduled date of the initiation of a series of launches, of intermediate-range missiles for the purpose of their elimination, including:

(i) the type of missiles to be eliminated;

(ii) the location of the launch, or, if elimination is by a series of launches, the location of such launches and the number of launches in the series;

(iii) the point of entry to be used by an inspection team conducting an inspection pursuant to paragraph 7 of Article XI of this Treaty; and

(iv) the estimated time of departure of an inspection team from the point of entry to the elimination facility;

(e) notification, no later than 48 hours after they occur, of changes in the number of intermediate-range and shorter-range missiles, launchers of such missiles and support structures and support equipment associated with such missiles and launchers resulting from elimination as described in the Protocol on Elimination, including:

(i) the number and type of items of a missile system which were eliminated; and

(ii) the date and location of such elimination; and

(f) notification of transit of intermediate-range or shorter-range missiles or launchers of such missiles, or the movement of training missiles or training launchers for such intermediate-range and shorter-range missiles, no later than 48 hours after it has been completed, including:

(i) the number of missiles or launchers;

(ii) the points, dates, and times of departure and arrival;

(iii) the mode of transport; and

(iv) the location and time at that location at least once every four days during the period of transit.

6. Upon entry into force of this Treaty and thereafter, each Party shall notify the other Party, no less than ten days in advance, of the scheduled date and location of the launch of a

research and development booster system as described in paragraph 12 of Article VII of this Treaty.

ARTICLE X

1. Each Party shall eliminate its intermediate-range and shorter-range missiles and launchers of such missiles and support structures and support equipment associated with such missiles and launchers in accordance with the procedures set forth in the Protocol on Elimination.

2. Verification by on-site inspection of the elimination of items of missile systems specified in the Protocol on Elimination shall be carried out in accordance with Article XI of this Treaty, the Protocol on Elimination and the Protocol on Inspection.

3. When a Party removes its intermediate-range missiles, launchers of such missiles and support equipment associated with such missiles and launchers from deployment areas to elimination facilities for the purpose of their elimination, it shall do so in complete deployed organizational units. For the United States of America, these units shall be Pershing II batteries and BGM-109G flights. For the Union of Soviet Socialist Republics, these units shall be SS-20 regiments composed of two or three battalions.

4. Elimination of intermediate-range and shorter-range missiles and launchers of such missiles and support equipment associated with such missiles and launchers shall be carried out at the facilities that are specified in the Memorandum of Understanding or notified in accordance with paragraph 5(b) of Article IX of this Treaty, unless eliminated in accordance with Sections IV or V of the Protocol on Elimination. Support structures, associated with the missiles and launchers subject to this Treaty, that are subject to elimination shall be eliminated *in situ*.

5. Each Party shall have the right, during the first six months after entry into force of this Treaty, to eliminate by means of launching no more than 100 of its intermediate-range missiles.

6. Intermediate-range and shorter-range missiles which have been tested prior to entry into force of this Treaty, but never deployed, and which are not existing types of intermediate-

range or shorter-range missiles listed in Article III of this Treaty, and launchers of such missiles, shall be eliminated within six months after entry into force of this Treaty in accordance with the procedures set forth in the Protocol on Elimination. Such missiles are:

(a) for the United States of America, missiles of the type designated by the United States of America as the Pershing IB, which is known to the Union of Soviet Socialist Republics by the same designation; and

(b) for the Union of Soviet Socialist Republics, missiles of the type designated by the Union of Soviet Socialist Republics as the RK-55, which is known to the United States of America as the SSC-X-4.

7. Intermediate-range and shorter-range missiles and launchers of such missiles and support structures and support equipment associated with such missiles and launchers shall be considered to be eliminated after completion of the procedures set forth in the Protocol on Elimination and upon the notification provided for in paragraph 5(e) of Article IX of this Treaty.

8. Each Party shall eliminate its deployment areas, missile operating bases and missile support facilities. A Party shall notify the other Party pursuant to paragraph 5(a) of Article IX of this Treaty once the conditions set forth below are fulfilled:

(a) all intermediate-range and shorter-range missiles, launchers of such missiles and support equipment associated with such missiles and launchers located there have been removed;

(b) all support structures associated with such missiles and launchers located there have been eliminated; and

(c) all activity related to production, flight-testing, training, repair, storage or deployment of such missiles and launchers has ceased there.

Such deployment areas, missile operating bases and missile support facilities shall be considered to be eliminated either when they have been inspected pursuant to paragraph 4 of Article XI of this Treaty or when 60 days have elapsed since the date of the scheduled elimination which was notified pursuant to paragraph 5(a) of Article IX of this Treaty. A deployment area, missile operating base or missile support facility listed in the Memorandum of Understanding that met the above conditions prior to entry into force of this Treaty, and is not included in the initial data exchange pursuant to paragraph 3 of Article IX of this Treaty, shall be considered to be eliminated.

9. If a Party intends to convert a missile operating base listed in the Memorandum of Understanding for use as a base associated with GLBM or GLCM systems not subject to this Treaty, then that Party shall notify the other Party, no less than 30 days in advance of the scheduled date of the initiation of the conversion, of the scheduled date and the purpose for which the base will be converted.

ARTICLE XI

1. For the purpose of ensuring verification of compliance with the provisions of this Treaty, each Party shall have the right to conduct on-site inspections. The Parties shall implement on-site inspections in accordance with this Article, the Protocol on Inspection and the Protocol on Elimination.

2. Each Party shall have the right to conduct inspections provided for by this Article both within the territory of the other Party and within the territories of basing countries.

3. Beginning 30 days after entry into force of this Treaty, each Party shall have the right to conduct inspections at all missile operating bases and missile support facilities specified in the Memorandum of Understanding other than missile production facilities, and at all elimination facilities included in the initial data update required by paragraph 3 of Article IX of this Treaty. These inspections shall be completed no later than 90 days after entry into force of this Treaty. The purpose of these inspections shall be to verify the number of missiles, launchers, support structures and support equipment and other data, as of the date of entry into force of this Treaty, provided pursuant to paragraph 3 of Article IX of this Treaty.

4. Each Party shall have the right to conduct inspections to verify the elimination, notified pursuant to paragraph 5(a) of Article IX of this Treaty, of missile operating bases and missile

support facilities other than missile production facilities, which are thus no longer subject to inspections pursuant to paragraph 5(a) of this Article. Such an inspection shall be carried out within 60 days after the scheduled date of the elimination of that facility. If a Party conducts an inspection at a particular facility pursuant to paragraph 3 of this Article after the scheduled date of the elimination of that facility, then no additional inspection of that facility pursuant to this paragraph shall be permitted.

5. Each Party shall have the right to conduct inspections pursuant to this paragraph for 13 years after entry into force of this Treaty. Each Party shall have the right to conduct 20 such inspections per calendar year during the first three years after entry into force of this Treaty, 15 such inspections per calendar year during the subsequent five years, and ten such inspections per calendar year during the last five years. Neither Party shall use more than half of its total number of these inspections per calendar year within the territory of any one basing country. Each Party shall have the right to conduct:

(a) inspections, beginning 90 days after entry into force of this Treaty, of missile operating bases and missile support facilities other than elimination facilities and missile production facilities, to ascertain, according to the categories of data specified in the Memorandum of Understanding, the numbers of missiles, launchers, support structures and support equipment located at each missile operating base or missile support facility at the time of the inspection; and

(b) inspections of former missile operating bases and former missile support facilities eliminated pursuant to paragraph 8 of Article X of this Treaty other than former missile production facilities.

6. Beginning 30 days after entry into force of this Treaty, each Party shall have the right, for 13 years after entry into force of this Treaty, to inspect by means of continuous monitoring:

(a) the portals of any facility of the other Party at which the final assembly of a GLBM using stages, any of which is outwardly similar to a stage of a solid-propellant

GLBM listed in Article III of this Treaty, is accomplished; or

(b) if a Party has no such facility, the portals of an agreed former missile production facility at which existing types of intermediate-range or shorter-range GLBMs were produced.

The Party whose facility is to be inspected pursuant to this paragraph shall ensure that the other Party is able to establish a permanent continuous monitoring system at that facility within six months after entry into force of this Treaty or within six months of initiation of the process of final assembly described in subparagraph (a). If, after the end of the second year after entry into force of this Treaty, neither Party conducts the process of final assembly described in subparagraph (a) for a period of 12 consecutive months, then neither Party shall have the right to inspect by means of continuous monitoring any missile production facility of the other Party unless the process of final assembly as described in subparagraph (a) is initiated again. Upon entry into force of this Treaty, the facilities to be inspected by continuous monitoring shall be: in accordance with subparagraph (b), for the United States of America, Hercules Plant Number 1, at Magna, Utah; in accordance with subparagraph (a), for the Union of Soviet Socialist Republics, the Votkinsk Machine Building Plant, Udmurt Autonomous Soviet Socialist Republic, Russian Soviet Federative Socialist Republic.

7. Each Party shall conduct inspections of the process of elimination, including elimination of intermediate-range missiles by means of launching, of intermediate-range and shorter-range missiles and launchers of such missiles and support equipment associated with such missiles and launchers carried out at elimination facilities in accordance with Article X of this Treaty and the Protocol on Elimination. Inspectors conducting inspections provided for in this paragraph shall determine that the processes specified for the elimination of the missiles, launchers and support equipment have been completed.

8. Each Party shall have the right to conduct inspections to confirm the completion of the process of elimination of intermediate-range and shorter-range missiles and launchers of

such missiles and support equipment associated with such missiles and launchers eliminated pursuant to Section V of the Protocol on Elimination, and of training missiles, training missile stages, training launch canisters and training launchers eliminated pursuant to Sections II, IV and V of the Protocol on Elimination.

ARTICLE XII

1. For the purpose of ensuring verification of compliance with the provisions of this Treaty, each Party shall use national technical means of verification at its disposal in a manner consistent with generally recognized principles of international law.

2. Neither Party shall:

(a) interfere with national technical means of verification of the other Party operating in accordance with paragraph 1 of this Article; or

(b) use concealment measures which impede verification of compliance with the provisions of this Treaty by national technical means of verification carried out in accordance with paragraph 1 of this Article. This obligation does not apply to cover or concealment practices, within a deployment area, associated with normal training, maintenance and operations, including the use of environmental shelters to protect missiles and launchers.

3. To enhance observation by national technical means of verification, each Party shall have the right until a Treaty between the Parties reducing and limiting strategic offensive arms enters into force, but in any event for no more than three years after entry into force of this Treaty, to request the implementation of cooperative measures at deployment bases for road-mobile GLBMs with a range capability in excess of 5500 kilometers, which are not former missile operating bases eliminated pursuant to paragraph 8 of Article X of this Treaty. The Party making such a request shall inform the other Party of the deployment base at which cooperative measures shall be implemented. The Party whose base is to be observed shall carry out the following cooperative measures:

(a) no later than six hours after such a request, the Party shall have opened the roofs of all fixed structures for launchers located at the base, removed completely all missiles on launchers from such fixed structures for launchers and displayed such missiles on launchers in the open without using concealment measures; and

(b) the Party shall leave the roofs open and the missiles on launchers in place until twelve hours have elapsed from the time of the receipt of a request for such an observation.

Each Party shall have the right to make six such requests per calendar year. Only one deployment base shall be subject to these cooperative measures at any one time.

ARTICLE XIII

1. To promote the objectives and implementation of the provisions of this Treaty, the Parties hereby establish the Special Verification Commission. The Parties agree that, if either Party so requests, they shall meet within the framework of the Special Verification Commission to:

(a) resolve questions relating to compliance with the obligations assumed; and

(b) agree upon such measures as may be necessary to improve the viability and effectiveness of this Treaty.

2. The Parties shall use the Nuclear Risk Reduction Centers, which provide for continuous communication between the Parties, to:

(a) exchange data and provide notifications as required by paragraphs 3, 4, 5 and 6 of Article IX of this Treaty and the Protocol on Elimination;

(b) provide and receive the information required by paragraph 9 of Article X of this Treaty;

(c) provide and receive notifications of inspections as required by Article XI of this Treaty and the Protocol on Inspection; and

(d) provide and receive requests for cooperative measures as provided for in paragraph 3 of Article XII of this Treaty.

ARTICLE XIV

The Parties shall comply with this Treaty and shall not assume any international obligations or undertakings which would conflict with its provisions.

ARTICLE XV

1. This Treaty shall be of unlimited duration.

2. Each Party shall, in exercising its national sovereignty, have the right to withdraw from this Treaty if it decides that extraordinary events related to the subject matter of this Treaty have jeopardized its supreme interests. It shall give notice of its decision to withdraw to the other Party six months prior to withdrawal from this Treaty. Such notice shall include a statement of the extraordinary events the notifying Party regards as having jeopardized its supreme interests.

ARTICLE XVI

Each Party may propose amendments to this Treaty. Agreed amendments shall enter into force in accordance with the procedures set forth in Article XVII governing the entry into force of this Treaty.

ARTICLE XVII

1. This Treaty, including the Memorandum of Understanding and Protocols, which form an integral part thereof, shall be subject to ratification in accordance with the constitutional procedures of each Party. This Treaty shall enter into force on the date of the exchange of instruments of ratification.

2. This Treaty shall be registered pursuant to Article 102 of the Charter of the United Nations.

DONE at Washington on December 8, 1987, in two copies, each in the English and Russian languages, both texts being equally authentic.

FOR THE UNITED STATES OF AMERICA:

Ronald Reagan

President of the United States of America

FOR THE UNION OF SOVIET SOCIALIST REPUBLICS:

Mikhail Gorbachev

General Secretary of the Central Committee of the CPSU

8

Treaty between the United States of America and the Union of Soviet Socialist Republics on Underground Nuclear Explosions for Peaceful Purposes

Signed at Washington and Moscow May 28, 1976
Entered into force December 11, 1990

The United States of America and the Union of Soviet Socialist Republics, hereinafter referred to as the Parties,

Proceeding from a desire to implement Article III of the Treaty Between the United States of America and the Union of Soviet Socialist Republics on the Limitation of Underground Nuclear Weapon Tests, which calls for the earliest possible conclusion of an agreement on underground nuclear explosions for peaceful purposes,

Reaffirming their adherence to the objectives and principles of the Treaty Banning Nuclear Weapon Tests in the Atmosphere, in Outer Space and Under Water, the Treaty on Non-Proliferation of Nuclear Weapons, and the Treaty on the Limitation of Underground Nuclear Weapon Tests, and their determination to observe strictly the provisions of these international agreements,

Desiring to assure that underground nuclear explosions for peaceful purposes shall not be used for purposes related to nuclear weapons,

Desiring that utilization of nuclear energy be directed only toward peaceful purposes,

Desiring to develop appropriately cooperation in the field of underground nuclear explosions for peaceful purposes,

Have agreed as follows:

ARTICLE I

1. The Parties enter into this Treaty to satisfy the obligations in Article III of the Treaty on the Limitation of Underground Nuclear Weapon Tests, and assume additional obligations in accordance with the provisions of this Treaty.

2. This Treaty shall govern all underground nuclear explosions for peaceful purposes conducted by the Parties after March 31, 1976.

ARTICLE II

For the purposes of this Treaty:

(a) "explosion" means any individual or group underground nuclear explosion for peaceful purposes;

(b) "explosive" means any device, mechanism or system for producing an individual explosion;

(c) "group explosion" means two or more individual explosions for which the time interval between successive individual explosions does not exceed five seconds and for which the emplacement points of all explosives can be interconnected by straight line segments, each of which joins two emplacement points and each of which does not exceed 40 kilometers.

ARTICLE III

1. Each Party, subject to the obligations assumed under this Treaty and other international agreements, reserves the right to:

(a) carry out explosions at any place under its jurisdiction or control outside the geographical boundaries of test sites specified under the provisions of the Treaty on the Limitation of Underground Nuclear Weapon Tests; and

(b) carry out, participate or assist in carrying out explosions in the territory of another State at the request of such other State.

2. Each Party undertakes to prohibit, to prevent and not to carry out at any place under its jurisdiction or control, and further undertakes not to carry out, participate or assist in carrying out anywhere:

(a) any individual explosion having a yield exceeding 150 kilotons;

(b) any group explosion:

(1) having an aggregate yield exceeding 150 kilotons except in ways that will permit identification of each individual explosion and determination of the yield of each individual explosion in the group in accordance with the provisions of Article IV of and the Protocol to this Treaty;

(2) having an aggregate yield exceeding one and one-half megatons;

(c) any explosion which does not carry out a peaceful application;

(d) any explosion except in compliance with the provisions of the Treaty Banning Nuclear Weapon Tests in the Atmosphere, in Outer Space and Under Water, the Treaty on the Non-Proliferation of Nuclear Weapons, and other international agreements entered into by that Party.

3. The question of carrying out any individual explosion having a yield exceeding the yield specified in paragraph 2(a) of this article will be considered by the Parties at an appropriate time to be agreed.

ARTICLE IV

1. For the purpose of providing assurance of compliance with the provisions of this Treaty, each Party shall:

(a) use national technical means of verification at its disposal in a manner consistent with generally recognized principles of international law; and

(b) provide to the other Party information and access to sites of explosions and furnish assistance in accordance with the provisions set forth in the Protocol to this Treaty.

2. Each Party undertakes not to interfere with the national technical means of verification of the other Party operating in accordance with paragraph 1(a) of this article, or with the implementation of the provisions of paragraph 1(b) of this article.

ARTICLE V

1. To promote the objectives and implementation of the provisions of this Treaty, the Parties shall establish promptly a Joint Consultative Commission within the framework of which they will:

(a) consult with each other, make inquiries and furnish information in response to such inquiries, to assure confidence in compliance with the obligations assumed;

(b) consider questions concerning compliance with the obligations assumed and related situations which may be considered ambiguous;

(c) consider questions involving unintended interference with the means for assuring compliance with the provisions of this Treaty;

(d) consider changes in technology or other new circumstances which have a bearing on the provisions of this Treaty; and

(e) consider possible amendments to provisions governing underground nuclear explosions for peaceful purposes.

2. The Parties through consultation shall establish, and may amend as appropriate, Regulations for the Joint Consultative Commission governing procedures, composition and other relevant matters.

ARTICLE VI

1. The Parties will develop cooperation on the basis of mutual benefit, equality, and reciprocity in various areas related to carrying out underground nuclear explosions for peaceful purposes.

2. The Joint Consultative Commission will facilitate this cooperation by considering specific areas and forms of

cooperation which shall be determined by agreement between the Parties in accordance with their constitutional procedures.

3. The Parties will appropriately inform the International Atomic Energy Agency of results of their cooperation in the field of underground nuclear explosions for peaceful purposes.

ARTICLE VII

1. Each Party shall continue to promote the development of the international agreement or agreements and procedures provided for in Article V of the Treaty on the Non-Proliferation of Nuclear Weapons, and shall provide appropriate assistance to the International Atomic Energy Agency in this regard.

2. Each Party undertakes not to carry out, participate or assist in the carrying out of any explosion in the territory of another State unless that State agrees to the implementation in its territory of the international observation and procedures contemplated by Article V of the Treaty on the Non-Proliferation of Nuclear Weapons and the provisions of Article IV of and the Protocol to this Treaty, including the provision by that State of the assistance necessary for such implementation and of the privileges and immunities specified in the Protocol.

ARTICLE VIII

1. This Treaty shall remain in force for a period of five years, and it shall be extended for successive five-year periods unless either Party notifies the other of its termination no later than six months prior to its expiration. Before the expiration of this period the Parties may, as necessary, hold consultations to consider the situation relevant to the substance of this Treaty. However, under no circumstances shall either Party be entitled to terminate this Treaty while the Treaty on the Limitation of Underground Nuclear Weapon Tests remains in force.

2. Termination of the Treaty on the Limitation of Underground Nuclear Weapon Tests shall entitle either Party to withdraw from this Treaty at any time.

3. Each Party may propose amendments to this Treaty. Amendments shall enter into force on the day of the exchange of instruments of ratification of such amendments.

ARTICLE IX

1. This Treaty, including the Protocol which forms an integral part hereof, shall be subject to ratification in accordance with the constitutional procedures of each Party. This Treaty shall enter into force on the day of the exchange of instruments of ratification which exchange shall take place simultaneously with the exchange of instruments of ratification of the Treaty on the Limitation of Underground Nuclear Weapon Tests.

2. This Treaty shall be registered pursuant to Article 102 of the Charter of the United Nations.

DONE at Washington and Moscow, on May 28, 1976, in duplicate, in the English and Russian languages, both texts being equally authentic.

FOR THE UNITED STATES OF AMERICA:
GERALD R. FORD
The President of the United States of America

FOR THE UNION OF SOVIET SOCIALIST REPUBLICS:
L. BREZHNEV
General Secretary of the Central Committee of the CPSU

9

Biological Weapons Convention Texts

Convention on the Prohibition of the Development, Production and Stockpiling of Bacteriological (Biological) and Toxin Weapons and on Their Destruction

Signed at Washington, London, and Moscow April 10, 1972
Ratification advised by U.S. Senate December 16, 1974
Ratified by U.S. President January 22, 1975
U.S. ratification deposited at Washington, London, and Moscow March 26, 1975
Proclaimed by U.S. President March 26, 1975
Entered into force March 26, 1975

The States Parties to this Convention,

Determined to act with a view to achieving effective progress towards general and complete disarmament, including the prohibition and elimination of all types of weapons of mass destruction, and convinced that the prohibition of the development, production and stockpiling of chemical and bacteriological (biological) weapons and their elimination, through effective measures, will facilitate the achievement of general and complete disarmament under strict and effective international control,

Recognizing the important significance of the Protocol for the Prohibition of the Use in War of Asphyxiating, Poisonous or

Other Gases, and of Bacteriological Methods of Warfare, signed at Geneva on June 17, 1925, and conscious also of the contribution which the said Protocol has already made, and continues to make, to mitigating the horrors of war,

Reaffirming their adherence to the principles and objectives of that Protocol and calling upon all States to comply strictly with them,

Recalling that the General Assembly of the United Nations has repeatedly condemned all actions contrary to the principles and objectives of the Geneva Protocol of June 17, 1925,

Desiring to contribute to the strengthening of confidence between peoples and the general improvement of the international atmosphere,

Desiring also to contribute to the realization of the purposes and principles of the Charter of the United Nations,

Convinced of the importance and urgency of eliminating from the arsenals of States, through effective measures, such dangerous weapons of mass destruction as those using chemical or bacteriological (biological) agents,

Recognizing that an agreement on the prohibition of bacteriological (biological) and toxin weapons represents a first possible step towards the achievement of agreement on effective measures also for the prohibition of the development, production and stockpiling of chemical weapons, and determined to continue negotiations to that end,

Determined, for the sake of all mankind, to exclude completely the possibility of bacteriological (biological) agents and toxins being used as weapons,

Convinced that such use would be repugnant to the conscience of mankind and that no effort should be spared to minimize this risk,

Have agreed as follows:

ARTICLE I

Each State Party to this Convention undertakes never in any circumstances to develop, produce, stockpile or otherwise acquire or retain:

(1) Microbial or other biological agents, or toxins whatever their origin or method of production, of types and in quantities that have no justification for prophylactic, protective or other peaceful purposes;

(2) Weapons, equipment or means of delivery designed to use such agents or toxins for hostile purposes or in armed conflict.

ARTICLE II

Each State Party to this Convention undertakes to destroy, or to divert to peaceful purposes, as soon as possible but not later than nine months after the entry into force of the Convention, all agents, toxins, weapons, equipment and means of delivery specified in article I of the Convention, which are in its possession or under its jurisdiction or control. In implementing the provisions of this article, all necessary safety precautions shall be observed to protect populations and the environment.

ARTICLE III

Each State Party to this Convention undertakes not to transfer to any recipient whatsoever, directly or indirectly, and not in any way to assist, encourage, or induce any State, group of States or international organizations to manufacture or otherwise acquire any of the agents, toxins, weapons, equipment or means of delivery specified in article I of the Convention.

ARTICLE IV

Each State Party to this Convention shall, in accordance with its constitutional processes, take any necessary measures to prohibit and prevent the development, production, stockpiling, acquisition, or retention of the agents, toxins, weapons, equipment and means of delivery specified in article I of the Convention, within the territory of such State, under its jurisdiction or under its control anywhere.

ARTICLE V

The States Parties to this Convention undertake to consult one another and to cooperate in solving any problems which may arise in relation to the objective of, or in the application of the provisions of, the Convention. Consultation and cooperation pursuant to this article may also be undertaken through appropriate international procedures within the framework of the United Nations and in accordance with its Charter.

ARTICLE VI

(1) Any State Party to this Convention which finds that any other State Party is acting in breach of obligations deriving from the provisions of the Convention may lodge a complaint with the Security Council of the United Nations. Such a complaint should include all possible evidence confirming its validity, as well as a request for its consideration by the Security Council.

(2) Each State Party to this Convention undertakes to cooperate in carrying out any investigation which the Security Council may initiate, in accordance with the provisions of the Charter of the United Nations, on the basis of the complaint received by the Council. The Security Council shall inform the States Parties to the Convention of the results of the investigation.

ARTICLE VII

Each State Party to this Convention undertakes to provide or support assistance, in accordance with the United Nations Charter, to any Party to the Convention which so requests, if the Security Council decides that such Party has been exposed to danger as a result of violation of the Convention.

ARTICLE VIII

Nothing in this Convention shall be interpreted as in any way limiting or detracting from the obligations assumed by any State under the Protocol for the Prohibition of the Use in War of Asphyxiating, Poisonous or Other Gases, and of Bacteriological Methods of Warfare, signed at Geneva on June 17, 1925.

ARTICLE IX

Each State Party to this Convention affirms the recognized objective of effective prohibition of chemical weapons and, to this end, undertakes to continue negotiations in good faith with a view to reaching early agreement on effective measures for the prohibition of their development, production and stockpiling and for their destruction, and on appropriate measures concerning equipment and means of delivery specifically designed for the production or use of chemical agents for weapons purposes.

ARTICLE X

(1) The States Parties to this Convention undertake to facilitate, and have the right to participate in, the fullest possible exchange of equipment, materials and scientific and technological information for the use of bacteriological (biological) agents and toxins for peaceful purposes. Parties to the Convention in a position to do so shall also cooperate in contributing individually or together with other States or international organizations to the further development and application of scientific discoveries in the field of bacteriology (biology) for prevention of disease, or for other peaceful purposes.

(2) This Convention shall be implemented in a manner designed to avoid, hampering the economic or technological development of States Parties to the Convention or international cooperation in the field of peaceful bacteriological (biological) activities, including the international exchange of bacteriological (biological) agents and toxins and equipment for the processing, use or production of bacteriological (biological) agents and toxins for peaceful purposes in accordance with the provisions of the Convention.

ARTICLE XI

Any State Party may propose amendments to this Convention. Amendments shall enter into force for each State Party accepting the amendments upon their acceptance by a majority of the States Parties to the Convention and thereafter for each remaining State Party on the date of acceptance by it.

ARTICLE XII

Five years after the entry into force of this Convention, or earlier, if it is requested by a majority of Parties to the Convention by submitting a proposal to this effect to the Depositary Governments, a conference of States Parties to the Convention shall be held at Geneva, Switzerland, to review the operation of the Convention, with a view to assuring that the purposes of the preamble and the provisions of the Convention, including the provisions concerning negotiations on chemical weapons, are being realized. Such review shall take into account any new scientific and technological developments relevant to the Convention.

ARTICLE XIII

(1) This Convention shall be of unlimited duration.

(2) Each State Party to this Convention shall, in exercising its national sovereignty, have the right to withdraw from the Convention if it decides that extraordinary events related to the subject matter of the Convention, have jeopardized the supreme interests of its country. It shall give notice of such withdrawal to all other States Parties to the Convention and to the United Nations Security Council three months in advance. Such notice shall include a statement of the extraordinary events it regards as having jeopardized its supreme interests.

ARTICLE XIV

(1) This Convention shall be open to all States for signature. Any State which does not sign the Convention before its entry into force in accordance with paragraph (3) of this Article may accede to it at any time.

(2) This Convention shall be subject to ratification by signatory States. Instruments of ratification and instruments of accession shall be deposited with the Governments of the United States of America, the United Kingdom of Great Britain and Northern Ireland and the Union of Soviet Socialist Republics, which are hereby designated the Depositary Governments.

(3) This Convention shall enter into force after the deposit of instruments of ratification by twenty-two Governments, including the Governments designated as Depositaries of the Convention.

(4) For States whose instruments of ratification or accession are deposited subsequent to the entry into force of this Convention, it shall enter into force on the date of the deposit of their instruments of ratification or accession.

(5) The Depositary Governments shall promptly inform all signatory and acceding States of the date of each signature, the date of deposit of each instrument of ratification or of accession and the date of the entry into force of this Convention, and of the receipt of other notices.

(6) This Convention shall be registered by the Depositary Governments pursuant to Article 102 of the Charter of the United Nations.

ARTICLE XV

This Convention, the English, Russian, French, Spanish and Chinese texts of which are equally authentic, shall be deposited in the archives of the Depositary Governments. Duly certified copies of the Convention shall be transmitted by the Depositary Governments to the Governments of the signatory and acceding states.

IN WITNESS WHEREOF the undersigned, duly authorized, have signed this Convention.

DONE in triplicate, at the cities of Washington, London and Moscow, this tenth day of April, one thousand nine hundred and seventy-two.

Parties and Signatories of the Biological Weapons Convention State (Country)

Afghanistan
Albania
Argentina
Armenia
Australia
Austria (1)
Bahamas
Bahrain (1)
Bangladesh
Barbados
Belarus
Belgium
Belize
Benin
Bhutan
Bolivia
Bosnia Herzegovina
Botswana
Brazil
Brunei Darussalam (2)
Bulgaria
Burkina Faso
Cambodia (Kampuchea)
Canada
Cape Verde
Chile
China, People's Republic of (3)
Colombia
Congo
Costa Rica
Croatia
Cuba
Cyprus
Czech Republic
Denmark
Dominica (2)
Dominican Republic
Ecuador

El Salvador
Equatorial Guinea
Estonia
Ethiopia
Fiji
Finland
France
Gambia, The
Georgia
Germany Ghana
Greece
Grenada
Guatemala
Guinea-Bissau
Honduras
Hungary
Iceland
India
Indonesia
Iran
Iraq
Ireland
Italy
Jamaica
Japan
Jordan
Kenya
Korea, Democratic People's Republic of
Korea, Republic of
Kuwait
Kyrgyzstan (4)
Laos
Latvia
Lebanon
Lesotho
Libya
Liechtenstein
Lithuania
Luxembourg
Macedonia, Former Yugoslav Republic of
Malaysia (1)
Maldives
Malta
Mauritius
Mexico
Monaco
Mongolia
Netherlands (5)
New Zealand
Nicaragua
Niger
Nigeria
Norway
Oman
Pakistan
Panama
Papua New Guinea
Paraguay
Peru
Philippines
Poland
Portugal
Qatar
Romania
Russian Federation
Rwanda
St. Kitts and Nevis
St. Lucia
St. Vincent and the Grenadines
San Marino
Sao Tome and Principe
Saudi Arabia
Senegal
Serbia-Montenegro (Formerly Yugoslavia)
Seychelles
Sierra Leone
Singapore
Slovak Republic
Slovenia
Solomon Islands (2)
South Africa
Spain
Sri Lanka
Surinam
Swaziland
Sweden
Switzerland
Thailand
Togo
Tonga
Tunisia
Turkey
Turkmenistan
Uganda
Ukraine
United Kingdom (6)
United States
Uruguay
Uzbekistan
Vanuatu
Venezuela
Vietnam
Yemen
Zaire
Zimbabwe

SIGNATORY COUNTRIES

Burundi
Central African Republic
Cote d'Ivoire
Egypt
Gabon
Guyana
Haiti
Liberia
Madagascar
Malawi
Mali
Morocco
Myanmar (Burma)
Nepal
Somalia
Syria
Tanzania
United Arab Emirates (6)

(1) With reservation

(2) Based on general declarations concerning Treaty obligations applicable prior to independence.

(3) Effective January 1, 1979, the United States recognized the government of the People's Republic of China as the sole government of China. The authorities on Taiwan state they will continue to abide by the provisions of the Convention, and the United States regards them as bound by its obligations.

(4) Formerly part of the Soviet Union who signed and ratified the Convention on behalf of Kyrgyzstan. Date of accession is unknown but Confidence Building Measures Data Declaration submitted to the UN in 1993.

(5) Applicable to Netherlands Antilles and Aruba.

(6) Extended to territories under the territorial sovereignty of the United Kingdom. Also extended to New Hebrides; continued application to Vanuatu not determined.

The United Arab Emirates which did not ratify the Convention is listed as one country.

10

Treaty between the United States of America and the Union of Soviet Socialist Republics on the Limitation of Underground Nuclear Weapon Tests

Signed at Moscow July 3, 1974
Ratified December 8, 1990
Entered into force December 11, 1990

The United States of America and the Union of Soviet Socialist Republics, hereinafter referred to as the Parties,

Declaring their intention to achieve at the earliest possible date the cessation of the nuclear arms race and to take effective measures toward reductions in strategic arms, nuclear disarmament, and general and complete disarmament under strict and effective international control,

Recalling the determination expressed by the Parties to the 1963 Treaty Banning Nuclear Weapon Tests in the Atmosphere, in Outer Space and Under Water in its Preamble to seek to achieve the discontinuance of all test explosions of nuclear weapons for all time, and to continue negotiations to this end,

Noting that the adoption of measures for the further limitation of underground nuclear weapon tests would contribute to the achievement of these objectives and would meet the interests of strengthening peace and the further relaxation of international tension,

Reaffirming their adherence to the objectives and principles of the Treaty Banning Nuclear Weapon Tests in the Atmosphere, in Outer Space and Under Water and of the Treaty on the Non-Proliferation of Nuclear Weapons,

Have agreed as follows:

ARTICLE I

1. Each Party undertakes to prohibit, to prevent, and not to carry out any underground nuclear weapon test having a yield exceeding 150 kilotons at any place under its jurisdiction or control, beginning March 31, 1976.

2. Each Party shall limit the number of its underground nuclear weapon tests to a minimum.

3. The Parties shall continue their negotiations with a view toward achieving a solution to the problem of the cessation of all underground nuclear weapon tests.

ARTICLE II

1. For the purpose of providing assurance of compliance with the provisions of this Treaty, each Party shall use national technical means of verification at its disposal in a manner consistent with the generally recognized principles of international law.

2. Each Party undertakes not to interfere with the national technical means of verification of the other Party operating in accordance with paragraph 1 of this Article.

3. To promote the objectives and implementation of the provisions of this Treaty the Parties shall, as necessary, consult with each other, make inquiries and furnish information in response to such inquiries.

ARTICLE III

The provisions of this Treaty do not extend to underground nuclear explosions carried out by the Parties for peaceful purposes. Underground nuclear explosions for peaceful purposes shall be governed by an agreement which is to be negotiated and concluded by the Parties at the earliest possible time.

ARTICLE IV

This Treaty shall be subject to ratification in accordance with the constitutional procedures of each Party. This Treaty shall enter into force on the day of the exchange of instruments of ratification.

ARTICLE V

1. This Treaty shall remain in force for a period of five years. Unless replaced earlier by an agreement in implementation of the objectives specified in paragraph 3 of Article I of this Treaty, it shall be extended for successive five-year periods unless either Party notifies the other of its termination no later than six months prior to the expiration of the Treaty. Before the expiration of this period the Parties may, as necessary, hold consultations to consider the situation relevant to the substance of this Treaty and to introduce possible amendments to the text of the Treaty.

2. Each Party shall, in exercising its national sovereignty, have the right to withdraw from this Treaty if it decides that extraordinary events related to the subject matter of this Treaty have jeopardized its supreme interests. It shall give notice of its decision to the other Party six months prior to withdrawal from this Treaty. Such notice shall include a statement of the extraordinary events the notifying Party regards as having jeopardized its supreme interests.

3. This Treaty shall be registered pursuant to Article 102 of the Charter of the United Nations.

DONE at Moscow on July 3, 1974, in duplicate, in the English and Russian languages, both texts being equally authentic.

FOR THE UNITED STATES OF AMERICA:

RICHARD NIXON

The President of the United States of America

FOR THE UNION OF SOVIET SOCIALIST REPUBLICS:

L. BREZHNEV

General Secretary of the Central Committee of the CPSU

11

Treaty between the United States of America and the Union of Soviet Socialist Republics on the Limitation of Anti-ballistic Missile Systems

Signed at Moscow May 26, 1972
Ratification advised by U.S. Senate August 3, 1972
Ratified by U.S. President September 30, 1972
Proclaimed by U.S. President October 3, 1972
Instruments of ratification exchanged October 3, 1972
Entered into force October 3, 1972

The United States of America and the Union of Soviet Socialist Republics, hereinafter referred to as the Parties,

Proceeding from the premise that nuclear war would have devastating consequences for all mankind,

Considering that effective measures to limit anti-ballistic missile systems would be a substantial factor in curbing the race in strategic offensive arms and would lead to a decrease in the risk of outbreak of war involving nuclear weapons,

Proceeding from the premise that the limitation of anti-ballistic missile systems, as well as certain agreed measures with respect to the limitation of strategic offensive arms, would contribute to the creation of more favorable conditions for further negotiations on limiting strategic arms,

Mindful of their obligations under Article VI of the Treaty on the Non-Proliferation of Nuclear Weapons,

Declaring their intention to achieve at the earliest possible date the cessation of the nuclear arms race and to take effective measures toward reductions in strategic arms, nuclear disarmament, and general and complete disarmament,

Desiring to contribute to the relaxation of international tension and the strengthening of trust between States,

Have agreed as follows:

ARTICLE I

1. Each Party undertakes to limit anti-ballistic missile (ABM) systems and to adopt other measures in accordance with the provisions of this Treaty.

2. Each Party undertakes not to deploy ABM systems for a defense of the territory of its country and not to provide a base for such a defense, and not to deploy ABM systems for defense of an individual region except as provided for in Article III of this Treaty.

ARTICLE II

1. For the purpose of this Treaty an ABM system is a system to counter strategic ballistic missiles or their elements in flight trajectory, currently consisting of:

(a) ABM interceptor missiles, which are interceptor missiles constructed and deployed for an ABM role, or of a type tested in an ABM mode;

(b) ABM launchers, which are launchers constructed and deployed for launching ABM interceptor missiles; and

(c) ABM radars, which are radars constructed and deployed for an ABM role, or of a type tested in an ABM mode.

2. The ABM system components listed in paragraph 1 of this Article include those which are:

(a) operational;

(b) under construction;

(c) undergoing testing;

(d) undergoing overhaul, repair or conversion; or

(e) mothballed.

ARTICLE III

Each Party undertakes not to deploy ABM systems or their components except that:

(a) within one ABM system deployment area having a radius of one hundred and fifty kilometers and centered on the Partys national capital, a Party may deploy: (1) no more than one hundred ABM launchers and no more than one hundred ABM interceptor missiles at launch sites, and (2) ABM radars within no more than six ABM radar complexes, the area of each complex being circular and having a diameter of no more than three kilometers; and

(b) within one ABM system deployment area having a radius of one hundred and fifty kilometers and containing ICBM silo launchers, a Party may deploy: (1) no more than one hundred ABM launchers and no more than one hundred ABM interceptor missiles at launch sites, (2) two large phased-array ABM radars comparable in potential to corresponding ABM radars operational or under construction on the date of signature of the Treaty in an ABM system deployment area containing ICBM silo launchers, and (3) no more than eighteen ABM radars each having a potential less than the potential of the smaller of the above-mentioned two large phased-array ABM radars.

ARTICLE IV

The limitations provided for in Article III shall not apply to ABM systems or their components used for development or testing, and located within current or additionally agreed test ranges. Each Party may have no more than a total of fifteen ABM launchers at test ranges.

ARTICLE V

1. Each Party undertakes not to develop, test, or deploy ABM systems or components which are sea-based, air-based, space-based, or mobile land-based.

2. Each Party undertakes not to develop, test or deploy ABM launchers for launching more than one ABM interceptor missile at a time from each launcher, not to modify deployed launchers to provide them with such a capacity, not to develop, test, or

deploy automatic or semi-automatic or other similar systems for rapid reload of ABM launchers.

ARTICLE VI

To enhance assurance of the effectiveness of the limitations on ABM systems and their components provided by the Treaty, each Party undertakes:

(a) not to give missiles, launchers, or radars, other than ABM interceptor missiles, ABM launchers, or ABM radars, capabilities to counter strategic ballistic missiles or their elements in flight trajectory, and not to test them in an ABM mode; and

(b) not to deploy in the future radars for early warning of strategic ballistic missile attack except at locations along the periphery of its national territory and oriented outward.

ARTICLE VII

Subject to the provisions of this Treaty, modernization and replacement of ABM systems or their components may be carried out.

ARTICLE VIII

ABM systems or their components in excess of the numbers or outside the areas specified in this Treaty, as well as ABM systems or their components prohibited by this Treaty, shall be destroyed or dismantled under agreed procedures within the shortest possible agreed period of time.

ARTICLE IX

To assure the viability and effectiveness of this Treaty, each Party undertakes not to transfer to other States, and not to deploy outside its national territory, ABM systems or their components limited by this Treaty.

ARTICLE X

Each Party undertakes not to assume any international obligations which would conflict with this Treaty.

ARTICLE XI

The Parties undertake to continue active negotiations for limitations on strategic offensive arms.

ARTICLE XII

1. For the purpose of providing assurance or compliance with the provisions of this Treaty, each Party shall use national technical means of verification at its disposal in a manner consistent with generally recognized principles of international law.

2. Each Party undertakes not to interfere with the national technical means of verification of the other Party operating in accordance with paragraph 1 of this Article.

3. Each Party undertakes not to use deliberate concealment measures which impede verification by national technical means of compliance with the provisions of this Treaty. This obligation shall not require changes in current construction, assembly, conversion, or overhaul practices.

ARTICLE XIII

1. To promote the objectives and implementation of the provisions of this Treaty, the Parties shall establish promptly a Standing Consultative Commission, within the framework of which they will:

(a) consider questions concerning compliance with the obligations assumed and related situations which may be considered ambiguous;

(b) provide on a voluntary basis such information as either Party considers necessary to assure confidence in compliance with the obligations assumed;

(c) consider questions involving unintended interference with national technical means of verification;

(d) consider possible changes in the strategic situation which have a bearing on the provisions of this Treaty;

(e) agree upon procedures and dates for destruction or dismantling of ABM systems or their components in cases provided for by the provisions of this Treaty;

(f) consider, as appropriate, possible proposals for further increasing the viability of this Treaty; including proposals for amendments in accordance with the provisions of this Treaty;

(g) consider, as appropriate, proposals for further measures aimed at limiting strategic arms.

2. The Parties through consultation shall establish, and may amend as appropriate, Regulations for the Standing Consultative Commission governing procedures, composition and other relevant matters.

ARTICLE XIV

1. Each Party may propose amendments to this Treaty. Agreed amendments shall enter into force in accordance with the procedures governing the entry into force of this Treaty.

2. Five years after entry into force of this Treaty, and at five-year intervals thereafter, the Parties shall together conduct a review of this Treaty.

ARTICLE XV

1. This Treaty shall be of unlimited duration.

2. Each Party shall, in exercising its national sovereignty, have the right to withdraw from this Treaty if it decides that extraordinary events related to the subject matter of this Treaty have jeopardized its supreme interests. It shall give notice of its decision to the other Party six months prior to withdrawal from the Treaty. Such notice shall include a statement of the extraordinary events the notifying Party regards as having jeopardized its supreme interests.

ARTICLE XVI

1. This Treaty shall be subject to ratification in accordance with the constitutional procedures of each Party. The Treaty shall enter into force on the day of the exchange of instruments of ratification.

2. This Treaty shall be registered pursuant to Article 102 of the Charter of the United Nations.

DONE at Moscow on May 26, 1972, in two copies, each in the English and Russian languages, both texts being equally authentic.

FOR THE UNITED STATES OF AMERICA:
RICHARD NIXON
President of the United States of America
FOR THE UNION OF SOVIET SOCIALIST REPUBLICS:
L.I. BREZHNEV
General Secretary of the Central Committee of the CPSU

12

Strategic Arms Limitation Talk (Salt I)

Interim Agreement between The United States of America and The Union of Soviet Socialist Republics on Certain Measures with Respect to The Limitation of Strategic Offensive Arms

Signed at Moscow May 26, 1972
Approval authorized by U.S. Congress September 30, 1972
Approved by U.S. President September 30, 1972
Notices of acceptance exchanged October 3, 1972
Entered into force October 3, 1972

The United States of America and the Union of Soviet Socialist Republics, hereinafter referred to as the Parties,

Convinced that the Treaty on the Limitation of Anti-Ballistic Missile Systems and this Interim Agreement on Certain Measures with Respect to the Limitation of Strategic Offensive Arms will contribute to the creation of more favorable conditions for active negotiations on limiting strategic arms as well as to the relaxation of international tension and the strengthening of trust between States,

Taking into account the relationship between strategic offensive and defensive arms,

Mindful of their obligations under Article VI of the Treaty on the Non-Proliferation of Nuclear Weapons,

Have agreed as follows:

ARTICLE I

The Parties undertake not to start construction of additional fixed land-based intercontinental ballistic missile (ICBM) launchers after July 1, 1972.

ARTICLE II

The Parties undertake not to convert land-based launchers for light ICBMs, or for ICBMs of older types deployed prior to 1964, into land-based launchers for heavy ICBMs of types deployed after that time.

ARTICLE III

The Parties undertake to limit submarine-launched ballistic missile (SLBM) launchers and modern ballistic missile submarines to the numbers operational and under construction on the date of signature of this Interim Agreement, and in addition to launchers and submarines constructed under procedures established by the Parties as replacements for an equal number of ICBM launchers of older types deployed prior to 1964 or for launchers on older submarines.

ARTICLE IV

Subject to the provisions of this Interim Agreement, modernization and replacement of strategic offensive ballistic missiles and launchers covered by this Interim Agreement may be undertaken.

ARTICLE V

1. For the purpose of providing assurance of compliance with the provisions of this Interim Agreement, each Party shall use national technical means of verification at its disposal in a manner consistent with generally recognized principles of international law.

2. Each Party undertakes not to interfere with the national technical means of verification of the other Party operating in accordance with paragraph 1 of this Article.

3. Each Party undertakes not to use deliberate concealment measures which impede verification by national technical means of compliance with the provisions of this Interim Agreement. This obligation shall not require changes in current construction, assembly, conversion, or overhaul practices.

ARTICLE VI

To promote the objectives and implementation of the provisions of this Interim Agreement, the Parties shall use the Standing Consultative Commission established under Article XIII of theTreaty on the Limitation of Anti-Ballistic Missile Systems in accordance with the provisions of that Article.

ARTICLE VII

The Parties undertake to continue active negotiations for limitations on strategic offensive arms.The obligations provided for in this Interim Agreement shall not prejudice the scope or terms of the limitations on strategic offensive arms which may be worked out in the course of further negotiations.

ARTICLE VIII

1. This Interim Agreement shall enter into force upon exchange of written notices of acceptance by each Party, which exchange shall take place simultaneously with the exchange of instruments of ratification of the Treaty on the Limitation of Anti-Ballistic Missile Systems.

2. This Interim Agreement shall remain in force for a period of five years unless replaced earlier by an agreement on more complete measures limiting strategic offensive arms. It is the objective of the Parties to conduct active follow-on negotiations with the aim of concluding such an agreement as soon as possible.

3. Each Party shall, in exercising its national sovereignty, have the right to withdraw from this Interim Agreement if it decides that extraordinary events related to the subject matter of this Interim Agreement have jeopardized its supreme interests. It shall give notice of its decision to the other Party six months prior to withdrawal from this Interim Agreement. Such notice shall include a statement of the extraordinary events the notifying Party regards as having jeopardized its supreme interests.

DONE at Moscow on May 26, 1972, in two copies, each in the English and Russian languages, both texts being equally authentic.

FOR THE UNITED STATES OF AMERICA:

RICHARD NIXON

President of the United States of America

FOR THE UNION OF SOVIET SOCIALIST REPUBLICS:

L.I. BREZHNEV

General Secretary of the

Central Committee of the CPSU

13

Convention on the Prohibition of the Development, Production and Stockpiling of Bacteriological (Biological) and Toxin Weapons and on their Destruction

Signed at Washington, London, and Moscow April 10,1972
Ratification advised by U.S. Senate December 16, 1974
Ratified by U.S. President January 22, 1975
U.S. ratification deposited at Washington, London, and Moscow March 26, 1975
Proclaimed by U.S. President March 26, 1975
Entered into force March 26, 1975

The States Parties to this Convention,

Determined to act with a view to achieving effective progress towards general and complete disarmament, including the prohibition and elimination of all types of weapons of mass destruction, and convinced that the prohibition of the development, production and stockpiling of chemical and bacteriological (biological) weapons and their elimination, through effective measures, will facilitate the achievement of general and complete disarmament under strict and effective international control,

Recognizing the important significance of the Protocol for the Prohibition of the Use in War of Asphyxiating, Poisonous or Other Gases, and of Bacteriological Methods of Warfare, signed at Geneva on June 17, 1925, and conscious also of the contribution which the said Protocol has already made, and continues to make, to mitigating the horrors of war,

Reaffirming their adherence to the principles and objectives of that Protocol and calling upon all States to comply strictly with them,

Recalling that the General Assembly of the United Nations has repeatedly condemned all actions contrary to the principles and objectives of the Geneva Protocol of June 17, 1925,

Desiring to contribute to the strengthening of confidence between peoples and the general improvement of the international atmosphere,

Desiring also to contribute to the realization of the purposes and principles of the Charter of the United Nations,

Convinced of the importance and urgency of eliminating from the arsenals of States, through effective measures, such dangerous weapons of mass destruction as those using chemical or bacteriological (biological) agents,

Recognizing that an agreement on the prohibition of bacteriological (biological) and toxin weapons represents a first possible step towards the achievement of agreement on effective measures also for the prohibition of the development, production and stockpiling of chemical weapons, and determined to continue negotiations to that end,

Determined, for the sake of all mankind, to exclude completely the possibility of bacteriological (biological) agents and toxins being used as weapons,

Convinced that such use would be repugnant to the conscience of mankind and that no effort should be spared to minimize this risk,

Have agreed as follows:

ARTICLE I

Each State Party to this Convention undertakes never in any circumstances to develop, produce, stockpile or otherwise acquire or retain:

(1) Microbial or other biological agents, or toxins whatever their origin or method of production, of types and in quantities that have no justification for prophylactic, protective or other peaceful purposes;

(2) Weapons, equipment or means of delivery designed to use such agents or toxins for hostile purposes or in armed conflict.

ARTICLE II

Each State Party to this Convention undertakes to destroy, or to divert to peaceful purposes, as soon as possible but not later than nine months after the entry into force of the Convention, all agents, toxins, weapons, equipment and means of delivery specified in article I of the Convention, which are in its possession or under its jurisdiction or control. In implementing the provisions of this article all necessary safety precautions shall be observed to protect populations and the environment.

ARTICLE III

Each State Party to this Convention undertakes not to transfer to any recipient whatsoever, directly or indirectly, and not in any way to assist, encourage, or induce any State, group of States or international organizations to manufacture or otherwise acquire any of the agents, toxins, weapons, equipment or means of delivery specified in article I of the Convention.

ARTICLE IV

Each State Party to this Convention shall, in accordance with its constitutional processes, take any necessary measures to prohibit and prevent the development, production, stockpiling, acquisition, or retention of the agents, toxins, weapons, equipment and means of delivery specified in article I of the Convention, within the territory of such State, under its jurisdiction or under its control anywhere.

ARTICLE V

The States Parties to this Convention undertake to consult one another and to cooperate in solving any problems which may arise in relation to the objective of, or in the application of the provisions of, the Convention. Consultation and cooperation pursuant to this article may also be undertaken through appropriate international procedures within the framework of the United Nations and in accordance with its Charter.

ARTICLE VI

(1) Any State Party to this Convention which finds that any other State Party is acting in breach of obligations deriving from the provisions of the Convention may lodge a complaint with the Security Council of the United Nations. Such a complaint should include all possible evidence confirming its validity, as well as a request for its consideration by the Security Council.

(2) Each State Party to this Convention undertakes to cooperate in carrying out any investigation which the Security Council may initiate, in accordance with the provisions of the Charter of the United Nations, on the basis of the complaint received by the Council. The Security Council shall inform the States Parties to the Convention of the results of the investigation.

ARTICLE VII

Each State Party to this Convention undertakes to provide or support assistance, in accordance with the United Nations Charter, to any Party to the Convention which so requests, if the Security Council decides that such Party has been exposed to danger as a result of violation of the Convention.

ARTICLE VIII

Nothing in this Convention shall be interpreted as in any way limiting or detracting from the obligations assumed by any State under the Protocol for the Prohibition of the Use in War of Asphyxiating, Poisonous or Other Gases, and of Bacteriological Methods of Warfare, signed at Geneva on June 17, 1925.

ARTICLE IX

Each State Party to this Convention affirms the recognized objective of effective prohibition of chemical weapons and, to this end, undertakes to continue negotiations in good faith with a view to reaching early agreement on effective measures for the prohibition of their development, production and stockpiling and for their destruction, and on appropriate measures concerning equipment and means of delivery specifically designed for the production or use of chemical agents for weapons purposes.

ARTICLE X

(1) The States Parties to this Convention undertake to facilitate, and have the right to participate in, the fullest possible exchange of equipment, materials and scientific and technological information for the use of bacteriological (biological) agents and toxins for peaceful purposes. Parties to the Convention in a position to do so shall also cooperate in contributing individually or together with other States or international organizations to the further development and application of scientific discoveries in the field of bacteriology (biology) for prevention of disease, or for other peaceful purposes.

(2) This Convention shall be implemented in a manner designed to avoid hampering the economic or technological development of States Parties to the Convention or international cooperation in the field of peaceful bacteriological (biological) activities, including the international exchange of bacteriological (biological) agents and toxins and equipment for the processing, use or production of bacteriological (biological) agents and toxins for peaceful purposes in accordance with the provisions of the Convention.

ARTICLE XI

Any State Party may propose amendments to this Convention. Amendments shall enter into force for each State Party accepting the amendments upon their acceptance by a majority of the States Parties to the Convention and thereafter for each remaining State Party on the date of acceptance by it.

ARTICLE XII

Five years after the entry into force of this Convention, or earlier if it is requested by a majority of Parties to the Convention by submitting a proposal to this effect to the Depositary Governments, a conference of States Parties to the Convention shall be held at Geneva, Switzerland, to review the operation of the Convention, with a view to assuring that the purposes of the preamble and the provisions of the Convention, including the provisions concerning negotiations on chemical weapons, are being realized. Such review shall take into account any new scientific and technological developments relevant to the Convention.

ARTICLE XIII

(1) This Convention shall be of unlimited duration.

(2) Each State Party to this Convention shall in exercising its national sovereignty have the right to withdraw from the Convention if it decides that extraordinary events, related to the subject matter of the Convention, have jeopardized the supreme interests of its country. It shall give notice of such withdrawal to all other States Parties to the Convention and to the United Nations Security Council three months in advance. Such notice shall include a statement of the extraordinary events it regards as having jeopardized its supreme interests.

ARTICLE XIV

(1) This Convention shall be open to all States for signature. Any State which does not sign the Convention before its entry into force in accordance with paragraph (3) of this Article may accede to it at any time.

(2) This Convention shall be subject to ratification by signatory States. Instruments of ratification and instruments of accession shall be deposited with the Governments of the United States of America, the United Kingdom of Great Britain and Northern Ireland and the Union of Soviet Socialist Republics, which are hereby designated the Depositary Governments.

(3) This Convention shall enter into force after the deposit of instruments of ratification by twenty-two Governments, including the Governments designated as Depositaries of the Convention.

(4) For States whose instruments of ratification or accession are deposited subsequent to the entry into force of this Convention, it shall enter into force on the date of the deposit of their instruments of ratification or accession.

(5) The Depositary Governments shall promptly inform all signatory and acceding States of the date of each signature, the date of deposit of each instrument of ratification or of accession and the date of the entry into force of this Convention, and of the receipt of other notices.

(6) This Convention shall be registered by the Depositary Governments pursuant to Article 102 of the Charter of the United Nations.

ARTICLE XV

This Convention, the English, Russian, French, Spanish and Chinese texts of which are equally authentic, shall be deposited in the archives of the Depositary Governments. Duly certified copies of the Convention shall be transmitted by the Depositary Governments to the Governments of the signatory and acceding states.

IN WITNESS WHEREOF the undersigned, duly authorized, have signed this Convention.

DONE in triplicate, at the cities of Washington, London and Moscow, this tenth day of April, one thousand nine hundred and seventy-two.

PARTIES AND SIGNATORIES OF THE BIOLOGICAL WEAPONS CONVENTION

STATE (COUNTRY)

Afghanistan
Albania
Argentina
Armenia
Australia
Austria(1)
Bahamas
Bahrain(1)
Bangladesh
Barbados
Belarus
Belgium
Belize
Benin
Bhutan
Bolivia
Bosnia Herzegovina
Botswana
Brazil
Brunei Darussalam(2)
Bulgaria
Burkina Faso
Burundi(S)
Cambodia (Kampuchea)
Canada
Cape Verde
Central African Republic(S)
Chile
China, People's Republic of
Colombia
Congo
Costa Rica
Cote d'Ivoire(S)
Croatia
Cuba
Cyprus
Czech Republic
Denmark

Dominica(2)
Dominican Republic
Ecuador
Egypt(S)
El Salvador
Equatorial Guinea
Estonia
Ethiopia
Fiji
Finland
France
Gabon(S)
Gambia, The Georgia
Germany
Ghana
Greece
Grenada
Guatemala
Guinea-Bissau
Guyana(S)
Haiti(S)
Honduras
Hungary
Iceland
India
Indonesia
Iran
Iraq
Ireland
Italy
Jamaica
Japan
Jordan
Kenya
Korea, Democratic
People's Republic of
Korea, Republic of
Kuwait
Laos
Latvia
Lebanon
Lesotho
Liberia(S)
Libya
Liechtenstein
Luxembourg
Macedonia, Former
Yugoslav Republic of
Madagascar(S)
Malawi(S)
Malaysia(1)
Maldives
Mali(S)
Malta
Mauritius
Mexico
Mongolia
Morocco(S)
Myanmar (Burma)(S)
Nepal(S)
Netherlands(4)
New Zealand
Nicaragua
Niger
Nigoria
Norway
Oman
Pakistan Panama
Papua New Guinea
Paraguay
Peru
Philippines
Poland
Portugal
Qatar
Romania
Russian Federation
Rwanda
St. Kitts and Nevis
St. Lucia
San Marino
Sao Tome and Principe

Saudi Arabia
Senegal
Serbia-Montenegro
(Formerly Yugoslavia)
Seychelles
Sierra Leone
Singapore
Slovak Republic
Slovenia
Solomon Islands(2)
Somalia(S)
South Africa
Spain
Sri Lanka
Suriname
Swaziland
Sweden
Switzerland
Syria(S)
Tanzania(S)
Thailand
Togo
Tonga
Tunisia
Turkey
Turkmenistan
Uganda
Ukraine
United Arab
Emirates (S)(5)
United Kingdom(6)
United States
Uruguay
Uzbekistan
Vanuatu
Venezuela
Vietnam
Yemen
Zaire
Zimbabwe

(S) Signatory

(1) With reservation

(2) Based on general declarations concerning Treaty obligations applicable prior to independence.

(3) Effective January 1, 1979, the United States recognized the government of the People's Republic of China as the sole government of China. The authorities on Taiwan state they will continue to abide by the provisions of the Convention, and the United States regards them as bound by its obligations.

(4) Applicable to Netherlands Antilles and Aruba.

(5) The United Arab Emirates which did not ratify the Convention is listed as one country.

(6) Extended to territories under the territorial sovereignty of the United Kingdom. Also extended to New Hebrides; continued application to Vanuatu not determined.

14

Treaty on the Non-proliferation of Nuclear Weapons

Signed at Washington, London, and Moscow July 1, 1968
Ratification advised by U.S. Senate March 13, 1969
Ratified by U.S. President November 24, 1969
U.S. ratification deposited at Washington, London, and Moscow March 5, 1970
Proclaimed by U.S. President March 5, 1970
Entered into force March 5, 1970

The States concluding this Treaty, hereinafter referred to as the "Parties to the Treaty",

Considering the devastation that would be visited upon all mankind by a nuclear war and the consequent need to make every effort to avert the danger of such a war and to take measures to safeguard the security of peoples,

Believing that the proliferation of nuclear weapons would seriously enhance the danger of nuclear war,

In conformity with resolutions of the United Nations General Assembly calling for the conclusion of an agreement on the prevention of wider dissemination of nuclear weapons,

Undertaking to cooperate in facilitating the application of International Atomic Energy Agency safeguards on peaceful nuclear activities,

Expressing their support for research, development and other efforts to further the application, within the framework of the International Atomic Energy Agency safeguards system, of the principle of safeguarding effectively the flow of source and special fissionable materials by use of instruments and other techniques at certain strategic points,

Affirming the principle that the benefits of peaceful applications of nuclear technology, including any technological by-products which may be derived by nuclear-weapon States from the development of nuclear explosive devices, should be available for peaceful purposes to all Parties of the Treaty, whether nuclear-weapon or non-nuclear weapon States,

Convinced that, in furtherance of this principle, all Parties to the Treaty are entitled to participate in the fullest possible exchange of scientific information for, and to contribute alone or in cooperation with other States to, the further development of the applications of atomic energy for peaceful purposes,

Declaring their intention to achieve at the earliest possible date the cessation of the nuclear arms race and to undertake effective measures in the direction of nuclear disarmament,

Urging the cooperation of all States in the attainment of this objective,

Recalling the determination expressed by the Parties to the 1963 Treaty banning nuclear weapon tests in the atmosphere, in outer space and under water in its Preamble to seek to achieve the discontinuance of all test explosions of nuclear weapons for all time and to continue negotiations to this end,

Desiring to further the easing of international tension and the strengthening of trust between States in order to facilitate the cessation of the manufacture of nuclear weapons, the liquidation of all their existing stockpiles, and the elimination from national arsenals of nuclear weapons and the means of their delivery pursuant to a Treaty on general and complete disarmament under strict and effective international control,

Recalling that, in accordance with the Charter of the United Nations, States must refrain in their international relations from the threat or use of force against the territorial integrity or political independence of any State, or in any other manner inconsistent with the Purposes of the United Nations, and that the establishment and maintenance of international peace and security are to be promoted with the least diversion for armaments of the worlds human and economic resources,

Have agreed as follows:

ARTICLE I

Each nuclear-weapon State Party to the Treaty undertakes not to transfer to any recipient whatsoever nuclear weapons or other nuclear explosive devices or control over such weapons or explosive devices directly, or indirectly; and not in any way to assist, encourage, or induce any non-nuclear weapon State to manufacture or otherwise acquire nuclear weapons or other nuclear explosive devices, or control over such weapons or explosive devices.

ARTICLE II

Each non-nuclear-weapon State Party to the Treaty undertakes not to receive the transfer from any transferor whatsoever of nuclear weapons or other nuclear explosive devices or of control over such weapons or explosive devices directly, or indirectly; not to manufacture or otherwise acquire nuclear weapons or other nuclear explosive devices; and not to seek or receive any assistance in the manufacture of nuclear weapons or other nuclear explosive devices.

ARTICLE III

1. Each non-nuclear-weapon State Party to the Treaty undertakes to accept safeguards, as set forth in an agreement to be negotiated and concluded with the International Atomic Energy Agency in accordance with the Statute of the International Atomic Energy Agency and the Agencys safeguards system, for the exclusive purpose of verification of the fulfillment of its obligations assumed under this Treaty with a view to preventing diversion of nuclear energy from peaceful uses to nuclear weapons or other nuclear explosive devices. Procedures for the safeguards required by this article shall be followed with respect to source or special fissionable material whether it is being produced,

processed or used in any principal nuclear facility or is outside any such facility. The safeguards required by this article shall be applied to all source or special fissionable material in all peaceful nuclear activities within the territory of such State, under its jurisdiction, or carried out under its control anywhere.

2. Each State Party to the Treaty undertakes not to provide: (a) source or special fissionable material, or (b) equipment or material especially designed or prepared for the processing, use or production of special fissionable material, to any non-nuclear-weapon State for peaceful purposes, unless the source or special fissionable material shall be subject to the safeguards required by this article.

3. The safeguards required by this article shall be implemented in a manner designed to comply with article IV of this Treaty, and to avoid hampering the economic or technological development of the Parties or international cooperation in the field of peaceful nuclear activities, including the international exchange of nuclear material and equipment for the processing, use or production of nuclear material for peaceful purposes in accordance with the provisions of this article and the principle of safeguarding set forth in the Preamble of the Treaty.

4. Non-nuclear-weapon States Party to the Treaty shall conclude agreements with the International Atomic Energy Agency to meet the requirements of this article either individually or together with other States in accordance with the Statute of the International Atomic Energy Agency. Negotiation of such agreements shall commence within 180 days from the original entry into force of this Treaty. For States depositing their instruments of ratification or accession after the 180-day period, negotiation of such agreements shall commence not later than the date of such deposit. Such agreements shall enter into force not later than eighteen months after the date of initiation of negotiations.

ARTICLE IV

1. Nothing in this Treaty shall be interpreted as affecting the inalienable right of all the Parties to the Treaty to develop

research, production and use of nuclear energy for peaceful purposes without discrimination and in conformity with articles I and II of this Treaty.

2. All the Parties to the Treaty undertake to facilitate, and have the right to participate in, the fullest possible exchange of equipment, materials and scientific and technological information for the peaceful uses of nuclear energy. Parties to the Treaty in a position to do so shall also cooperate in contributing alone or together with other States or international organizations to the further development of the applications of nuclear energy for peaceful purposes, especially in the territories of non-nuclear-weapon States Party to the Treaty, with due consideration for the needs of the developing areas of the world.

ARTICLE V

Each party to the Treaty undertakes to take appropriate measures to ensure that, in accordance with this Treaty, under appropriate international observation and through appropriate international procedures, potential benefits from any peaceful applications of nuclear explosions will be made available to non-nuclear-weapon States Party to the Treaty on a non-discriminatory basis and that the charge to such Parties for the explosive devices used will be as low as possible and exclude any charge for research and development. Non-nuclear-weapon States Party to the Treaty shall be able to obtain such benefits, pursuant to a special international agreement or agreements, through an appropriate international body with adequate representation of non-nuclear-weapon States. Negotiations on this subject shall commence as soon as possible after the Treaty enters into force. Non-nuclear-weapon States Party to the Treaty so desiring may also obtain such benefits pursuant to bilateral agreements.

ARTICLE VI

Each of the Parties to the Treaty undertakes to pursue negotiations in good faith on effective measures relating to cessation of the nuclear arms race at an early date and to nuclear disarmament, and on a Treaty on general and complete disarmament under strict and effective international control.

ARTICLE VII

Nothing in this Treaty affects the right of any group of States to conclude regional treaties in order to assure the total absence of nuclear weapons in their respective territories.

ARTICLE VIII

1. Any Party to the Treaty may propose amendments to this Treaty. The text of any proposed amendment shall be submitted to the Depositary Governments which shall circulate it to all Parties to the Treaty. Thereupon, if requested to do so by one-third or more of the Parties to the Treaty, the Depositary Governments shall convene a conference, to which they shall invite all the Parties to the Treaty, to consider such an amendment.

2. Any amendment to this Treaty must be approved by a majority of the votes of all the Parties to the Treaty, including the votes of all nuclear-weapon States Party to the Treaty and all other Parties which, on the date the amendment is circulated, are members of the Board of Governors of the International Atomic Energy Agency. The amendment shall enter into force for each Party that deposits its instrument of ratification of the amendment upon the deposit of such instruments of ratification by a majority of all the Parties, including the instruments of ratification of all nuclear-weapon States Party to the Treaty and all other Parties which, on the date the amendment is circulated, are members of the Board of Governors of the International Atomic Energy Agency. Thereafter, it shall enter into force for any other Party upon the deposit of its instrument of ratification of the amendment.

3. Five years after the entry into force of this Treaty, a conference of Parties to the Treaty shall be held in Geneva, Switzerland, in order to review the operation of this Treaty with a view to assuring that the purposes of the Preamble and the provisions of the Treaty are being realized. At intervals of five years thereafter, a majority of the Parties to the Treaty may obtain, by submitting a proposal to this effect to the Depositary Governments, the convening of further conferences with the same objective of reviewing the operation of the Treaty.

ARTICLE IX

1. This Treaty shall be open to all States for signature. Any State which does not sign the Treaty before its entry into force in accordance with paragraph 3 of this article may accede to it at any time.

2. This Treaty shall be subject to ratification by signatory States. Instruments of ratification and instruments of accession shall be deposited with the Governments of the United States of America, the United Kingdom of Great Britain and Northern Ireland and the Union of Soviet Socialist Republics, which are hereby designated the Depositary Governments.

3. This Treaty shall enter into force after its ratification by the States, the Governments of which are designated Depositaries of the Treaty, and forty other States signatory to this Treaty and the deposit of their instruments of ratification. For the purposes of this Treaty, a nuclear-weapon State is one which has manufactured and exploded a nuclear weapon or other nuclear explosive device prior to January 1, 1967.

4. For States whose instruments of ratification or accession are deposited subsequent to the entry into force of this Treaty, it shall enter into force on the date of the deposit of their instruments of ratification or accession.

5. The Depositary Governments shall promptly inform all signatory and acceding States of the date of each signature, the date of deposit of each instrument of ratification or of accession, the date of the entry into force of this Treaty, and the date of receipt of any requests for convening a conference or other notices.

6. This Treaty shall be registered by the Depositary Governments pursuant to article 102 of the Charter of the United Nations.

ARTICLE X

1. Each Party shall in exercising its national sovereignty have the right to withdraw from the Treaty if it decides that extraordinary events, related to the subject matter of this Treaty, have jeopardized the supreme interests of its country. It shall

give notice of such withdrawal to all other Parties to the Treaty and to the United Nations Security Council three months in advance. Such notice shall include a statement of the extraordinary events it regards as having jeopardized its supreme interests.

2. Twenty-five years after the entry into force of the Treaty, a conference shall be convened to decide whether the Treaty shall continue in force indefinitely, or shall be extended for an additional fixed period or periods. This decision shall be taken by a majority of the Parties to the Treaty.

ARTICLE XI

This Treaty, the English, Russian, French, Spanish and Chinese texts of which are equally authentic, shall be deposited in the archives of the Depositary Governments. Duly certified copies of this Treaty shall be transmitted by the Depositary Governments to the Governments of the signatory and acceding States.

IN WITNESS WHEREOF the undersigned, duly authorized, have signed this Treaty.

DONE in triplicate, at the cities of Washington, London and Moscow, this first day of July one thousand nine hundred sixty-eight.

15

Treaty Banning Nuclear Weapon Tests in the Atmosphere, in Outer Space and Under Water

Signed at Moscow August 5, 1963
Ratification advised by U.S. Senate September 24, 1963
Ratified by U.S. President October 7, 1963
U.S. ratification deposited at Washington, London, and Moscow October 10, 1963
Proclaimed by U.S. President October 10, 1963
Entered into force October 10, 1963

The Governments of the United States of America, the United Kingdom of Great Britain and Northern Ireland, and the Union of Soviet Socialist Republics, hereinafter referred to as the "Original Parties,"

Proclaiming as their principal aim the speediest possible achievement of an agreement on general and complete disarmament under strict international control in accordance with the objectives of the United Nations which would put an end to the armaments race and eliminate the incentive to the production and testing of all kinds of weapons, including nuclear weapons,

Seeking to achieve the discontinuance of all test explosions of nuclear weapons for all time, determined to continue negotiations to this end, and desiring to put an end to the contamination of mans environment by radioactive substances,

Have agreed as follows:

ARTICLE I

1. Each of the Parties to this Treaty undertakes to prohibit, to prevent, and not to carry out any nuclear weapon test explosion, or any other nuclear explosion, at any place under its jurisdiction or control:

(a) in the atmosphere; beyond its limits, including outer space; or under water, including territorial waters or high seas; or

(b) in any other environment if such explosion causes radioactive debris to be present outside the territorial limits of the State under whose jurisdiction or control such explosion is conducted. It is understood in this connection that the provisions of this subparagraph are without prejudice to the conclusion of a Treaty resulting in the permanent banning of all nuclear test explosions, including all such explosions underground, the conclusion of which, as the Parties have stated in the Preamble to this Treaty, they seek to achieve.

2. Each of the Parties to this Treaty undertakes furthermore to refrain from causing, encouraging, or in any way participating in, the carrying out of any nuclear weapon test explosion, or any other nuclear explosion, anywhere which would take place in any of the environments described, or have the effect referred to, in paragraph 1 of this Article.

ARTICLE II

1. Any Party may propose amendments to this Treaty. The text of any proposed amendment shall be submitted to the Depositary Governments which shall circulate it to all Parties to this Treaty. Thereafter, if requested to do so by one-third or more of the Parties, the Depositary Governments shall convene a conference, to which they shall invite all the Parties, to consider such amendment.

2. Any amendment to this Treaty must be approved by a majority of the votes of all the Parties to this Treaty, including the votes of all of the Original Parties. The amendment shall

enter into force for all Parties upon the deposit of instruments of ratification by a majority of all the Parties, including the instruments of ratification of all of the Original Parties.

ARTICLE III

1. This Treaty shall be open to all States for signature. Any State which does not sign this Treaty before its entry into force in accordance with paragraph 3 of this Article may accede to it at any time.

2. This Treaty shall be subject to ratification by signatory States. Instruments of ratification and instruments of accession shall be deposited with the Governments of the Original Parties —the United States of America, the United Kingdom of Great Britain and Northern Ireland, and the Union of Soviet Socialist Republics—which are hereby designated the Depositary Governments.

3. This Treaty shall enter into force after its ratification by all the Original Parties and the deposit of their instruments of ratification.

4. For States whose instruments of ratification or accession are deposited subsequent to the entry into force of this Treaty, it shall enter into force on the date of the deposit of their instruments of ratification or accession.

5. The Depositary Governments shall promptly inform all signatory and acceding States of the date of each signature, the date of deposit of each instrument of ratification of and accession to this Treaty, the date of its entry into force, and the date of receipt of any requests for conferences or other notices.

6. This Treaty shall be registered by the Depositary Governments pursuant to Article 102 of the Charter of the United Nations.

ARTICLE IV

This Treaty shall be of unlimited duration.

Each Party shall in exercising its national sovereignty have the right to withdraw from the Treaty if it decides that extraordinary events, related to the subject matter of this Treaty, have jeopardized the supreme interests of its country. It shall give notice of such withdrawal to all other Parties to the Treaty three months in advance.

ARTICLE V

This Treaty, of which the English and Russian texts are equally authentic, shall be deposited in the archives of the Depositary Governments. Duly certified copies of this Treaty shall be transmitted by the Depositary Governments to the Governments of the signatory and acceding States.

IN WITNESS WHEREOF the undersigned, duly authorized, have signed this Treaty.

DONE in triplicate at the city of Moscow the fifth day of August, one thousand nine hundred and sixty-three.

For the Government of the United States of America

DEAN RUSK

For the Government of the United Kingdom of Great Britain and Northern Ireland

SIR DOUGLAS HOME

For the Government of the Union of

Soviet Socialist Republics

A. GROMYKO

Limited Test Ban Treaty

Country	Date 1 of Signature	Date of Deposit 1 of Ratification	Date of Deposit 1 of Accession
Afghanistan	08/08/63	03/12/64	
Algeria	08/14/63		
Argentina	08/08/63		11/21/86
Australia	08/08/63	11/12/63	
Austria	09/11/63	07/17/64	
Bahamas, The			07/16/76
Bangladesh			03/11/85
Belgium	08/08/63	03/01/66	
Benin	08/27/63	12/15/64	
Bhutan			06/08/78
Bolivia	08/08/63	08/04/65	
Botswana			01/05/68

Brazil	08/08/63	12/15/64	
Bulgaria	08/08/63	11/13/63	
Burkina Faso	08/30/63		
Burma	08/14/63	11/15/63	
Burundi	10/04/63		
Byelorussian S.S.R.2	10/08/63	12/16/63	
Cameroon	08/27/63		
Canada	08/08/63	01/28/64	
Cape Verde			10/24/79
Central African Republic			12/22/64
Chad	08/26/63	03/01/65	
Chile	08/08/63	10/06/65	
China (Taiwan) 4	08/23/63	05/18/64	
Colombia	08/16/63	10/17/85	
Costa Rica	08/09/63	07/10/67	
Cote d'Ivoire	09/05/63	07/05/65	
Cyprus	08/08/63	04/15/65	
Czechoslovakia	08/08/63	10/14/63	
Denmark	08/09/63	01/15/64	
Dominican Republic	09/16/63	06/03/64	
Ecuador	09/27/63	05/06/64	
Egypt	08/08/63	01/10/64	
El Salvador	08/21/63	12/03/64	
Ethiopia	08/09/63		
Fiji			07/18/72
Finland	08/08/63	01/09/64	
Gabon	09/10/63	02/20/64	
Gambia, The			04/27/65
German Democratic Republic	08/08/63	12/30/63	
Germany, Federal Republic of	08/19/63	12/01/64	
Ghana	08/08/63	11/27/63	
Greece	08/08/63	12/18/63	
Guatemala	09/23/63	01/06/64	
Haiti	10/09/63		
Honduras	08/08/63	10/02/64	
Hungary	08/08/63	10/21/63	
Iceland	08/12/63	04/29/64	
India	08/08/63	10/10/63	
Indonesia	08/23/63	01/20/64	

Iran	08/08/63	05/05/64	
Iraq	08/13/63	11/30/64	
Ireland	08/08/63	12/18/63	
Israel	08/08/63	01/15/64	
Italy	08/08/63	12/10/64	
Jamaica	08/13/63		11/22/91
Japan	08/14/63	06/15/64	
Jordan	08/12/63	05/29/64	
Kenya			06/10/65
Korea, Republic of	08/30/63	07/24/64	
Kuwait	08/20/63	05/20/65	
Laos	08/12/63	02/10/65	
Lebanon	08/12/63	05/14/65	
Liberia	08/08/63	05/19/64	
Libya	08/09/63	07/15/68	
Luxembourg	08/13/63	02/10/65	
Madagascar	09/23/63	03/15/65	
Malawi		11/26/64	
Malaysia	08/08/63	07/15/64	
Mali	08/23/63		
Malta			11/25/64
Mauritania	09/13/63	04/06/64	
Mauritius			04/30/69
Mexico	08/08/63	12/27/63	
Mongolia	08/08/63	11/01/63	
Morocco	08/27/63	02/01/66	
Nepal	08/26/63	10/07/64	
Netherlands	08/09/63	09/14/64	
New Zealand	08/08/63	10/10/63	
Nicaragua	08/13/63	01/26/65	
Niger	09/24/63	07/03/64	
Nigeria	08/30/63	02/17/67	
Norway	08/09/63	11/21/63	
Pakistan	08/14/63		03/03/88
Panama	09/20/63	02/24/66	
Papua New Guinea			03/16/81
Paraguay	08/15/63		
Peru	08/23/63	07/20/64	
Philippines	08/08/63	11/10/65	
Poland	08/08/63	10/14/63	
Portugal	10/09/63		

Romania	08/08/63	12/12/63	
Rwanda	09/19/63	12/27/63	
San Marino	09/17/63	07/03/64	
Senegal	09/20/63	05/06/64	
Seychelles			03/12/85
Sierra Leone	09/04/63	02/21/64	
Singapore			07/12/68
Somalia	08/19/63		
South Africa			10/10/63
Spain	08/13/63	12/17/64	
Sri Lanka	08/22/63	02/05/64	
Sudan	08/09/63	03/04/66	
Swaziland			05/29/69
Sweden	08/12/63	12/09/63	
Switzerland	08/26/63	01/16/64	
Syria	08/13/63	06/01/64	
Tanzania	09/16/63	02/06/64	
Thailand	08/08/63	11/15/63	
Togo	09/18/63	12/07/64	
Tonga			07/07/71
Trinidad & Tobago	08/12/63	07/14/64	
Tunisia	08/08/63	05/26/65	
Turkey	08/09/63	07/08/65	
Uganda	08/29/63	03/24/64	
Ukrainian S.S.R.[2]	10/08/63	12/30/63	
Union of Soviet Socialist Republics		08/05/63	10/10/63
United Kingdom	08/05/63	10/10/63	
United States	08/05/63	10/10/63	
Uruguay	08/12/63	02/25/63	
Venezuela	08/16/63	02/22/65	
Western Samoa	09/05/63	01/15/65	
Yemen Arab Republic (Sanaa)	08/13/63		
Yemen, People's Democratic Republic of (Aden)			06/01/79
Yugoslavia	08/08/63	01/15/64	
Zaire	08/08/63	10/28/63	
Zambia			1/11/65
Total[3]	108	94	23

Notes

1. Dates given are the earliest dates on which countries signed the agreements or deposited their ratifications or accessions—whether in Washington, London, Moscow, or New York. In the case of a country that was a dependent territory which became a party through succession, the date given is the date on which the country gave notice that it would continue to be bound by the terms of the agreement.
2. The United States regards the signature and ratification by the Byelorussian S.S.R. and the Ukrainian S.S.R. as already included under the signature and ratification of the Union of Soviet Socialist Republics.
3. This total does not include actions by the Byelorussian S.S.R. and the Ukrainian S.S.R. (See footnote 2.)
4. Effective January 1, 1979, the United States recognized the Government of the People's Republic of China as the sole government of China.

16

Remarks by U.S. Secretary of State, Hillary Rodham Clinton, at CTBT Article XIV Conference, New York, U.S.A.

24 September 2009

...I am delighted to be here on behalf of the United States. It has been a long time since our government was represented at this conference. We are glad to be back.

Earlier today, President Obama chaired a special session of the Security Council to adopt a resolution outlining comprehensive steps to strengthen the nuclear non-proliferation regime. This is part of a deliberative, ongoing effort by the Obama Administration to enhance our common security while moving us closer to the vision the President outlined in Prague: a world without nuclear weapons.

The Comprehensive Nuclear-Test-Ban Treaty is an integral part of our non-proliferation and arms control agenda, and we will work in the months ahead both to seek the advice and consent of the United States Senate to ratify the treaty, and to secure ratification by others so that the treaty can enter into force.

We believe that the CTBT contributes to our global nonproliferation and disarmament strategy as well as the President's long-range vision. It does so without jeopardizing the safety, security, or credibility of our nuclear arsenal. By pursuing these goals and supporting the CTBT, we are working in the interest of all nations committed to non-proliferation and to reducing the threat of nuclear attack.

The Obama Administration has already begun the work necessary to support U.S. ratification of the Treaty. We know this task will not be quick or easy. But as long as we are confronted with the prospect of nuclear testing by others, we will face the potential threat of newer, more powerful, and more sophisticated weapons that could cause damage beyond our imagination. A test ban treaty that has entered into force will permit the United States and others to challenge states engaged in suspicious testing activities—including the option of calling on-site inspections to be sure that no testing occurs on land, underground, underwater, or in space. CTBT ratification would also encourage the international community to move forward with other essential nonproliferation steps.

To put it plainly, we support this treaty because it strengthens the prospect of a peaceful, stable, and secure world and would enhance the security of the American people.

As we work with the Senate to ratify the CTBT, we will encourage other countries to play their part—including the eight remaining Annex 2 countries. Those who haven't signed should sign. Those, like us, who haven't ratified, should ratify. And the 150 countries that have already progressed to ratification can use this opportunity to continue preparations for CTBT implementation.

Even in these times of strained budgets, we are prepared to pay our share of the Preparatory Commission budget so that the global verification regime will be fully operational when the CTBT enters into force.

More than eighty percent of the monitoring stations that will constitute the International Monitoring System have already been installed and we urge all host countries to ensure that the data from these installations are reported to the International Data Center. In the coming months, we will look for new ways to support the monitoring system—including upgrades to the system and other verification capabilities of the CTBT—with the help of all nations, including those who have yet to ratify.

President Obama and I applaud Indonesian Foreign Minister Wirajuda's recent pledge that his country will move forward with ratification once we have done so. We look forward to similar statements from the remaining Annex 2 nations, while recognizing that today's Article XIV Conference provides an opportunity for all of us to pledge our support for the Treaty, reaffirm our commitment to the verification regime, and demonstrate the importance of this treaty to reducing the threat and role of nuclear weapons.

It will take our collective effort to develop a comprehensive, diplomatic strategy that lays the groundwork for eventual entry into force.

I am pleased that Under Secretary of State Ellen Tauscher will hold consultations with her many counterparts at this conference to discuss diplomatic efforts to move the process forward.

Mr. Chairman, after a ten year absence from this conference, America stands ready to renew its leadership role in the nonproliferation regime. As President Obama said yesterday, we have a shared responsibility for a global response to global challenges. We come to this conference with an optimistic spirit that all parties can make a contribution towards a world without nuclear weapons. That is the promise of the CTBT, and it is why we are rededicating ourselves to this effort.

17

Statement by Tibor Toth, CTBTO Executive Secretary: Towards a World Free of Nuclear Weapons—The Contribution of the Comprehensive Nuclear Test Ban Treaty

Over 2,000 nuclear tests had been conducted in the world before the CTBT "the longest sought, hardest fought prize in the history of arms control" opened for signature in 1996. The Treaty that bans all nuclear explosions on Earth constituted a milestone in the history of nuclear non-proliferation and disarmament.

Eleven years later, the Treaty has not yet entered into force. Despite this, it has already created a strong international norm. 178 countries have signed and 144 have ratified the Treaty, including the nuclear-weapon states Russia, France and the United Kingdom. Nine countries whose ratifications are necessary for entry into force remain. These are China, Democratic People's Republic of Korea, Egypt, India, Indonesia, Islamic Republic of Iran, Israel, Pakistan and the United States of America.

The CTBT verification regime set up to make sure that no nuclear explosion goes undetected, proved its worth in October 2006 when the DPRK announced that it had conducted a nuclear test. The explosion was low yield, the international monitoring system only 60% completed, and the noble gas system only 25% completed at that time. Despite all this, the system not only successfully detected and analyzed the explosion, but also showed that its verification capabilities were significantly better than what had been envisaged by the Treaty negotiators in 1996.

The CTBT verification regime, together with the Safeguards regime of the IAEA, demonstrates that **nuclear activities can be** monitored.

In 2008, the CTBTO Preparatory Commission will consolidate the on-site inspection capability. This will occur with the first integrated field exercise for on-site inspections which will take place at the former Soviet nuclear test site Semipalatinsk in Kazakhstan. The build up of the noble gas detection capability that was so crucial in detecting the nuclear explosion by the DPRK in October 2006 will continue. 35 monitoring stations, many areas in which stations are missing will be constructed. The stations in China will be integrated and several additional stations in Russia will be incorporated into the network. Stations installed in the United States, France and the United Kingdom have already reached an advanced stage. The plan is to have 90% of the 337 monitoring facilities up and running in the next couple of years. Stable and sufficient funding levels will be required in order not to jeopardize the build-up and the operation and maintenance of the IMS.

Today, we see that the discussion on the CTBT is intensifying, not the least due to the bi-partisan effort culminating in the op-ed pieces in the *Wall Street Journal* in January 2007 and 2008. Moreover, there is progress towards universalization of the Treaty. The year 2008 has already seen ratifications by three additional countries: Barbados, Malaysia and Colombia. Colombia's ratification is of particular importance since it belongs to the group of countries whose ratification is necessary for entry into force. Malaysia's ratification may well have tipped the balance in the ASEAN region where now only four countries have yet to ratify the CTBT; Indonesia whose ratification is needed for entry into force being one of them. Clearly, there is a momentum going.

US leadership on the CTBT is seen by many as crucial. The WMD Commission recommended that "the United States should reconsider its position and proceed to ratify the Treaty, recognizing that its ratification would trigger other required ratifications and be a step towards the treaty's entry into force." India—the only other state that has expressed opposition to the

Treaty—has repeatedly said that it will not stand in the way for the Treaty's entry into force.

The CTBT is not only a measure in its own right, but also a catalyst for progress in many nuclear non-proliferation and disarmament processes underway and in many proposals put on the table.

- The CTBT is crucial in a world in which we see the resurgence of nuclear energy. More and more states are mastering the nuclear fuel cycle. The decision between nuclear energy for peaceful or for weapons purposes will become more a political and legal issue rather than one of technology and know how. Legal instruments "upstream" of the nuclear fuel cycle are facing increasing difficulties when it comes to the delineation between prohibited and permitted activities. A nuclear test provides unquestionable "downstream" proof of the intentions of a state. The CTBT thus provides the last and clearly visible barrier between the two. This legal line needs to be drawn clear and irrevocably. A CTBT in force would also be an incentive for ending the production of fissile material for weapons use, pending the entry into force of a Fissile Material Cut-Off Treaty, as well as reducing the stocks of such materials.
- The CTBT is a strong instrument for non-proliferation. It limits the ability of countries that do not have nuclear weapons to develop these weapons. A country that does not have the capability beforehand and builds a nuclear device will face many uncertainties with regards to the performance of the device. Uncertainty will increase when trying to make it deliverable by cruise or ballistic missile when weight is a major factor. This in turn reduces greatly the possibility of integrating nuclear weapons in military planning or strategic doctrines.
- The CTBT is also a catalyst for nuclear disarmament. It provides a firm legal barrier against nuclear testing, thereby curbing the development of new types and new designs of nuclear weapons. This will be essential when

moving towards deeper arms reductions between Russia and the United States. It will also be essential when moving towards multilateral disarmament in a process involving all the nuclear armed states. In this context, it will be particularly important that the CTBT is a non-discriminatory instrument: the ban on testing is the same for everyone, nuclear weapon state and non-nuclear weapon state alike.

- The CTBT is a strong confidence and security building measure. In the US-Russia strategic relationship, additional confidence would be gained if the United States were to ratify the Treaty as Russia has done. This would assist arms control measures such as de-alerting, strategic and non-strategic arms reductions, and changes of strategic doctrines. The extension of the provisions of the START treaty, the completion of the SORT treaty and reductions beyond SORT would be facilitated with a CTBT in force.
- The CTBT could also serve as a regional confidence and security building measure. Referring to the regional situation, the WMD Commission recommended that Egypt, Iran and Israel joined other countries in the Middle East and ratified the Treaty. Such a step would be a positive catalyst for other security related issues affecting the region. The WMD Commission also recommended signing and ratification of India and Pakistan—the only states besides the DPRK that have broken the international norm against nuclear testing since the Treaty came about in 1996. There is obviously a need to engage India and Pakistan on a range of security and arms related issues. CTBT would naturally be one of them, providing a cap on the further development of nuclear weapons and thus on the further production of weapons materials to that end. The importance of a legally-binding commitment on nuclear testing in this regional context should not be downplayed. Similarly, it has been argued by many that

the CTBT is the next logical step after the present denuclearization stage is fulfilled in the deal with the DPRK. In a wider regional context, much would be gained for confidence and security building in Asia if the continent as a whole moved towards ratification.

- A consensus agreement on the CTBT and its entry into force will be essential if the Non-Proliferation Treaty and its current review process is to be successful. Looking back in history to the negotiations of the NPT in the 1960s with the inclusion of the permanent nuclear test ban in the preamble of the Treaty, and to the successful review conferences of 1995 and 2000 as well as the unsuccessful ones over the years, it becomes clear that advancement on the CTBT is crucial. Progress on a CTBT in 2009 or 2010 will be a catalyst for progress on other measures necessary for the strengthening of the non-proliferation regime.

The CTBT is certainly one of the measures around which an international consensus can be built. It would be relatively easy to gather around a CTBT since it is almost universally supported. In the past four years, the number of ratifying states has increased from around 100 to 144. This CTBT family now includes all of Europe, all Nato members except one, and the vast majority of states in Latin America, Africa, and Asia and the Pacific.

Last September, ratifying and signatory states adopted a Final Declaration at the UN Conference to facilitate the entry into force of the CTBT. This consensus declaration—a rare commodity in today's arms control environment—contained strong language on the importance of entry into force and was signed on to also by the non-ratifying states China, Egypt, Iran and Israel. It underscored the international community's commitment to establishing a universal and internationally and effectively verifiable CTBT as a major instrument in the field of nuclear disarmament and non-proliferation. It is clear that a CTBT in force is a logical and necessary element of the security architecture, if today's and future nuclear non-proliferation challenges are to be addressed credibly.

18

Statement by H.E. Mr. Heinz Fischer, Federal President of the Republic of Austria, at Security Council's High-Level Summit on Nuclear Non-proliferation and Nuclear Disarmament, New York, U.S.A.

24 September 2009

This is an auspicious moment: Today the Security Council of the UN pronounces its commitment to a world without nuclear weapons.

For more than half a century, this goal has been pursued by concerned citizens and political leaders around the world. The international community has undertaken efforts to contain the threat but many have adjusted to it, almost accepting the nuclear shadow as part of life.

But any such complacency is ill-founded:

We have arrived at a fork in the road: We can maintain our course and hope nothing happens. Or we can seek real change.

Future historians will assess whether today is a turning point. This will not depend on the words spoken today but on the deeds that follow. In May 2010 the international community will convene at the NPT-Review Conference in New York. There, we will have to agree on measures that enable progress toward a nuclear weapon free world.

For Austria, the following points will be paramount:

1. The prospect of a world without nuclear weapons must become a goal shared by all States. Austria supports the idea of a Nuclear Weapons Convention equipped with

a sophisticated verification mechanism. In the meantime, the NPT remains the core of the global nuclear disarmament and non-proliferation regime. But to fulfil its functions effectively, it must be strengthened, it must be institutionalized, and it must become universal.

2. The Nuclear-Weapons-States must reduce their arsenals. As you, Mr. President, noted in Prague, "Words must mean something". The words enshrined in Article VI of the NPT have to be taken seriously. There have been positive developments, yes, but Nuclear-Weapons-States must do more.

3. We must devise a process for entry into force of the Comprehensive Nuclear Test-Ban Treaty (CTBT). Austria and Costa Rica, as co-chairs of the Article XIV-Conference, worked hard to promote entry into force over the last two years. This will only be possible, however, with the political commitment of the 9 States that still need to ratify.

4. We must enable the Conference on Disarmament (CD) in Geneva to negotiate a Fissile Material Cut-Off-Treaty (FMCT). As current President of the Conference, Austria will make every effort to promote this goal. But to achieve progress the support of all its members is necessary.

5. Our capabilities to prevent nuclear materials from proliferating to States and non-state actors must improve. Security Council Resolution 15401 needs better implementation: Austria welcomes its comprehensive review next week. Most importantly, we must enhance the International Atomic Energy Agency's (IAEA) monitoring and verification capabilities and ensure strict export control for sensitive material and technologies. In view of the presence of Director General ElBaradei here today, let me thank him warmly for his excellent work as head of the Agency over the last 12 years.

6. Finally, we must strengthen trust and confidence. Nuclear weapon free zones contribute significantly to sustainable stability; regions like the Middle East would benefit from such a regime. Ensuring that arms control mechanisms operate in a fair and transparent manner is crucial. Austria's proposal to multilateralize the nuclear fuel cycle under the control of the IAEA could help

to avoid crises of trust such as those with regard to the Iranian and North Korean nuclear programs.

For clarification, I would like to underline that paragraph 11 of this Resolution refers to those countries that have decided to use nuclear energy for peaceful energy reasons, which is not the case for Austria.

Austria is very satisfied that the Resolution we just adopted is a strong text, a positive contribution to the ongoing disarmament process. But resolutions are not enough. Every State must accept responsibility and actively participate.

I promise: Austria's support will be there. You can also count on the European Union with its well-known position on these issues and its deep commitment to strengthening the multilateral system. And we can rely on civil society which throughout the years remained the motor behind disarmament efforts.

Today we identified our goals for the future. We now need the energy, the commitment and the persistence to move forward. The support by Heads of State and Government at this table today makes me confident that, together, we can reach our goal.

19

Speech by Rt. Hon. Peter Hain, MP, Minister for Foreign and Commonwealth Affairs, U.K., Opening the Meeting of the Independent Commission on the Verifiability of the CTBT

...

The fact that you are here in your individual capacities as independent experts is important in the light of the differing national views on the CTBT.

By banning all nuclear test explosions, the Treaty will constrain the development and qualitative improvement of nuclear weapons and the development of advanced new types of nuclear weapons. It will be a major step on the road towards ridding the world of the means to destroy itself.

The importance of this treaty and the desire of the International Community to see it enter into force has been underlined on numerous occasions this year such as the NPT Review Conference, the G8 Summit in Okinawa and the ongoing UNGA. There is widespread consensus that this treaty should and must enter into force as soon as possible.

Unfortunately, almost exactly four years after the Treaty was opened for signature, progress towards entry into force has been patchy. To date, only 30 out of the 44 States whose ratification is necessary for the Treaty to enter into force have deposited their Instruments of Ratification and three of those 44 States have yet to sign the Treaty. The U.K. is, of course, one of the 30 as are two other Nuclear Weapons States, France and

Russia. We take every opportunity to encourage others to join us and I would again today urge all States to sign and ratify the Treaty as soon as possible.

India and Pakistan have announced unilateral moratoria on further nuclear explosions. I welcome these announcements. But, they cannot be a substitute for signature and ratification of the CTBT. I hope that efforts in both countries to build consensus in favour of signature will soon result in a positive outcome.

We attach great importance to the push towards entry into force, the so-called Article XIV process, currently being ably guided by our Japanese colleagues. Last year's conference in Vienna, which I attended, was designed specifically to encourage further Treaty signatures and ratification, did just that. We are keen to see another Article XIV conference next year and encourage Ambassador Abe...in his efforts to take forward arrangements. We must use this Conference to maintain the political momentum in support of the Treaty.

Clearly, a major obstacle in persuading others to sign was the vote in October last year by the U.S. Senate not to ratify the Treaty. That was a matter of deep regret to us and an obvious set back to the Treaty. But it is important that it should be seen as no more than that: a set back. We must not let the Senate's decision be an excuse for others to delay their own signature and ratification of the Treaty.

Equally importantly, we must we not let the Senate's vote be an excuse to delay the work necessary to prepare for the Treaty's entry into force. We welcome and support the efforts being made by the US Administration to take forward the debate in their country, particularly the appointment of General Shalikashvili [General Shali] to head the Task Force. I hope that these efforts, together with the work of this Commission will clarify issues raised during the U.S. consideration of the Treaty. I further hope that the incoming Administration will continue these policies and make the ratification of the CTBT a priority.

The basis for the verification system is, as you well know, set out in the treaty itself

"In order to verify compliance with this Treaty, a verification regime shall be established consisting of the following elements:

(a) An International Monitoring System;

(b) Consultation and clarification;

(c) On-site inspections; and

(d) Confidence-building measures."

Britain is confident that the verification regime described in the Treaty will provide a credible, effective and cost effective way to monitor compliance with the Treaty. But, we acknowledge that others may not share that view. We also acknowledge that technology has changed, even in the short time since the CTBT was negotiated. We believe that it is right therefore for independent experts such as yourselves to take a fresh look at the verifiability of the Treaty and to give us the benefit of your expertise.

The CTBT exists because of the political will of the negotiating States to negotiate the treaty. But the work, the desire to see a functioning Treaty did not end with the conclusion of the negotiations. It only began. We must now address issues such as providing the Provisional Technical Secretariat with adequate resources to enable it to fulfil the requirement of the Treaty. The Provisional Technical Secretariat must be given the means to have a verification regime in place at entry into force capable of meeting the verification requirements of this treaty.

I know that the amount of financial resources that the Provisional Technical Secretariat needs to carry out its functions has been a subject of some debate in the course of the year and indeed in previous years. Britain has already made clear our belief that the level of budget and programme for 2001 as now proposed by the Provisional Technical Secretariat is reasonable. We will support this budget when it comes up for discussion at the Preparatory Commission in November. We hope that others, particularly those who are the leading proponents of nuclear disarmament will do likewise.

The work of establishing the verification system also means dealing with other issues such as how the key work of putting together the On Site Inspection Manual can gain badly needed momentum. I understand that there has been recent progress during discussions in Vienna in at least agreeing the process by which we can do this. Next year, it will be vital to tackle the substance.

Your work will by definition concentrate on technical aspects of CTBT verification. But Governments must maintain the political momentum which brought the CTBT into being. We must make sure that the technical discussions in Vienna do not become bogged down or delayed. Beyond that, we have a wider duty to create the conditions which remove the need to develop nuclear weapons and other weapons of mass destruction. We must build on the results achieved at the NPT Review Conference earlier this year to advance towards our common goal: the global elimination of nuclear weapons and other weapons of mass destruction. We must consolidate progress made towards eliminating chemical warfare—136 countries are now participating in the OPCW. We have a Verification Protocol for the Biological Weapons Convention that is within our grasp. We must ensure that humankind is denied the tools for selfdestruction. The British Government is committed to playing an active and positive role in achieving these goals. We will continue to play this role to the full.

All the WMD instruments are underpinned by verification systems. Each has their critics. But, I leave you with one thought. Those who criticise the Treaty need to consider whether they prefer the alternative: the proliferation of nuclear weapons. I prefer that our discussion today should be about how best to verify a Treaty banning nuclear test explosions than about how best to monitor the explosions that the absence of the treaty would permit.

20

Statement by President Hu Jintao, at the United Nations Security Council Summit, on Nuclear Non-proliferation and Nuclear Disarmament, New York, U.S.A.

24 September 2009

...

The current international security environment is complex and fluid. Nuclear proliferation remains a pressing issue and nuclear disarmament a long and arduous task. To build a safer world for all, we should endeavor to do the following:

- Foster a peaceful and stable international environment, resolve international disputes through peaceful means, and increase the sense of security for all countries. Promote development, eradicate poverty, and remove the root causes of conflict and instability.
- Fully respect and accommodate the legitimate and reasonable security concerns of all countries, refrain from pursuing one's own security at the expense of others, and ensure security for all through win-win cooperation.
- Build state-to-state relations of mutual understanding and mutual trust, resolve differences and dispel misgivings, and conduct dialogue and cooperation on an equal footing.

- Adhere to multilateralism. Consolidate the collective security system with the United Nations at its core and make the system more just and reasonable so that it can play a robust role in international security cooperation.

To realize a safer world for all, we must first and foremost remove the threat of nuclear war. I wish to propose, in this connection, that we make efforts in the following five areas:

First, maintain global strategic balance and stability and vigorously advance nuclear disarmament. All nuclear-weapon states should fulfill in good faith obligations under Article VI of the Treaty on the Non-Proliferation of Nuclear Weapons (NPT), and publicly undertake not to seek permanent possession of nuclear weapons. Countries with the largest nuclear arsenals should continue to take the lead in making drastic and substantive reductions in their nuclear weapons. The Comprehensive Nuclear Test Ban Treaty should be brought into force at an early date, and negotiations on the Fissile Material Cut-off Treaty should start as soon as possible. When conditions are ripe, other nuclear-weapon states should also join the multilateral negotiations on nuclear disarmament. To attain the ultimate goal of complete and thorough nuclear disarmament, the international community should develop, at an appropriate time, a viable, long-term plan composed of phased actions, including the conclusion of a convention on the complete prohibition of nuclear weapons.

Second, abandon the nuclear deterrence policy based on first use of nuclear weapons and take credible steps to reduce the threat of nuclear weapons. All nuclear-weapon states should make an unequivocal commitment of unconditionally not using or threatening to use nuclear weapons against non-nuclear-weapon states or nuclear-weapon-free zones, and conclude a legally-binding international instrument in this regard. In the meantime, nuclear-weapon states should negotiate and conclude a treaty on no-first-use of nuclear weapons against one another.

Third, consolidate the international nuclear non-proliferation regime and prevent proliferation of nuclear weapons. All countries should join the NPT and real efforts should be made to uphold and enhance its authority and effectiveness. The function of the

International Atomic Energy Agency (IAEA) in safeguards should be strengthened. All countries should strictly comply with non-proliferation obligations, refrain from double standards, and tighten and improve export control to prevent proliferation.

Fourth, fully respect the right of all countries to peaceful use of nuclear energy and carry out active international cooperation. Developed countries should actively assist developing countries in developing and using nuclear energy for peaceful purposes. The IAEA should increase input to promote technical cooperation and assistance in nuclear power, nuclear safety and security, and nuclear technology application.

Fifth, take strong measures to enhance nuclear security and reduce nuclear risks. Countries should act in strict observance of all international legal instruments governing nuclear security, take credible steps to ensure the security of their nuclear facilities and materials, and prevent the diversion of nuclear materials with effective means. The international community should intensify cooperation and combat nuclear terrorism through concerted efforts.

China has consistently stood for the complete prohibition and thorough destruction of nuclear weapons. I wish to take this opportunity to solemnly reiterate that China is firmly committed to a nuclear strategy of self-defense. We have adhered to the policy of no-first-use of nuclear weapons at any time and under any circumstances, and made the unequivocal commitment that we will unconditionally not use or threaten to use nuclear weapons against non-nuclear-weapon states or nuclear-weapon-free zones. China does not participate in any form of nuclear arms race. We will continue to keep our nuclear capabilities at the minimum level required for national security, and make effort to advance the international nuclear disarmament process. China will continue to play a constructive role in upholding the international nuclear non-proliferation regime.

21

WILPF Statement on the Comprehensive Test Ban Treaty's Entry into Force, on the Occasion of the CTBT's Sixth Article XIV Conference, New York, U.S.A.

24-25 September 2009

Since the first nuclear weapon test in New Mexico, USA in 1945, the Women's International League for Peace and Freedom (WILPF) has called for the cessation of all nuclear testing and for an international treaty banning such tests. WILPF welcomed the Partial Test Ban Treaty in 1963 but pushed for more—for a complete ban. In 1996, WILPF was encouraged by the opening for signature of the Comprehensive Test Ban Treaty (CTBT).

Unfortunately, thirteen years and 149 ratifications later, the Treaty has not yet entered into force. Three countries—India, Pakistan, and the Democratic People's Republic of Korea—have tested nuclear explosive devices in the interim. Since 1997, the United States has carried out over 20 subcritical nuclear tests at its Nevada Test Site.

It is unfortunate that the CTBT does not expressly forbid qualitative improvements to nuclear weapons through subcritical testing and other means. Its stated objectives, however, are disarmament and the prevention of further nuclear weapon modernization and subsequent arms races. Thus the entry into force of the CTBT would constitute an important step towards an equitable and secure nuclear free world envisioned by the vast majority of the world's citizens and governments. The CTBT provides measures both to determine compliance with the Treaty (i.e. to detect nuclear tests) and to remedy any situation of non-compliance. It is thus one of the best tools the international community currently has at its disposal to establish a process of complete nuclear disarmament.

China, the Democratic People's Republic of Korea, Egypt, India, Indonesia, Iran, Israel, Pakistan, and the United States are the nine states preventing the CTBT's entry into force. Their excuses vary, though many suggest, or expect, that US ratification would lead to a ricochet effect for other ratifications. The merits of this analysis are debatable; regardless, all current Washington discourse indicates that the price of US ratification will be high—too high.

A Congressional Research Service report from June 2009[1] explains that when the US Senate ratified the Partial Test Ban Treaty, the Joint Chiefs of Staff conditioned their support for the Treaty on four safeguards: an aggressive nuclear test program; maintaining nuclear weapon laboratories; maintaining the ability to resume atmospheric tests promptly; and improving intelligence and nuclear explosion monitoring capabilities. The report emphasises that safeguards were key to securing Senate ratification of the 1963 Treaty. The report goes on to explain that updated safeguards have been part of CTBT ratification negotiations in the Senate. The report's author notes, "Safeguards could be updated, such as by adding Safeguards for the nuclear weapon production plants and strategic forces, and could be augmented with implementation measures" that enforce the updated safeguards and prevent any erosion of the anti-disarmament scheme behind ratification.

Furthermore, as Greg Mello of the Los Alamos Study Group argues, the opposition in the Senate to ratifying the Treaty is not about preserving the United States' ability to test a nuclear weapon—it has no reason to ever test a nuclear weapon again and if there were such a circumstance, it would be able to withdraw from the Treaty under its withdrawal clause. Mello writes, "Any ratification deal would be aimed, in part, precisely at negating the Treaty's disarmament impact.... In this shifting and uncertain scene, the CTBT ratification process will be viewed by many actors—defense ideologues, nuclear contractors, and pork-barrel politicians—as a means to protect the U.S. nuclear establishment against the vicissitudes of time."[2]

Other governments and international civil society advocates need to be wary of the process underway in the United States toward CTBT ratification and in their advocacy must emphasise core value of the Treaty: that a ban on nuclear weapon testing is intended to prevent the design, development, or modernisation of nuclear weapons. While WILPF welcomes US President Obama's interest in achieving US ratification, there is such a thing as a price too high. Any deals given in trade for ratification will only serve to undermine the Treaty and cannot be accepted.

Nuclear testing is a message from a government to the world that it is willing to use nuclear weapons. So to is a government's refusal to ratify the test ban. WILPF calls upon all states that have not yet ratified the CTBT to do so. If the eight other Annex II states ratified the Treaty without waiting for the United States, they would isolate the United States as the sole outlier. WILPF also calls on the US Senate to ratify the Treaty without conditions, without safeguards, and without undermining the Treaty's goals of preventing the development of new or "better" nuclear weapons. Conditions to sustain existing nuclear forces and infrastructure are not part of the ban on nuclear testing for a reason.

WILPF also calls upon the nuclear weapon possessors to maintain their testing moratoriums and to cease subcritical testing immediately. A special emphasis should be put on the United Kingdom and Russia, who have ratified the CTBT, yet undermine its efficacy by continuing to conduct these tests. In addition, the United States and the United Kingdom should be condemned for their nuclear weapon modernization and extension programmes, which also weaken the CTBT.

Notes

1. Jonathan Medalia, "Comprehensive Nuclear-Test-Ban Treaty: Updated 'Safeguards' and Net Assessments," Congressional Research Service, 3 June 2009, at <http://assets.opencrs.com/rpts/R40612_20090603.pdf>.
2. Greg Mello, "Obama and CTBT Ratification: Dangerous Distraction," Reaching Critical Will's NPT News in Review, 5 May 2009, at <http://www.reachingcriticalwill.org/legal/npt/NIR2009/No5.pdf>.

22

Statement by the Head of Delegation of the Russian Federation, Deputy Minister of Foreign Affairs Sergey Ryabkov, at the 6th Conference on Facilitating the Entry into Force, of the Comprehensive Nuclear Test Ban Treaty, New York, U.S.A.

24 September 2009

...

Let me congratulate you and the representative of France with the appointment as Co-Chairs of our Forum and express my confidence in the successful outcome of the 6th Conference on Facilitating the Entry into Force of the Comprehensive Nuclear-Test-Ban Treaty (CTBT) under your able leadership.

Definitely, the earliest entry into force of the CTBT is our priority. Russia ratified the CTBT as early as in 2000 and as a matter of principle strongly supports this instrument and works actively towards this goal. The CTBT is called on to become an essential element of the international legal system of security as an important link for other non-proliferation and disarmament instruments.

President of the Russian Federation Dmitry Medvedev emphasized the need for the earliest entry into force of the CTBT at the Security Council Summit meeting on nuclear non-proliferation and disarmament. A provision in support of the CTBT has been included in the UN Security Council resolution 1887 adopted today.

At present, 181 States have signed and 150 of them have already ratified the CTBT. We look with optimism at positive developments in connection with the CTBT. We welcome the intent of the US administration to ratify the CTBT, as it was stated in London on April 1, 2009 in the Joint Statement of President Dmitry Medvedev of the Russian Federation and President Barack Obama of the United States of America.

However, thirteen years since the opening of the CTBT for signature this Treaty has not yet entered into force. The prospects of entry into force of this important international legal instrument remain blurred and this gives all reasons for concern. The future of this Treaty in many respects will be an indicator of the readiness of the international community to move towards a noble goal of creating a world free of nuclear weapons. Therefore, we believe that the remaining 9 States of the so-called "List of 44", whose signing and/or ratifying the Treaty is essential for its entry into force, bear special responsibility for the future of the CTBT. We call upon those States to act accordingly without delay and without preconditions.

In the present situation the States who support the CTBT must continue their efforts to promote the treaty.

Russia continues to advocate the CTBT in the United Nations, and to repeatedly stress the role and significance of the CTBT in the course of preparatory work for the 2010 NPT Review Conference and in other relevant multilateral fora. In April 2009 we supported the non-proliferation resolution of the Interparliamentary Union with a special emphasis on the CTBT.

Russia along with other participants in the 2009 G8 Aquila Summit initiated the inclusion of a section on the support by the G8 of the CTBT's early entry into force and its universalization to the statement on non-proliferation. We actively advocate the CTBT through our bilateral contacts.

We would like to draw your attention to the need for all States to adhere to the letter and spirit of the treaty before its entry into force. It is essential that within this period the nuclear test moratorium is observed. Russia intends to further comply with this commitment if other nuclear weapon States do likewise. We believe and we would like to stress it once again that voluntary moratorium on nuclear testing, no matter how important, cannot substitute the primary goal—the earliest entry into force of the CTBT in strict accordance with the provisions of its Article XIV. After all, unilateral political commitments of some States cannot be compared with the international legal obligations under the CTBT.

Russia supports the efforts of the CTBTO Preparatory Commission to establish a Treaty verification mechanism and actively participates in this work. The progress is obvious—more than two thirds of the International monitoring system (IMS) facilities have been certified. Most of these facilities are fully operational. A large-scale on-site inspection Integrated field exercise, conducted in August-September 2008 in Kazakhstan was a landmark event. The existing high level of alert of the CTBT verification mechanism has been confirmed by timely recording of the notorious event in the DPRK on May 25, 2009 using technical means of verification mechanism and timely notification of the States Parties. This is another point in case that the Treaty is verifiable, which cannot but compel the States who have not yet ratified the CTBT under the pretext of its unverifiability to reconsider their position.

The Russian Federation closely cooperates with the CTBTO Preparatory Commission in establishing the IMS facilities on its territory. We are satisfied with the level and quality of the existing cooperation between us and the Commission in the deployment of the Russian IMS segment. Half of its stations have already been certified and are functioning.

We would like to state that the Russian delegation supports the draft Final declaration of the Conference and draft Measures to promote the entry into force of the Comprehensive Nuclear-Test-Ban Treaty contained there. We are ready to participate actively in its implementation. We hope that of our joint efforts will lead to a qualitative shift towards the transformation of the CTBT into a functioning international legal instrument.

In conclusion, we once again call upon all States that have not yet signed or ratified the CTBT, and first of all those on whom its entry into force depend, to do so without delay or any preconditions.

23

Final Declaration and Measures to Promote the Entry into Force, of the Comprehensive Nuclear Test Ban Treaty

24 September 2009

Final Declaration

1. We the ratifiers, together with the States Signatories, met in New York on 24 and 25 September 2009 to promote the entry into force of the Comprehensive Nuclear-Test-Ban Treaty at the earliest possible date. In accordance with the mandate given to us in Article XIV of the Treaty, we decided by consensus what measures consistent with international law may be undertaken to accelerate the ratification process in order to facilitate the early entry into force of the Treaty, thus ridding the world of nuclear weapon test explosions.

2. We reaffirm that the ultimate objective of the efforts of States in the disarmament process is general and complete disarmament under strict and effective international control. We reiterate that the cessation of all nuclear weapon test explosions and all other nuclear explosions, by constraining the development and qualitative improvement of nuclear weapons and ending the development of advanced new types of nuclear weapons, constitutes an effective measure of nuclear disarmament and non-proliferation in all its aspects. The end to all nuclear weapons testing is, thus, a meaningful step in the realization of a systematic process to achieve nuclear disarmament.

3. The international community is committed to establishing a universal and internationally and effectively verifiable comprehensive nuclear-test-ban treaty as a major instrument in the field of nuclear disarmament and non-proliferation. The overwhelming support for the Treaty and its early entry into force has been expressed by the United Nations General Assembly and other multilateral and regional organs and initiatives, which have called for signature and ratification of the Treaty as soon as possible, and have urged all States to remain seized of the issue at the highest political level. We affirmed the importance and urgency of signatures and ratifications without delay to achieve early entry into force of the Treaty as one of the practical steps for the systematic and progressive efforts towards nuclear disarmament and nuclear nonproliferation, which were agreed to by the participating States at international forums dealing with nuclear disarmament and nuclear non-proliferation.

4. We note that significant progress has been made in signing and ratifying the CTBT, which has achieved near universal adherence with signature by 181 States and ratification by 150. States as of today, of which four have signed and ten, including one listed in Annex 2 to the Treaty, whose ratification is required for its entry into force, have ratified since the 2007 Conference on Facilitating the Entry into Force of the CTBT. This progress demonstrates the strong determination of the vast majority of States not to carry out any nuclear weapon test explosion or any other nuclear explosion, and to prohibit and prevent any such nuclear explosion at any place under their jurisdiction or control. Of the 44 States listed in Annex 2 to the Treaty, 41 have signed and of these, 35 have also ratified the Treaty. A list of those States is provided in the Appendix.

5. Despite the progress made and the near universal international support that exists for the Treaty, we note with concern that it has not entered into force thirteen years after its opening for signature on 24 September 1996. Relevant international developments since the 2007 Conference on Facilitating the Entry into Force of the CTBT make entry into force of the Treaty more urgent today than ever before, within the broader framework of multilateral disarmament, arms control

and non-proliferation efforts. Noting the improved prospects for ratification in several Annex 2 countries, we renew our strong conviction that entry into force of the CTBT will enhance international peace and security.

6. We call upon all States which have not yet done so, to sign and ratify the Treaty without delay, in particular, those States whose ratification is needed for entry into force. We strongly encourage such Annex 2 States to take individual initiatives to ratify the Treaty. We also commend efforts to create conditions facilitating ratification by such Annex 2 States, including confidence building measures through which such States could be encouraged to consider, as an option, ratifying the Treaty in a coordinated manner. At the same time, we renew our commitment to work for universal ratification of the Treaty and its early entry into force.

7. We recognize the extensive range of bilateral and joint outreach efforts by signatories and ratifiers to encourage and assist States that have not yet signed and ratified the Treaty to do so, and agreed to intensify our efforts to encourage ratification. Such efforts should pay special attention to States listed in Annex 2 to the Treaty. We expressed appreciation for the efforts of the Special Representative in promoting entry into force of the Treaty.

8. In accordance with the letter and spirit of the Treaty, we reaffirm our firm determination to end nuclear weapon test explosions and any other nuclear explosions. We call upon all States not to carry out such explosions. Continuing and sustained voluntary adherence to a moratorium is of the highest importance, but does not have the same effect as the entry into force of the Treaty, which offers the global community the prospect of a permanent and legally binding commitment to end nuclear weapon test explosions or any other nuclear explosions. We reaffirm our commitment to the Treaty's basic obligations and call on all States to refrain from acts which would defeat the object and purpose of the Treaty pending its entry into force. With respect to the nuclear tests announced by the Democratic People's Republic of Korea on 9 October 2006 and 25 May 2009, bearing in mind the United Nations General Assembly

Resolutions (A/RES/61/104 and A/RES/63/87) and other relevant United Nations resolutions including the latest (S/RES/1874 (2009)), we underline the need for a peaceful solution of the nuclear issues through successful implementation of the Joint Statement agreed upon in the framework of the Six-Party Talks. We also believe that the aforementioned events, internationally condemned, highlighted the urgent need for the early entry into force of the Treaty and hence the completion of the CTBT verification regime at its entry into force, in accordance with the provisions of the Treaty and the mandate of the Preparatory Commission for the Comprehensive Nuclear-Test-Ban Treaty Organization.

9. We reaffirmed our strong belief that it is essential to maintain momentum in building all elements of the verification regime, which will be capable of verifying compliance with the Treaty at its entry into force. The verification regime will be unprecedented in its global reach after entry into force of the Treaty and will thereby ensure confidence that States are maintaining their Treaty commitments. In this context, we will continue to provide the tangible support required to enable the Preparatory Commission for the Comprehensive Nuclear-Test-Ban Treaty Organization to complete all its tasks in the most efficient and cost-effective way, including the On-Site Inspection programme and the progressive development and coverage of the International Monitoring System, which will be capable of meeting the verification requirements of the Treaty at its entry into force. In this regard we note the progress achieved in the establishment of the International Monitoring System, which has currently 249 certified facilities, and the satisfactory functioning of the International Data Centre.

10. We agree that in addition to its essential function, the CTBT verification system currently being built up would be capable of bringing scientific and civil benefits, including for tsunami warning systems and possibly other disaster alert systems. We will continue to consider ways to ensure that these benefits can be broadly shared by the international community in conformity with the Treaty.

11. We reaffirm our determination to continue to work towards early entry into force of the Treaty and to this end adopt the following measures.

Measures to Promote the Entry into Force of the Comprehensive Nuclear-Test-Ban Treaty

Convinced of the importance of achieving universal adherence to the Treaty, we:

(a) Will spare no efforts and use all avenues open to us in conformity with international law to encourage further signature and ratification of the Treaty, and urge all States to sustain the momentum generated by this Conference to remain seized of the issue at the highest political level;

(b) Support and encourage bilateral, regional and multilateral initiatives by interested countries and the Preparatory Commission for the Comprehensive Nuclear-Test-Ban Treaty Organization to promote the entry into force of the Treaty;

(c) Agree that ratifying States will continue the practice of selecting coordinators to promote cooperation, through informal consultations with all interested countries, aimed at promoting further signatures and ratifications;

(d) Will maintain a contact list of countries among ratifiers which volunteer to assist the coordinators in various regions in promoting activities enhancing the entry into force of the Treaty;

(e) Encourage the organization of regional seminars in conjunction with other regional meetings in order to increase the awareness of the important role that the Treaty plays;

(f) Call upon the Preparatory Commission for the Comprehensive Nuclear-Test-Ban Treaty Organization to continue its international cooperation activities and organizing workshops, seminars and training programmes in the legal and technical fields;

(g) Call upon the Preparatory Commission for the Comprehensive Nuclear-Test-Ban Treaty Organization to continue promoting understanding of the Treaty and demonstrating, on a provisional basis, the benefits of the civil and scientific applications of the verification technologies, inter alia, in such areas as environment, earth science and technology, tsunami warning systems and possibly other disaster alert systems;

(h) Recommend that the Provisional Technical Secretariat continue to provide States with legal assistance with respect to the ratification process and implementation measures and, in order to enhance these activities and their visibility, maintain a contact point for the exchange and dissemination of relevant information and documentation;

(i) Request the Provisional Technical Secretariat to continue to act as a 'focal point' for collecting information on outreach activities undertaken by ratifiers and signatories, and to maintain an updated overview of the information based on inputs provided by States Signatories for this purpose on the public web site of the Preparatory Commission for the Comprehensive Nuclear-Test-Ban Treaty Organization, thereby assisting in promoting the entry into force of the Treaty;

(j) Encourage cooperation with inter-governmental and non-governmental organizations and other elements of civil society to raise awareness of and support for the Treaty and its objectives, as well as the need for its early entry into force.

Appendix to the Final Declaration and Measures to Promote the Entry into Force of the Comprehensive Nuclear-Test-Ban Treaty

List of States

A. States that have ratified the Treaty

Afghanistan	Eritrea	Mexico
Albania	Estonia	Micronesia (Federated States of)
Algeria	Ethiopia	Moldova
Andorra	Fiji	Monaco
Antigua and Barbuda	Finland	Mongolia

Argentina
Armenia
Australia
Austria
Azerbaijan
Bahamas
Bahrain
Bangladesh
Barbados
Belarus
Belgium
Belize
Benin
Bolivia (Plurinational State of)
Bosnia and Herzegovina
Botswana
Brazil
Bulgaria
Burkina Faso
Burundi
Cambodia
Cameroon
Canada
Cape Verde
Chile
Colombia
Cook Islands
Costa Rica
Côte d'Ivoire
Croatia
Cyprus
Czech Republic
Democratic Republic of the Congo
Denmark
Djibouti
Dominican
Ecuador
El Salvador
Sudan
Suriname
Sweden
Switzerland
Tajikistan
The former Yugoslav Republic of Macedonia
Togo

France
Gabon
Georgia
Germany
Greece
Grenada
Guyana
Haiti
Holy See
Honduras
Hungary
Iceland
Ireland
Italy
Jamaica
Japan
Jordan
Kazakhstan
Kenya
Kiribati
Kuwait
Kyrgyzstan
Lao People's Democratic Republic
Latvia
Lebanon
Lesotho
Liberia
Libyan Arab Jamahiriya
Liechtenstein
Lithuania
Luxembourg
Madagascar
Malawi
Malaysia
Maldives
Republic Mali
Malta
Mauritania
Tunisia
Turkey
Turkmenistan
Uganda
Ukraine
United Arab Emirates
United Kingdom of Great Britain and Northern Ireland

Montenegro
Morocco
Mozambique
Namibia
Nauru
Netherlands
New Zealand
Nicaragua
Niger
Nigeria
Norway
Oman
Palau
Panama
Paraguay
Peru
Philippines
Poland
Portugal
Qatar
Republic of Korea
Romania
Russian Federation
Rwanda
Saint Kitts and Nevis
Saint Lucia
Saint Vincent and the Grenadines
Samoa
San Marino
Senegal
Serbia
Seychelles
Sierra Leone
Singapore
Slovakia
Slovenia
South Africa
Spain
United Republic of Tanzania
Uruguay
Uzbekistan
Vanuatu
Venezuela (Bolivarian Republic of)
Viet Nam
Zambia

B. The following 44 States, whose ratification is required for the entry into force of the Treaty in accordance with Article XIV, are listed in Annex 2 to the Treaty

Algeria
Argentina
Australia
Austria
Bangladesh
Belgium
Brazil

Egypt
Finland
France
Germany
Hungary
India
Indonesia

Poland
Republic of Korea
Romania
Russian Federation
Slovakia
South Africa
Spain

Bulgaria
Canada
Chile
China
Colombia
Democratic People's Republic of Korea
Democratic Republic of the Congo
Iran (Islamic Republic of)
Israel
Italy
Japan
Mexico
Netherlands
Norway
Pakistan
Peru
Sweden
Switzerland
Turkey
Ukraine
United Kingdom of Great Britain and Northern Ireland
United States of America
Viet Nam

1. States listed in Annex 2 to the Treaty that have signed and ratified the Treaty

Algeria
Argentina
Australia
Austria
Bangladesh
Belgium
Brazil
Bulgaria
Canada
Chile
Colombia
Democratic Republic of the Congo
Finland
France
Germany
Hungary
Italy
Japan
Mexico
Netherlands
Norway
Peru
Poland
Republic of Korea
Romania
Russian Federation
Slovakia
South Africa
Spain
Sweden
Switzerland
Turkey
Ukraine
United Kingdom of Great Britain and Northern Ireland
Viet Nam

2. States listed in Annex 2 to the Treaty that have signed but not ratified the Treaty

China
Egypt
Indonesia
Iran (Islamic Republic of)
Israel
United States of America

3. States listed in Annex 2 to the Treaty that have not signed the Treaty

Democratic People's Republic of Korea
India
Pakistan

24

Statement by the New Zealand Minister of Foreign Affairs Hon. Murray McCully, at the 6th CTBT Article XIV Conference, New York, U.S.A.

24-25 September 2009

...

New Zealanders have a proud record of opposition to nuclear weapons and nuclear weapons testing. We strongly support the Comprehensive Nuclear-Test-Ban Treaty as an important milestone along the path to a world free of nuclear weapons.

A nuclear-weapons-free world remains the ultimate goal for New Zealand. We do not believe that goal is unattainable. The global community can make it happen, with practical, concrete steps which build confidence among nuclearweapons states and between them and those who do not possess nuclear weapons. The CTBT is a fundamental part of this process. It makes it clear that the development of new nuclear weapons is unacceptable.

The nuclear disarmament and non-proliferation regime is still confronted with many unprecedented challenges. The nuclear test conducted by the DPRK in...struck again at the heart of the CTBT. It challenged the moratorium on nuclear testing observed by others in the absence of the entry into force of the Treaty. But it is precisely for that reason that we need to redouble our efforts to encourage those States whose ratification is required for entry into force to ratify the Treaty without delay. Such action would make a significant and positive contribution to international security.

The DPRK test also served to highlight the important role that the CTBT's International Monitoring System can and will play in verifying adherence to the ban on nuclear testing. The provision of high-quality and timely analysis by the Provisional Technical Secretariat to state signatories was an important demonstration that the global verification mandate of the CTBT works and will be operational when the Treaty enters into force. The build-up of the IMS has been a key priority for New Zealand.

The CTBT has a vital place in today's multilateral framework for nuclear disarmament and non-proliferation. It already contributes to global stability. Its entry into force would be a major step towards a world free of nuclear weapons—which must be our ultimate destination. New Zealand would like to see this happen without delay. We stand ready to work with all, large and small, for a goal which will benefit all of mankind.

25

NGO Statement on the Comprehensive Nuclear Test Ban Treaty (CTBT), for the Fifth Article XIV Conference on Facilitating Entry into Force

18 September 2007

...

1. For more than half a century, countless nongovernmental organizations, scientific experts, political leaders, and ordinary citizens have pursued the goal of a more secure world free of the dangers of nuclear weapon test explosions. A decade ago, the 1996 Comprehensive Nuclear Test Ban Treaty (CTBT) was negotiated and opened for signature. Today, over 176 states have signed. Installation of the Treaty's extensive and sophisticated monitoring system and preparations for on-site inspections to verify compliance are advancing. Yet, after almost fifty years of hard work and advocacy, we have not crossed the finish line. More must be done to achieve the CTBT's entry into force.

2. We, the representatives of nongovernmental organizations from across the globe, applaud the 10 states that have ratified the treaty since 2005. We call on all states that have not done so to sign and ratify the treaty we call upon all states to commit themselves to take the final step toward securing signatures and ratifications of the 10 remaining Annex II states that are necessary to bring the CTBT into force.

3a. The CTBT is important to all states—North and South, East and West, large and small, with nuclear weapons and without. The CTBT is essential to the prevention of nuclear arms races, the development of increasingly more destructive weapons, the prevention of more states acquiring nuclear arsenals, and the protection of human health and the global environment from the devastating effects of nuclear weapons production and testing.

3b. CTBT entry into force would also shore up support for the increasingly beleaguered nuclear Nonproliferation Treaty (NPT) regime. The nuclear-weapon states' commitment to the test ban's entry into force was vital in securing the indefinite extension of the NPT in 1995. NPT states-parties unanimously endorsed signature and ratification of the CTBT as part of the 2000 NPT Review Conference. The continued failure by a few states to move forward with the CTBT undermines the confidence in the nonproliferation bargain and perpetuates the outdated 20th century belief that nuclear weapons are necessary and legitimate tools of foreign policy.

4. Achieving CTBT entry into force is no easy or ordinary task. Since the Article XIV Conference of 2005 in New York, new hurdles have emerged. North Korea conducted a nuclear weapon test explosion, more than a few states are failing to meet their financial obligations to support the CTBT Provisional Secretariat and the task of global test ban verification and monitoring, and some CTBT adherents have put forward proposals to engage in civil nuclear trade with states that have not yet signed the CTBT.

5a. As a result, CTBT entry into force is even more urgent and overdue. We respectfully call upon the CTBT member states to demonstrate more determined leadership and steadfast fidelity to the principles of the treaty so that entry into force can be achieved at the earliest possible date.

5b. Specifically, we strongly urge this conference to: (a) reiterate that a state's signature of the treaty constitutes an obligation not to conduct a nuclear test explosion, and that the CTBT establishes a norm of behavior that applies to states that have not yet signed the treaty; (b) call upon all signatory states to provide necessary support to the construction and maintenance of the CTBTO monitoring and verification system, including on-site inspection; c) honor treaty and political commitments not to engage in nuclear trade with countries that have not yet joined the CTBT regime; and d) call upon *de facto* and *de jure* nuclear-armed states to cease and desist from research and development activities that may create pressure to test in the future.

5c. We urge the 10 remaining Annex II states that either have not signed or ratified the treaty to do so without further delay. We remind those hold-out states that their delay not only is holding the entire treaty hostage, but is also undermining their own security.

6a. Since the CTBT opened for signature, many states have advanced the cause of the treaty in ways that extend beyond their ratification. We gratefully acknowledge the support that has been offered to the test ban by individual governments, the EU, the NAM, and the OAS in policy statements and political pronouncements at this conference and in other international fora.

6b. We urge governments of CTBT signatories to maintain their public support, which helps reinforce the test ban norm, and to translate that support into action through meetings with representatives of hold-out states and in the implementation of each signatory state's foreign and security policies. Rhetoric alone is not enough. Consistent, high-level pressure is necessary to move states to sign and/or ratify the treaty.

7a. In these conversations, it must be emphasized that a global test ban can help head-off and deescalate destabilizing nuclear arms competition. Short-sighted arguments that nuclear testing and improved nuclear weapons capabilities may be needed to enhance the credibility of a state's nuclear retaliatory capabilities or its ability to execute preemptive strikes must be addressed directly and forcefully.

7b. Such arguments are at times voiced by diplomats from the Middle East, South Asia, and East Asia, where the entry into force of the treaty would be a signal contribution to nuclear-risk reduction. With no shortage of conflict and hostility in the

Middle East, ratification by Israel, Egypt, and Iran would reduce nuclear weapons-related security concerns and bring these states further into the nuclear nonproliferation mainstream. Egyptian and Iranian steps to build and allow the operation of monitoring stations on their territories also would be helpful. The Pakistan-India nuclear arms race could be contained to the benefit of both countries if they signed and ratified the CTBT.

8. The world's patience is wearing thin with signatory states that do not appear to be exerting a good-faith effort to ratify. The two remaining NPT weapon-states stand out in particular. The leadership in Beijing must fulfill its repeated and now somewhat empty promise to conclude the ratification process. It claimed at the last two Article XIV Conferences that it has submitted the treaty to the Standing Committee of People's National Congress for approval and that "all necessary work is underway in a serious and orderly fashion." There does not appear to be any domestic political obstacle in the way that should prevent China's ratification within a few months. In the absence of such action, China owes a detailed explanation for its continued delay and a timetable for its ratification process. China could demonstrate it is a true leader and not simply a follower by finally ratifying the CTBT.

9. Despite U.S. leadership for the treaty's negotiation, the current U.S. presidential administration does not support CTBT entry into force. However, there are new and hopeful signs that a bipartisan process may be initiated as early as 2009 to reconsider ratification of the CTBT. We note that former Secretaries of State George Shultz and Henry Kissinger, along with former Secretary of Defense Bill Perry, former Senator Sam Nunn, and other prominent Democratic and Republican foreign policy experts have joined many NGOs in calling on the Senate "to achieve ratification of the Comprehensive Test Ban Treaty, taking advantage of recent technical advances, and working to secure ratification by other key states." Some leading presidential candidates support this approach. Key senators can do this through hearings, by working with their colleagues, and through exchanges with technical experts and allied governments.

10. Other states also must do their part and ratify. There is no compelling reason why states such as Indonesia and Colombia, which consistently profess their support for the CTBT, should continue to dither.

11. We express our most serious concern over the October 2006 nuclear detonation in the Democratic People's Republic of Korea (DPRK). This dangerous and irresponsible act has damaged the international non-testing norm. The restraint exhibited by the DPRK's neighbors and their strategic partners is commendable and we strongly urge them to continue to build on progress with the DPRK toward establishing a nuclear-weapon free and more secure Korean peninsula. We call upon this conference to condemn the North Korean test as an affront and danger to international security and urge the states engaged in the six-party process to accelerate their efforts to implement their September 2005 Joint Statement for the denuclearization of the Korean Peninsula.

12a. The unwelcome North Korean nuclear test explosion, however, demonstrated once more the robust nature of the treaty's verification and monitoring system. The International Monitoring System (IMS) and its experimental noble gas monitoring network successfully observed and provided data that helped identify the event as a nuclear detonation, despite a relatively small explosive yield of approximately half a kiloton TNT equivalent.

12b. We commend the valuable work of the CTBT PrepCom and the Provisional Technical Secretariat in developing the IMS, the International Data Center (IDC), and an On-Site Inspection capability but are deeply concerned about the failure of certain signatories to fully fund the CTBT Organization (CTBTO). As of September 4th, the largest contributor, the United States, is now more than $28.5 million behind in fulfilling its assessed contributions, while Brazil is almost $12 million in arrears, and Argentina is more than $6.5 million in arrears. The U.S. Congress, for its part, should ensure that the United States fully funds the international test ban verification system. All of the several signatory states that are behind in their assessed contributions must act now to become part of the solution rather than a part of the problem. Other states must not use this as an excuse to renege on their payments, but should press the United States and others to fulfill their obligations as a signatory to support the CTBTO.

13a. Continued budget shortfalls will hinder the remaining construction and provisional operation of international monitoring and verification facilities, which are crucial in maintaining the capability to confidently detect noncompliance. A robust verification system in turn alleviates concerns about risks involved in ratification because no other state can conduct secret nuclear test explosions to gain an advantage.

13b. Ongoing activities at the test sites of China, Russia, and the United States also have the potential to ignite concerns about noncompliance with the CTBT. Current subcritical experiments, contained chemical explosions, and tunneling activities are unnecessary. We call on China, Russia, the United States, and others to permanently close their test sites or else negotiate transparency and confidence building visits to decrease concerns about activities not compliant with the CTBT.

14a. We also are deeply concerned that certain CTBT signatory states are pursuing nuclear trade arrangements with India, which has refused to join the NPT and the CTBT.

14b. We urge CTBT signatory governments that are also members of the Nuclear Suppliers Group (NSG) to establish CTBT signature as a condition of nuclear trade before they agree to exempt India from the NSG's full-scope international safeguards condition of nuclear supply. If India is, as Prime Minister Manmohan Singh said in July 2005, prepared to take on the responsibilities expected of other advanced nuclear nations, it is reasonable to expect that India can sign the CTBT, as the five original nuclear-weapon states have already done. If India and the other states that are not members of the NPT are to enjoy the benefits of NPT membership, they should at least make meaningful, legally binding commitments to core nonproliferation and disarmament undertakings, including the CTBT.

14c. We also note that the proposed U.S.-India agreement for nuclear cooperation does not explicitly state that the United States would terminate civil nuclear trade with India in the event that New Delhi were to renew nuclear testing. Incredibly, the agreement also commits the United States to support the creation of a strategic fuel reserve for India and to help India gain access to fuel supplies from other suppliers such as the United Kingdom, France, or Russia, if nuclear fuel supplies are interrupted—even if the interruption is due to an Indian nuclear test or a violation of its safeguards agreements. It would be highly irresponsible for NSG member states to approve of changes to their guidelines for nuclear trade that do not stipulate that any exemption for India from the full-scope safeguards requirement would be revoked if India were to resume testing.

15. We are particularly disappointed that some states that have in the past strongly advocated for CTBT entry into force appear to have abandoned their CTBT principles and their duty to support UN Resolution 1172, which was the international community's response to the 1998 Indian and Pakistani nuclear tests. Not only have the United States, France, Russia, and the United Kingdom failed to condition their support for renewed nuclear trade with India on New Delhi's support for the test ban, but Australia has also apparently abandoned its CTBT efforts vis-à-vis India by considering the sale of uranium to India. Only two years ago, Australian Foreign Minister Alexander Downer chaired the fourth Article XIV Conference and said of states like India that are obstructing entry into force: "We have over the years heard many reasons as to why this is so. The time for excuses is past. It is time for them to act." Indeed, the time is now for all states to act in support of the CTBT.

16a. We note with concern that CTBT signatories possessing nuclear weapons—France, China, Russia, the United States, and the United Kingdom—also continue to pursue nuclear weapons research activities that are not consistent with the CTBT's goal of "constraining the development and qualitative improvement of nuclear weapons."

16b. In particular, the Bush administration's pursuit of a new, so-called reliable replacement warhead (also known as RRW) could undermine the CTBT and provide other states with a cynical excuse to pursue new nuclear weapons capabilities and to keep their nuclear testing options open. The Bush administration claims that the new warhead and related modernization of the U.S. nuclear weapons production infrastructure can improve confidence in the reliability of the U.S. stockpile and reduce the likelihood the United States would resume nuclear testing.

16c. Such claims are unfounded and misleading. The production of new nuclear warheads is unnecessary to maintain existing nuclear weapons stockpiles under the CTBT and is contrary to the spirit of the CTBT and the commitments of states under Article VI of the NPT. We note that since the United States ceased nuclear testing 15 years ago this month, its ability to maintain its existing stockpile without testing has only improved. Recent U.S. government studies found that the plutonium primaries of most U.S. nuclear weapons will have minimum lifetimes of 85 years, about twice as long as previous estimates.

16d. We urge states gathered at this Article XIV Conference to formally call upon states possessing nuclear weapons to refrain from research and development efforts that could lead to new warheads and possibly the resumption of nuclear testing.

17a. The treaty's broader political and security benefits are clear. But at its most basic level, the treaty exists to ban the explosive testing of nuclear weapons and to prevent the devastating effects of such tests on human health and the environment.

17b. Since 1945, eight countries have conducted 2,051 nuclear test explosions. Most of those tests were conducted at U.S. test sites in Nevada and the Marshall Islands, the Soviet Union's test sites in Kazakhstan and Novaya Zemlya, France's test sites on the Polynesian atolls of Fangataufa and Moruroa, China's Lop Nor test site, and in Algeria and Australia. Most of the test sites are on the lands of indigenous peoples and far from the capitals of the testing governments. The 528 atmospheric tests delivered radioactive materials that produced approximately 430,000 additional cancer fatalities by the year 2000, according to a 1990 report by the International Physicians for the Prevention of Nuclear War. The U.S. National Cancer Institute estimated in a 1997 report that the 90 dirtiest U.S. tests could cause 7,500-75,000 additional cases of thyroid cancer.

17c. While underground nuclear explosions pose a smaller radioactive hazard than atmospheric tests, there has been widespread venting from underground explosions. This was especially true at the Semipalatinsk test site in Kazakhstan. The United States has acknowledged that 433 of its 824 underground tests released radioactive material into the atmosphere. In addition, underground nuclear blasts produce large amounts of radioactive contamination in situ, which over time leak into the surrounding environment.

18. We have presented political and technical reasons in support of the comprehensive and verifiable ban on nuclear testing. But as we discuss the policy issues, diplomatic steps, and financial needs for the CTBT, we must not lose sight of the moral dimension of the CTBT—a dimension equal to that of national and international security. Your citizens and future generations depend on your wisdom and courage to protect them from the effects of the most dangerous weapons ever to curse humanity. No government should stand in the way of this indispensable step toward eliminating the threat of nuclear weapons and preventing nuclear war.

19. We express our gratitude for the opportunity to address the conference, to the secretariat and other organizers, and to the hard work and dedication of the staff and leadership of the CTBTO.

20. This presentation was prepared and supported by the NGOs that have been working for the banning of nuclear tests for many years, in many countries, and in many ways. We look forward to the day when all of our efforts bring about the entry into force of the CTBT.

1. Abolition 2000 (New Zealand)
2. Alliance for Nuclear Accountability (U.S.A.)

3. Acronym Institute for Disarmament Diplomacy (U.K.)
4. Action des Citoyens pour le Désarmement Nucléaire (France)
5. Arms Control Association (U.S.A.)
6. British American Security Information Council
7. Boundary Peace Initiative (Canada)
8. Canadian Federation of University Women (Canada)
9. Canadian Peace Alliance (Canada)
10. Canadian Voice of Women for Peace (Canada)
11. Center for Arms Control and Non-Proliferation (U.S.A.)
12. Center for Encounters and Active Non-Violence (Austria)
13. Círculo Latinoamericano de Estudios Internacionales (Mexico)
14. Citizens' Nuclear Information Center (Japan)
15. Coalition for Nuclear Disarmament and Peace (India)
16. Council for a Livable World (U.S.A.)
17. Friedens- und Begegnungsstätte Mutlangen e.V. (Germany)
18. Friedenswerkstatt Mutlangen e.V. (Germany)
19. Friends Committee on National Legislation (U.S.A.)
20. Amb. George Bunn, first general counsel for the U.S. Arms Control and Disarmament Agency who helped negotiate the NPT
21. Global Action to Prevent War (U.S.A.)
22. Global Anti-Nuclear Alliance
23. Global Security Institute (U.S.A.)
24. International Physicians for the Prevention of Nuclear War
25. Lawyers' Committee on Nuclear Policy (U.S.A.)
26. Mayors for Peace
27. Nuclear Age Peace Foundation (U.S.A.)
28. Pax Christi Aotearoa (New Zealand)

29. Peace Depot (Japan)
30. Peace Foundation Disarmament & Security Centre (New Zealand)
31. Peace Movement Aotearoa (New Zealand)
32. Peace Movement Aotearoa, Wellington (New Zealand)
33. Peace Union of Finland (Finland)
34. Physicians for Social Responsibility (U.S.A.)
35. Proposition One Committee (U.S.A.)
36. Science for Peace (Canada)
37. Simon's Centre for Disarmament and Nonproliferation Research (Canada)
38. Toronto Hiroshima Day Coalition (Canada)
39. Tri-Valley Citizens Against a Radioactive Environment (U.S.A.)
40. Women's Federation for World Peace International
41. Women's International League for Peace and Freedom
42. Women's International League for Peace and Freedom (U.S.A.)
43. Women's International League for Peace and Freedom, Aotearoa (New Zealand)
44. World Conference of Religions for Peace (Canada)

26

Speech by State Secretary Frank Belfrage, Sweden, at the CTBT Conference in Vienna, on Facilitating the Entry into Force, of the Comprehensive Nuclear Test Ban Treaty

17-18 September 2007

...

Let me first congratulate you on your election as President of this conference.

Sweden fully associates itself with the statement made by Portugal on behalf of the European Union.

It is with somewhat mixed feelings that I address this forum today. The need to convene a fifth conference to facilitate the entry into force of the Comprehensive Nuclear-Test-Ban Treaty is a sad reminder of the lack of progress in the field of arms control and disarmament during the decade that has passed since the Treaty opened for signature. At the same time, it is a manifestation of the continued commitment to ban nuclear weapon tests once and for all by an overwhelming majority of states. We knew from the outset that this was no easy task—but we remain committed.

We remain committed to fulfil the promise to future generations, that the age of nuclear testing is a closed chapter in history. Honouring the efforts of those who tirelessly negotiated the Treaty we must now push this five-decade long process the last mile to completion.

We remain committed because we know the importance of the CTBT for the overall non-proliferation regime:

- Raising the threshold for acquisition of nuclear weapons;
- Preventing a qualitative arms race; and
- Building confidence through an effective verification system.

We remain committed in pursuit of our long-term vision of a world free from weapons of mass destruction, convinced of the urgent need to revive international non-proliferation and disarmament efforts.

Mr. President,

When new threats to global and human security emerge, we must resist the temptation of reaching for traditional tools and means of defence. Today, it is indeed difficult to imagine a situation in which the use of a nuclear weapon would pass the tests of military necessity, proportionality, and humanity. Yet, there are still some 27000 nuclear warheads in the world and new weapons systems are contemplated. If nuclear weapon states continue to rely on their nuclear arsenals as a guarantor for security, there is a real risk that other states will seek nuclear weapons for the same reason.

And here I quote from the January 4th article in the *Wall Street Journal*, signed by former US Secretaries of State Henry Kissinger, and George Schultz, former Secretary of Defence William Perry, and former Senator Sam Nunn:

> Reliance on nuclear weapons for [deterrence] is becoming increasingly hazardous and decreasingly effective.

Preventing the proliferation of nuclear weapons is one of the major challenges of this generation of international leaders. The confidence gap regarding the nuclear ambitions of Iran, and the negotiations over the nuclear weapons program in North Korea, are the two most prominent examples. The risk that non-state groups and terrorist networks acquire nuclear weapons or sensitive materials is another. In dealing with these urgent cases, we should not lose sight of the ultimate goal of eliminating all nuclear weapons. Global challenges call for multilateral responses—and the most effective way to ensure a certain conduct by some states, is that all states adhere to the same principles.

In June 2006, the Weapons of Mass Destruction Commission, chaired by Dr. Hans Blix, delivered its report "Weapons of Terror: Freeing the world of Nuclear Biological and Chemical Arms", representing a welcome contribution to the international discourse on disarmament, arms control and non-proliferation. Sweden joins the Commission in urging that "all states that have not already done so should sign and ratify the Comprehensive Test-Ban Treaty unconditionally and without delay."

A particular responsibility rests with the remaining ten states whose ratification is necessary for the Treaty to enter into force. To them, the CTBT represents an extraordinary opportunity for international leadership. Ratifications by key states—such as China and the United States—could potentially spark a positive chain reaction. The US was the first country to sign the CTBT in 1996 and renewed US leadership for the entry into force of the Treaty would be immensely important.

Regional approaches to secure ratifications by Egypt, Iran, and Israel—and signatures and ratifications by India and Pakistan—should also be further explored. China could play an important role as a catalyst in South Asia. Finally, the framework of the six-party talks offers an opportunity to influence North Korea to adhere to the Treaty. In the face of a positive chain reaction, Colombia and Indonesia would no doubt follow suite.

Even though three states—India, Pakistan and North Korea —have conducted nuclear tests since the CTBT opened for signature in 1996, there is reason to be optimistic. The international community, including the Security Council, has unanimously condemned all these tests. In combination with the voluntary abstention from nuclear testing by all recognized nuclear weapon states, we denote a virtually universal consensus that nuclear testing is unacceptable.

Let us be clear—aside from keeping the door open for future nuclear tests, there is no valid reason to remain outside the treaty or to bar it from entering into force. We are here to call for a confirmation that no such plans exist. We are determined to close the door to future nuclear tests—and we remain committed.

27

Statement by Representatives of Non-Governmental Organizations, on the Comprehensive Nuclear Test Ban Treaty (CTBT), to the Preparatory Meeting for the 2010 Review Conference for the Treaty on the Non-proliferation of Nuclear Weapons

5 May 2009

...

The history of the nuclear age makes clear that opportunities to reduce the risks posed by nuclear weapons are often fleeting. When the right political conditions are in place, government leaders must seize the chance to make progress.

Now is such a time.

Entry into force of the Comprehensive Nuclear Test Ban Treaty (CTBT) is within sight. Since the idea of a ban on nuclear testing was first proposed in the 1950s, it has stood among the highest priorities on the international nonproliferation and disarmament agenda. The CTBT is more important now than ever.

By banning all nuclear weapon test explosions, including very low-yield hydronuclear explosions, the CTBT limits the ability of established nuclear-weapon states to field more sophisticated warheads and makes it far more difficult for newer members of the club to perfect smaller, more easily deliverable warheads.

For this reason, CTBT ratification has long been considered essential to the fulfillment of Article VI of the NPT and the goal of "effective measures relating to cessation of the nuclear arms race at an early date and to nuclear disarmament."

The CTBT also serves to reinforce the nonproliferation system by acting as a downstream confidence-building measure about a state's nuclear intentions and, in this regard, it can help head-off and de-escalate regional tensions. With no shortage of conflict and hostility in the Middle East, ratification by Israel, Egypt and Iran would reduce nuclear-weapons-related security concerns in the region. It would also help create the conditions necessary for the realization of a zone free of nuclear weapons and other weapons of mass destruction in the Middle East, as called for in the Middle East Resolution adopted by the 1995 NPT Review Conference.

India and Pakistan could substantially ease regional tensions and demonstrate nuclear restraint by converting their unilateral test moratoria into a legally-binding commitment to end nuclear testing through the CTBT.

With the CTBT in force, global and national capabilities to detect and deter possible clandestine nuclear testing by other states will be significantly greater. Entry-into-force is essential to making short-notice, on-site inspections possible and maintaining long-term political and financial support from other nations for the operation of the International Monitoring System and International Data Center.

The CTBT has near-universal support: 180 nations have signed and 148 have ratified the Treaty. Last fall, the UN General Assembly voted 175-1 in favor of The CTBT and we expect that the one "no" vote by the United States to become a "yes" vote this year. We applaud those states that support of the Treaty and make their full financial contribution to the build-up and operation of the international monitoring and verification system.

Unfortunately, broad support is not enough. Article XIV of the Treaty provides that in order to enter into force, ratification is needed from a number of key players. Nine necessary states have failed to ratify the CTBT and are therefore delaying its entry into force.

Ratification by the United States and China is particularly important. Given their existing nuclear test moratoria and 1996 signature of the CTBT, Washington and Beijing already bear most CTBT-related responsibilities, yet their failure to ratify has denied them and others the full security benefits of CTBT entry into force.

The United States is poised to be a leader on the CTBT once again as President Barack Obama has pledged to achieve ratification "as soon as practical." We applaud his April 5 statement in Prague in which he said:

> To achieve a global ban on nuclear testing, my administration will immediately and aggressively pursue U.S. ratification of the Comprehensive Test Ban Treaty. After more than five decades of talks, it is time for the testing of nuclear weapons to finally be banned.

To do so, President Obama must convince two-thirds of the Senate that the treaty enhances U.S. security, is effectively verifiable, and would not compromise future efforts to maintain the reliability, safety, or security of the United States' remaining stockpile of nuclear warheads. Technical advances in each of these areas over the past decade should make the case for the CTBT even stronger than it was in 1999 when the Senate failed to provide its advice and consent for ratification.

The Obama administration's effort will require sustained, top-level leadership. His efforts will have the full support of a wide array of NGOs in the United States and around the globe.

For years, Chinese government representatives have reported that the CTBT is before the National People's Congress for consideration but has apparently taken no action to win legislative approval needed for ratification.

Washington's renewed pursuit of CTBT ratification opens up opportunities for China and other Annex II states, such as Indonesia, to lead the way toward entry into force by ratifying before the United States does. Action by Beijing would increase its credibility as a nonproliferation leader and improve the chances that other states in Asia, as well as the United States, would follow suit. Ratification by Indonesia would enhance its reputation as a world leader and agent for international security.

If Israel were to ratify the CTBT, it would bring that nation closer to the nuclear nonproliferation mainstream and help encourage other states in the region to do so.

Iranian ratification would help reduce concerns that its nuclear program could be used to develop and deploy deliverable nuclear warheads. Continued failure by Iran to ratify the CTBT raises further questions about the nature of its sensitive nuclear fuel cycle activities.

The recent decision of the government of the Democratic Peoples Republic of North Korea to suspend its participation in the Six-Party Denuclearization process is deeply disappointing. We sincerely urge the Pyonyang to refrain from further nuclear testing and we urge the effective and rapid implementation of the commitments made pursuant to the Six-Party agreements by all involved as a step toward mutual security, as well as CTBT entry into force.

If India and Pakistan wish to be regarded as responsible states with advanced nuclear technology, they need to engage more widely and deeply with the international community in support of meaningful and legally-binding nuclear nonproliferation and disarmament measures, particularly the CTBT, as well those outlined in UN Security Council Resolution 1172 of June 1998. The decision last year by the Nuclear Suppliers Group to adopt a proposal by the United States and other key supplier states to grant India—a non-signatory to the NPT and the CTBT—a once-off exemption from NSG nuclear trading restrictions was deeply disappointing to many and contrary to the 1995 NPT Review Conference commitment to engage in nuclear trade only with those states that accept full-scope safeguards.

In the wake of that episode, leading states have a responsibility to work much harder to encourage India to meet the same nonproliferation and disarmament standards expected of other states, including ratification of the CTBT. Responsible nuclear supplier states should also make it clear to Indian officials, as the

United States has already done, that as a matter of national policy they will terminate nuclear trade with any state that conducts a nuclear test explosion regardless of the circumstances.

To help put the CTBT over the finish line, we also strongly urge that like-minded pro-CTBT states work together to develop a common diplomatic strategy to persuade the remaining states to sign and/or ratify the treaty. Pro-CTBT states should announce their intention to execute that strategy at the September 23-25 Conference on Facilitating the Entry into Force of the CTBT at the United Nations here New York. To reinforce their commitment to the purpose and objectives of the CTBT, we also call upon all nuclear-armed nations to adopt clear policies not to develop or produce new design warheads or to modify existing warhead types in a manner that creates new military capabilities. The Obama administration has taken an important step in this direction by stating that it will "stop the development of new nuclear weapons."

To increase confidence in their commitment to the CTBT, we urge nuclear-armed states to seriously consider joining France in closing their test sites to all nuclear weapons-related research activities and experiments, particularly those involving fissile material, and, in the meantime, to adopt additional transparency measures at their test sites.

CTBT entry into force is within reach. The next one to two years may represent the best opportunity to secure the future of this long-awaited and much-needed treaty. We urge you to act now and to act with boldness.

This statement was coordinated by the Arms Control Association and has been endorsed by the following individuals and organizations:

Irma Arguello, Chair, Nonproliferation for Global Security Foundation (Argentina)

Prof. Mashahiko Asada, Graduate School of Law, Kyoto University

Hideyuki Ban, Co-Director, Citizens' Nuclear Information Center (Japan)

Cara Bautista, Coordinator, Campaign for a Nuclear Weapons Free World (United States)

Barry Blechman, Distinguished Fellow, Henry L. Stimson Center (United States)

Jay Coughlin, Director, Nuclear Watch New Mexico (United States)

David Culp, Legislative Director, Friends Committee on National Legislation (United States)

Ambassador Jonathan Dean, former arms control negotiator, U.S. Department of State

Prof. Trevor Findlay, Director, Canadian Centre for Treaty Compliance, Carleton University

Jonathan Granoff, President, Global Security Institute (United States)

Ambassador Robert Grey, former U.S. Representative to the Conference on Disarmament

John Hallam, Coordinator, Nuclear Flashpoints (Australia)

Mort Halperin, Director of Policy Planning, Department of State 1996-2001 (United States)

Prof. Frank von Hippel, Program on Science and Global Security, Princeton University

Paul Ingram, Executive Director, British-American Security Information Council (United Kingdom - United States)

Dr. Rebecca Johnson, Founding Director, Acronym Institute for Disarmament Diplomacy (United Kingdom)

Daryl G. Kimball, Executive Director, Arms Control Association (United States)

Kevin Knobloch, President, Union of Concerned Scientists (United States)

David Krieger, President, Nuclear Age Peace Foundation (United States)

John Rainwater, Executive Director, Peace Action West (United States)

Lawrence Scheinman, Distinguished Professor, Monterey Institute of International Studies

Susi Snyder, Secretary General, Women's International League for Peace and Freedom

Vappu Taipale, M.D., Co-President, International Physicians for the Prevention of Nuclear War

Hiromichi Umebayashi, Special Adviser, Peace Depot (Japan)

Paul Walker, Director, Security and Sustainability, Global Green USA (United States)

Peter Wilk, MD, Executive Director, Physicians for Social Responsibility (United States)

Angela Woodward, Executive Director, Verification, Research, Training, and Information Centre (United Kingdom)

28

Statement by Ambassador Tibor Toth, Executive Secretary of the Preparatory Commission for the Comprehensive Nuclear Test Ban Treaty Organization: Third Session of the Preparatory Committee for the 2010 NPT Review Conference, New York, U.S.A.

4-15 May 2009

...

1. Allow me to express my appreciation for the opportunity to address this Third Preparatory Committee session. The last time that the Commission addressed an NPT review forum in a sustained way was back in the 2000 cycle. Because of that I will provide a more comprehensive overview of the progress achieved by the Organization.

2. Firstly, however, I would like to thank all delegations that have expressed their support for the Comprehensive Nuclear-Test-Ban Treaty (CTBT) and the Commission in their statements during the past few days. This is an overwhelming verdict on the part of the international community, including all five NPT nuclear weapon States, in favour of putting an end to the era of nuclear testing.

3. The Treaty has endured politically stormy times since it first opened for signature in 1996. Yet, despite the challenges, and probably because of them, support for it has grown continuously. At the time of the 2000 review conference 56 States had ratified it. As of today, 180 countries have signed the CTBT, and 148 States have also ratified it. Since 2000 nearly 100 States by the virtue of their ratification voted with their feet.

It is the most genuine demonstration that the international community is not just a fairweather companion of this Treaty. Nine Annex II countries still need to ratify the Treaty for it to enter into force. There is further and renewed hope. An important manifestation of such a hope is the goal stated by President Obama and his administration, reiterated at this Preparatory Committee session by the U.S. delegation.

4. In this context, I would like to draw your attention to the upcoming Conference on Facilitating the Entry into Force of the CTBT (also known as the Article XIV conference). It will take place in New York from 24 to 25 September 2009. Previous Article XIV conferences have been attended by Foreign Ministers and other senior representatives of CTBT Signatories. They have thus become the largest high-level gathering in the non-proliferation and disarmament arena during the past decade.

Moreover, Article XIV conferences have traditionally adopted a consensus declaration with a programme of action—another scarce commodity in this field. This year's conference will be of particular importance. It will offer a unique opportunity to capitalize on the fresh political momentum and to send a high level signal of unity of purpose for the entry into force of the Treaty. I sincerely hope that all State Signatories will seize this exceptional opportunity and attend this conference at the highest possible level.

5. Back in the spring of 2000 the build-up the Treaty's verification regime was still at an early stage. The International Monitoring System (IMS) was more a concept than reality. We reported then that none of the stations in the four verification technologies had been officially certified. A first generation Global Communications Infrastructure (GCI) had been in place to transmit data from our stations to the International Data Centre (IDC) in Vienna. Data distribution to State Signatories was still in a testing phase. And we reported that some experiments and training activities to establish the Treaty's on-site inspection (OSI) were being undertaken. Much progress has been achieved since.

6. Today the CTBT verification regime is nearing completion. From the 2000 level we have moved to 236 certified stations.

Thus 75 percent of the system's 321 global monitoring stations already send data to headquarters in Vienna. Ten radionuclide laboratories have been certified. Several more IMS stations have been built and are in the process of being certified and many more are under construction.

7. A new Global Communication Infrastructure "GCI II" is now up and running and relaying data back and forth across the globe. The volume of data being transmitted from monitoring facilities to the international data centre has tripled just in the last five years. The daily content of data analysis, so-called data products, provided to States Signatories has doubled in the same period. Software improvements have led to the delivery of more detailed and significantly higher quality data products. 110 countries and 1100 institutions are beneficiaries of the data and the data products generated by this unprecedented joint venture.

8. Great strides have been made towards achieving on-site inspection readiness. The first integrated on-site inspection field exercise took place in September 2009 in the former Soviet Union nuclear test site of Semipalatinsk, Kazakhstan. The parameters of the exercise speak for themselves: 1000 square kilometres of inspection area, a team of 40 inspectors, overall logistical support for nearly 200 participants, four weeks of activities, 50 tonnes of equipment, comprising a dozen different verification technologies. Many valuable lessons were learned. They will be fed into our OSI preparations as we move forward towards operational readiness.

9. We are coming within sight of the fulfilment of our mandate as a Preparatory Commission for the CTBTO. Our main task it is to establish the global verification regime so that it is fully operational once the Treaty enters into force. Theory is moving in to the realm of established fact.

10. The CTBT verification regime was validated two and a half years ago when the Democratic People's Republic of Korea (DPRK) conducted its nuclear test. Only half of the CTBT's International Monitoring System had been installed at the time. But the verification system exceeded the expectations of the Treaty negotiators in 1996 in terms of sensitivity, reliability,

precision and characterization. The technical capability—the quality of the information and data generated by the system—was proven. The low yield explosion was detected by over 20 of the IMS seismic stations worldwide, which registered the shock waves in the ground. Traces of radioactive noble gas were picked up and could be attributed to the DPRK test. This is a technology which was at an early experimental stage at the time of the conception of the CTBT verification regime. It has significantly increased the ability to detect and identify nuclear explosions. And when combined with the final arm of the verification regime—on-site inspections—which can only be invoked after entry into force, no country today can be confident of being able to evade detection.

11. The recent threat by the DPRK to conduct another nuclear test underscores the urgent need for establishing a legally binding universal ban on nuclear testing through the early entry into force of the CTBT. All States should refrain from acts that would defeat the object and purpose of the Treaty.

12. But you need not take our word for it that the CTBT is verifiable. The constant close interaction with the scientific community is one of the key challenges for the Preparatory Commission, given the highly specialized technological focus of our verification mandate. We have initiated the "International Scientific Studies" (ISS) project. It aims to assess and evaluate the readiness and capability of the CTBT verification regime in a coordinated international effort. Scientific institutions worldwide have conducted independent scientific work for more than a year, and will present their results at the International Scientific Studies Conference, to be held in Vienna from 10 to 12 June 2009. The build up of the CTBT verification regime has reached such an advanced stage. Thus the ISS project is of particular relevance for our ability to stay abreast with the latest scientific developments in our field.

13. The CTBT will only enter into force if States, in particular the remaining Annex II States, see it as being fundamental to their national interest. Essentially, they must ask themselves: is it better to keep the door open for testing in the future and thereby also keep it open for others? Or should a cap be placed

on the development of nuclear weapons by possessors and non-possessors alike in the implementation of a universal barrier? Compared to 2000 they have to make this judgement in a strategically different environment: one in which there is greatly heightened attention to non-state actors, their potential access to nuclear weapons, devices, fissile material, technology and expertise. I am convinced that the Treaty has a key role to play in today's security environment. A strong and verifiable final barrier on the road to a nuclear weapons capability is of vital importance for a comprehensive approach to address our common security challenges. This contribution goes beyond establishing the norm against nuclear test explosions or any other nuclear explosions.

14. The CTBT is a strong instrument for non-proliferation; its credentials in this regard are clear. Testing is necessary for the development of new and more sophisticated nuclear weapons by established nuclear weapon possessors. It is also essential for establishing technical and scientific confidence in any developing programme on the part of wouldbe possessors. Making the *de-facto* international norm against nuclear testing legally binding through the entry into force of the Treaty will close this door once and for all.

15. Once the CTBT's unprecedented verification regime is fully operationalized, issues of non-compliance can then be addressed properly, in a pre-determined and pre-agreed manner, as foreseen in the Treaty. There are increased concerns over non-compliance in other quarters of the nuclear non-proliferation regime, including with the NPT. Against this background the compliance mechanisms built into the Treaty are of extreme importance in strengthening the overall objectives of the NPT.

16. The CTBT is also a catalyst for nuclear disarmament. It provides a firm legal barrier against nuclear testing, thereby curbing the development of new types and new designs of nuclear weapons by possessors.

17. Moreover, the CTBT is a strong confidence and security building measure. A CTBT in place will be an essential element for a process in which deeper arms reductions are being discussed

and pursued by nuclear weapons States. A CTBT in force will be equally essential when moving towards multilateral disarmament in a process involving all the nuclear armed States. Also, the CTBT could serve as a regional confidence and security building measure, for example in the Middle East and in Asia.

18. As we have all witnessed in the past years, the NPT-based nuclear non-proliferation and disarmament regime is challenged on many fronts. There is a common enemy in the very real prospect of some form of nuclear terrorism. We stand united against this common enemy—States and international organizations alike. Moreover, the challenges are taking place in the face of a global nuclear energy renaissance. With much more fissile material in circulation, and more actors handling that material, as predicted, we urgently need a strengthened comprehensive system of barriers against misuse. Such a systemic approach to address the challenges of the nuclear regime requires—as the last barrier against nuclear weapons—would be the CTBT in force.

19. I am convinced that the Treaty represents one of the key elements on which effective international consensus can be built in advance of the 2010 NPT Review Conference. Its entry into force and full implementation are achievable and doable. It means progress on each of the three main pillars. It bridges the divide between the different emphases placed on each of these pillars by the NPT's different parties. It signals commitment to disarmament. It strengthens non-proliferation. It facilitates peaceful uses. Of course, it is not sufficient. But it is necessary for success.

20. Progress on the CTBT's entry into force is one of the most important catalysts. It could drive the international community's resolve to address the multitude of challenges facing the non-proliferation regime. As such it is a measure where progress can be achieved in a relatively short time. The Treaty already exists. It has been signed by 180 and ratified by almost 150 States. Its verification regime is close to completion. And it has been tried and tested.

21. The CTBT is, of course, not the only answer to concerns generated by nuclear weapons. It is to be an integral part of a

strengthened comprehensive nuclear non-proliferation and disarmament regime. The Treaty's entry into force will pave the way to solving many of the current and future challenges facing the regime.

29

Remarks by Ban Ki-moon, UN Secretary-General, to the Third Session of the Preparatory Committee for the 2010 NPT Review Conference

4 May 2009

...

For too long, the nuclear disarmament and non-proliferation agenda has been stagnating in a Cold War mentality.

In 2005, the world experienced what might be called a disarmament depression. The NPT Review Conference that year ended in disappointment. The UN World Summit outcome contained not even a single line on weapons of mass destruction.

Today, we seem to be emerging from that low point. The change has come in recent weeks. But it is unfolding against a backdrop of multiple threats that, while urgent, tend to obscure the urgency of the disarmament and non-proliferation agenda.

The global economic crisis, climate change and the outbreak of the H1N1 flu virus are all reminders that we live in an interdependent world. They demand a full and forceful multilateral response.

At the same time, nuclear weapons remain an apocalyptic threat. We cannot afford to place disarmament and non-proliferation on a backburner. Let us not be lulled into complacency. Let us not miss the opportunity to make our societies safer and more prosperous.

I have been using every opportunity to push for progress. I discussed non-proliferation and disarmament with Russian President Medvedev and U.S. President Obama. I welcome the joint commitment they announced...to fulfill their obligations under article VI of the NPT.

I am particularly encouraged that both countries are committed to rapidly pursuing verifiable reductions in their strategic offensive arsenals by replacing the Strategic Arms Reduction Treaty with a new, legally-binding pact. I hope their example will serve as a catalyst in inspiring other nuclear powers to follow suit.

Other developments also merit attention.

On Iran, I encourage the country's leaders to continue their cooperation with the IAEA with a view to demonstrating the entirely peaceful nature of Iran's nuclear programme.

I also encourage them to re-engage in the negotiating process with the EU 3+3 and the EU High Representative on the basis of the relevant Security Council resolutions, and in line with the package of proposals for cooperation with Iran.

With respect to the Democratic People's Republic of Korea, despite the current serious challenges, I continue to believe that the Six-Party process is the best mechanism to achieve the verifiable denuclearization of the Korean Peninsula in a peaceful manner.

I therefore urge the DPRK to return to these talks so that everybody can resolve their respective concerns through dialogue and cooperation, based on the relevant Security Council resolutions as well as multilateral and bilateral agreements.

I also urge all states to end the stalemate that has marked the international disarmament machinery for too long. To strengthen the NPT regime, it is essential that the Comprehensive Nuclear-Test-Ban Treaty enters into force without further delay, and that the Conference on Disarmament begins negotiations on a verifiable fissile material treaty. I commend President Obama's commitment to ratify the CTBT, and urge all countries that have not done so to ratify the Treaty without conditions.

Hopes for a breakthrough on the deadlocked disarmament agenda have been building. We have seen a cascade of proposals. Elder statesmen, leaders of nuclear-weapon states, regional groups, various commissions and civil society representatives have elaborated proposals for slaying the nuclear monster.

Their voices may be varied, but they are all part of the same rising chorus demanding action on nuclear disarmament and non-proliferation. Concerns about nuclear terrorism, a new rush by some to possess nuclear arms, and renewed interest in nuclear power as an alternative to fossil fuels have only heightened the need for urgent action.

The work you do...will be critical. You must seize the moment and show your seriousness.

This preparatory session must generate agreements on key procedural issues and substantive recommendations to the Review Conference.

The Review Conference must produce a clear commitment by all NPT states parties to comply fully with all of their obligations under this vital Treaty.

I urge you to work in a spirit of compromise and flexibility. I hope you will avoid taking absolute positions that have no chance of generating consensus. Instead, build bridges, and be part of a new multilateralism.

People understand intuitively that nuclear weapons will never make us more secure.

They know that real security lies in responding to poverty, climate change, armed conflict and instability.

They want governments to invest in plans for growth and development, not weapons of mass destruction.

If you can set us on a course towards achieving a nuclear-weapon-free world, you will send a message of hope to the world.

We desperately need this message at this time. I am counting on you, and I am supporting all of your efforts to succeed, now and at the Review Conference in 2010.

30

Statement by H.E. Boniface Chidyausiku, Permanent Representative of Zimbabwe to the United Nations, and Chairman of the Third Preparatory Committee for the 2010 NPT Review Conference, New York, U.S.A.

4 May 2009

...

We have a lot of work to accomplish...and I intend to do my best to chair proceedings in a manner that will bring us to a successful fulfillment of these mandates. First and foremost, ...I see my role as a facilitator, but I am always in your hands and will depend and count on your cooperation, advice and assistance to fulfill the mandates which we have been given.

...

While delegations have contributed to shaping my vision for the Prep COM, I wish to indicate that my lenses are heavily coated with ambition to achieve the utmost possible.

We are meeting at an opportune time in the history of the NPT. There is abundant political and goodwill from all States Parties for the Review Conference to succeed. I want to appeal to this meeting that we should not lose this great opportunity before us. Let us focus on the core business of the NPT in order to prepare for a successful Review

Conference which will strengthen and make our treaty more effective.

In conclusion, let me reiterate that I remain in your hands and look forward to your utmost support in order for us to successfully fulfill the challenging task before us.

In this regard, I would like to remind the Prep COM that we should make sure that we provide an agenda for the 2010 NPT Review Conference so as to avoid the repeat of what happened at the 2005 NPT Review Conference.

31

General Statement on behalf of the European Union, by H.E. Mr. Tomáš POJAR, First Deputy Minister of Foreign Affairs, at the Preparatory Committee for the 2010 Non-proliferation Treaty Review Conference, Third Session, New York, U.S.A.

4 May 2009

...

The Candidate Countries Turkey, Croatia* and the former Yugoslav Republic of Macedonia*, the Countries of the Stabilisation and Association Process and potential candidates Albania, Bosnia and Herzegovina, Montenegro and Serbia, as well as Ukraine and the Republic of Moldova align themselves with this declaration.

We support you in your endeavours as the Chairman of this Preparatory Committee at its third session as well as your wise request to limit statements and avoid repetitions.

1. The NPT, based on the three mutually reinforcing pillars of non-proliferation, disarmament and the peaceful uses of nuclear energy, represents a unique and irreplaceable framework for maintaining and strengthening international peace, security and stability. Given the current challenges in the field of international security, in particular the risk of proliferation, we are convinced that the NPT is more important now than ever. It is our duty to maintain and strengthen its authority and integrity, to continue

* Croatia and the former Yugoslav Republic of Macedonia continue to be part of the Stabilisation and Association Process.

to advocate its universality. To this end, the EU will continue to promote all the objectives contained in the Treaty.

2. The EU is conscious of new opportunities for the NPT, in particular with the renewed US-Russia engagement, renewed commitment to ensure the entry into force of the Comprehensive Test Ban Treaty (CTBT) and to international negotiations for a verifiable Treaty to end the production of fissile materials for nuclear weapons (FMCT). The EU also notes with interest the renewed international public debate on ways to advance all the objectives enshrined in the Treaty.

3. The year 2009 presents serious proliferation challenges for the NPT and will be decisive in finding negotiated solutions especially for the Iranian nuclear issue.

4. The EU calls upon all States Parties to live up to both challenges and opportunities and work constructively towards reaffirming the fundamental principles underlying the Treaty, in particular through renewed consensus on ways to strengthen it.

5. The EU has come to this meeting with a clear vision of the 2010 review cycle. The current review cycle should help us to foster the sense of common purpose among States parties and create a more secure international context by expressing renewed support from the entire international community for the NPT's goals and obligations, by addressing the main issues at stake, and by demonstrating the capacity of the review cycle to give appropriate responses to these challenges. We are ready to continue to work for its successful outcome, with a view to strengthening the international nuclear non-proliferation regime, in particular all three pillars of the Treaty, as underlined in the EU Common Position of 25 April 2005.

6. We continue to support the decisions and the resolution on the Middle East adopted at the 1995 NPT Review and Extension Conference as well as the Final Document of the 2000 NPT Review Conference and shall bear in mind the current situation. We continue to work towards the universality of the NPT and call on those States not yet party to the NPT to join the Treaty as a Non Nuclear Weapon State.

7. To this end, the EU intends to work together with all States Parties at this session of the PrepCom

(a) on agreement during this PrepCom on the provisional agenda and rules of procedure for the 2010 Review Conference and the nomination of the President,

(b) on identifying areas of convergence under each of the three pillars where concrete progress could be made,

(c) aiming at achieving consensus wherever possible on realistic, balanced and effective recommendations from the Preparatory Committee to Review Conference.

8. Our vision for a meaningful outcome of the review process comprises the following principles:

(a) A balanced approach of the Review Process between the three pillars is essential.

(b) The 2010 Review Conference should adopt a set of concrete, effective, pragmatic, and consensual measures for stepping up international efforts against proliferation, pursuing disarmament and ensuring a responsible development of peaceful uses of nuclear energy by countries wishing to develop their capacities in this field.

9. To achieve these goals, the EU has elaborated a set of forward-looking proposals on all three pillars of the NPT, to be part of an action plan adopted by the RevCon. We will address those elements in a detailed manner in our cluster statements. Let me briefly comment on their main axis.

Non-proliferation

10. Strengthening the non-proliferation regime is a key priority for us. We shall continue to promote the universalisation and effective implementation of rules and instruments preventing the proliferation of WMD and their means of delivery.

11. If we want to preserve the central role of the NPT in promoting security for all, we must reaffirm that all States Parties must take concerted and resolute action to ensure strict compliance with their non-proliferation obligations and respond quickly and effectively to non-compliance. Non-compliance and

the proliferation of nuclear weapons undermine the security of all nations. They imperil prospects for progress on disarmament, in particular for nuclear disarmament. They hurt prospects for expanding international nuclear co-operation.

12. The proliferation risks presented in particular by the nuclear programs of Iran and DPRK continue to be a matter of ongoing serious concern to us. A negotiated solution to the Iranian nuclear issue is of cardinal importance for the EU, since if Iran were to acquire a military nuclear capability, this would constitute an unacceptable threat to regional and international security.

13. Universalisation and strengthening of the IAEA safeguards system including the Additional Protocol are of particular importance to us.

14. To be effective, our action against proliferation must also be based on resolute operational cooperation. To this end in 2008, the EU adopted "New Lines for Action by the EU in Combating the Proliferation of Weapons of Mass Destruction and their Delivery Systems" which will further enhance the effectiveness of the EU's 2003 Strategy against proliferation of WMD.

Disarmament

15. The EU is committed to the pursuit of nuclear disarmament and the final objective enshrined in Article VI of the NPT. This issue is of particular relevance to the EU, two of whose members have nuclear weapons. We are working for general disarmament and notably nuclear disarmament. Keenly aware of the fact that its own security benefits from the pursuit of global disarmament efforts, the EU is prepared to do more. Our ambition extends to every aspect of disarmament.

16. The EU highly appreciates the reductions of strategic and non-strategic nuclear weapons and their delivery systems since the end of the Cold War. We warmly welcome the commitment expressed by the USA and Russia to replace START with a new legally binding treaty before it expires in December 2009. The EU has already done much for disarmament. The EU supports the nuclear disarmament measures taken by the two

EU nuclear-weapon states and welcomes their new initiatives in this field.

17. The EU calls on the international community to work on promoting the concrete and realistic disarmament initiatives endorsed by our 27 Heads of State and Government which we submitted to the United Nations General Assembly in 2008. It is in particular essential in the short-term to achieve the entry into force of the CTBT and to launch negotiations without preconditions in the Conference on Disarmament on a FMCT including verification provisions.

Peaceful uses of nuclear energy

18. In accordance with Article IV of the NPT, the EU reaffirms its support for the inalienable right of all Parties to the Treaty to develop research, production and use of nuclear energy for peaceful purposes, without discrimination and in conformity with Articles I, II and III of the Treaty. In this regard, the EU supports the important activities of the IAEA in the field of technical cooperation and assistance. The EU is the prime contributor to the IAEA's technical cooperation fund.

19. It is important that the development of nuclear energy for peaceful uses takes place in the best safety, security and non-proliferation conditions. The EU is committed to strengthened international cooperation in this respect both within the next NPT Review Conference and in other fora. The EU supports and financially assists the work of the IAEA related to assisting states to develop the adequate infrastructures in these areas. The EU has also set up an important Instrument for Nuclear Safety Cooperation to help countries benefit from its important experience in this field.

20. International efforts aimed at establishing multilateral mechanisms, by helping to strengthen energy security, can also offer a credible alternative to the development of national capabilities for sensitive fuel cycle technologies. We have taken specific measures along these lines, with our announcement that the European Union stands ready to contribute financially up to EUR 25 million to the creation of a nuclear fuel bank under the control of the IAEA. This proposal is complementary to other

proposals for supply guarantees or multilateral installations developed by some EU Member States and other NPT State Parties. We welcome their further elaboration and look forward discussing them.

21. We reaffirm our full support for the work of the IAEA as a unique and indispensable organization for peaceful nuclear co-operation, nuclear safety, preventing the spread of nuclear weapons and countering new threats of nuclear terrorism.

Regional Issues, including with respect to the Middle East and implementation of the 1995 Middle East Resolution

22. The EU also remains committed to the full implementation of the resolutions on the Middle East adopted by the United Nations Security Council and the 1995 NPT Review and Extension Conference, and the IAEA General Conference. The EU calls upon the States of the region to establish an effectively verifiable zone free of nuclear weapons, as well as of other weapons of mass destruction and their means of delivery. We will refer to this issue in more detail in a separate statement.

23. In conclusion, we must not fail to seize the opportunity of the 2010 Review Conference to move toward a safer world, one in which it is possible to meet all the objectives enshrined in the NPT, whether they be disarmament, non-proliferation, or the peaceful uses of nuclear energy. We should advance on all fronts, pragmatically, so that we can achieve a successful and balanced conclusion of the review process in 2010.

32

Statement by H.E. Mr. Cheng Jingye, Head of the Chinese Delegation, at the Third Session of the Preparatory Committee for the 2010 Review Conference of the Parties to the Treaty on the Non-proliferation of Nuclear Weapons, New York, U.S.A.

4 May 2009

...

As the cornerstone of the international nuclear non-proliferation regime, the Treaty on the Non-Proliferation of Nuclear Weapons (NPT) has over the years played an important role in maintaining international security. Nowadays, we have witnessed a number of initiatives in the area of nuclear disarmament. More and more countries start to develop nuclear energy. Meanwhile, the nuclear non-proliferation situation is still grave.

It is now a common task for the entire international community to seize the opportunity of the 2010 NPT Review Conference and to promote, in a comprehensive and balanced way, the NPT's three major objectives—nuclear disarmament, non-proliferation, and the peaceful uses of nuclear energy.

Nuclear Disarmament

Complete prohibition and thorough destruction of nuclear weapons for the establishment of a world free of nuclear weapons, is not only the shared aspiration of the international community, but also the goal that China has advocated and worked for over the years. As early as in the 1960s, the Chinese Government by its statements solemnly proposed the convocation of a world summit to address the issue of complete prohibition and thorough destruction of nuclear weapons. It is encouraging to see that today a growing number of countries around the world have expressed their support to a nuclear-weapon-free world. Mankind was able to make nuclear weapons in the 20th century. We believe they are equally able to eliminate such weapons in the 21st century.

As a nuclear-weapon state, China has made relentless efforts to push forward complete prohibition and thorough destruction of nuclear weapons.

- Ever since the first day when it came into possession of nuclear weapons, China has solemnly declared that it will not be the first to use nuclear weapons at any time and under any circumstances. China also undertakes unconditionally not to use or threaten to use nuclear weapons against non-nuclear-weapon states or nuclear-weapon-free zones. China is the only one among the five nuclear-weapon states who has made such commitments.
- China adheres to a self-defensive nuclear strategy and has exercised extreme restraint on the development of nuclear weapons. China has never deployed any nuclear weapon in other countries, and has never participated and would never participate in nuclear arms races in any form.
- China is among the first to sign the Comprehensive Test Ban Treaty (CTBT) and has always honoured its commitment on nuclear test moratorium. China supports early entry into force of the CTBT and will continue to make its efforts to this end.
- China supports an early start of negotiations on a non-discriminatory, multilateral and internationally verifiable fissile material cut-off treaty, on the basis of an agreed programme of work at the Conference on Disarmament in Geneva.

China is ready to work with other countries to make further contributions to the lofty goal of establishing a world free of nuclear weapons.

China believes that nuclear disarmament should be a fair and reasonable process of gradual reductions towards a downward balance. All disarmament measures should follow the guidelines of "promoting international strategic stability" and "undiminished security for all". Countries concerned should work towards nuclear disarmament in the following ways.

- Nuclear-weapon states should commit themselves unequivocally to complete prohibition and thorough destruction of nuclear weapons. In this respect, they should negotiate and conclude an international legal instrument at an early date.
- Pending achievement of the above-mentioned goal, nuclear-weapon states should reduce the role of nuclear weapons in their national security policies. They should undertake unequivocally not to be the first to use nuclear weapons, and conclude an international legal instrument on not to use or threaten to use nuclear weapons against non-nuclear-weapon states or nuclear-weapons-free zones.
- As states with largest nuclear arsenals, the United States and the Russian Federation bear special and primary responsibilities. They should continue to drastically cut their nuclear arsenals, which is indispensable for advancing the nuclear disarmament process and realizing the ultimate goal of complete and thorough nuclear disarmament. In this regard, China welcomes the agreement of the United States and the Russian Federation to start negotiations on a new bilateral nuclear disarmament treaty and we hope the two countries will further reduce their nuclear arsenals in a verifiable and irreversible manner.

Nuclear disarmament is closely linked to international strategic stability. Deployment of weapons in outer space or development of global ballistic missile defence systems and cooperation in this field is neither conducive to maintaining international strategic stability, nor beneficial to international arms control and non-proliferation efforts. The Conference on Disarmament should negotiate and conclude a new international legal instrument on prohibiting the deployment of weapons in outer space at an early date. On the issue of ABM systems, the countries concerned should take the security interests of others into serious consideration and refrain from taking actions that may undermine the international nuclear disarmament process.

Establishing nuclear-weapon-free zones is an important step in promoting the international nuclear disarmament and non-proliferation process. China respects and supports efforts by relevant countries and regions to establish nuclear-weapon-free zones on the basis of consultations among themselves and voluntary agreement in light of their actual conditions. We welcome the...entry into force of the Central Asian Nuclear-Weapon-Free Zone Treaty. We support the early establishment of a nuclear-weapon-free zone in the Middle East. The resolution on the Middle East issue adopted by the 1995 NPT Review Conference is very important. The international community should continue to make every effort to facilitate the implementation of the above resolutions.

Nuclear Non-proliferation

Strengthening the international nuclear non-proliferation regime and eliminating the risks of proliferation is a pressing task for the international community. The problem of proliferation of nuclear weapons is caused by complex factors, and requires a holistic approach which addresses both the symptoms and the root causes.

- Efforts should be made to build an international environment of cooperation and trust, respect each other's security interests, and seek collective security. This will help eliminate the root causes for seeking nuclear weapons.
- Regional nuclear issues should be addressed through dialogues and negotiations. Imposing sanctions or resorting to force would only exacerbate tension instead of leading to a proper solution of relevant issues.

- The universality and integrity of the international non-proliferation regime should be further reinforced. Any practice of selectivity should be discarded.

China supports the strengthening of IAEA's safeguards function and is in favour of promoting the universality of the Comprehensive Safeguards Agreement and the Additional Protocol.

As a permanent member of the UN Security Council, China has made great efforts to promote peaceful settlement of nuclear issues in relevant regions through dialogues and negotiations.

China believes that the Six-Party-Talks still serves as an important mechanism for addressing the Korean Peninsula nuclear issue. The parties concerned, proceeding from overall perspective, should keep calm and exercise restraint, and work together to maintain the Six-Party Talks process and safeguard peace and stability of the Peninsula.

China stands for a proper solution of the Iranian nuclear issue through diplomatic negotiations. Now the situation concerning this issue is at a crucial juncture. Parties concerned should seize the opportunity, step up their diplomatic efforts, and restart negotiations at an early date between Iran and EU3+3, with a view to seeking a comprehensive, proper and long-term solution.

Peaceful Uses of Nuclear Energy

Peaceful uses of nuclear energy is an inalienable right by non-nuclear-weapon states under the NPT. At present, development of nuclear energy is attracting growing attention around the world. It is all the more important that the right of non-nuclear weapon states to the peaceful uses of nuclear energy is fully respected and effectively safeguarded. This is of great importance to the integrity and effectiveness of the NPT.

China believes that the relationship between the peaceful uses of nuclear energy and non-proliferation should be handled in a balanced manner to ensure that they mutually reinforce rather than conflict with each other. We are against any attempt to restrict or deprive the right of non-nuclear weapon states to peaceful uses of nuclear energy under the pretext of non-proliferation. And we are also against any attempt to engage in proliferation activities under the disguise of peaceful use.

Currently some countries have put forward a number of initiatives on establishing multilateral nuclear fuel supply mechanism. China supports in general the objectives and purposes of relevant initiatives and has taken an active part in relevant international discussions. Since those initiatives involve various political, economical, technical, and legal factors, the international community should continue in-depth and extensive consultations so as to seek a practical solution that is acceptable to all.

China appreciates the positive role of the IAEA in promoting peaceful uses of nuclear energy. We encourage and support the IAEA to make further inputs to promote international exchanges and cooperation in this field, so as to advance common prosperity and development.

The three major pillars of the NPT are closely linked and of equal importance. They should be advanced in a comprehensive and balanced way. We hope this will be reflected in the agenda, organizational structure, time allocation and documents of the NPT Review Conference.

This session of the Preparatory Committee is highly important to the Review Conference. It's our hope that all parties will intensify their efforts to reach agreement on the agenda of the Review Conference as soon as possible. Meanwhile, we are looking forward to further in-depth exchange of views among parties on how to promote nuclear disarmament, non-proliferation and peaceful uses of nuclear energy, so as to build up consensus and lay the ground work for substantive achievements at the Review Conference.

33

Statement on behalf of the New Agenda Coalition, by H.E. Mr. Christer Ahlstrom, Head of Delegation, Sweden, to Preparatory Committee for 2010 Review Conference of the Parties to the Treaty on Non-proliferation of Nuclear Weapons, New York, U.S.A.

4 May 2009

...

The New Agenda Coalition remains fully committed to the objectives of the NPT and its three fundamental pillars: nuclear disarmament, nuclear non-proliferation and the peaceful use of nuclear energy. The NPT is an essential bedrock of our global security regime. All aspects of the Treaty need to be fully implemented and strengthened. The current challenges to the Treaty must be met with a common purpose and concrete action, demonstrating progress on all three pillars of the Treaty, The long-term success of the Treaty is dependent on the delivery of all its objectives.

Our common task at this Third Prepcom is twofold: to fmalize the procedural arrangements for the Eighth Review Conference, and to make every effort to agree substantive input and recommendations to the Review Conference. We must at least agree a shared framework for approaching the Review Conference. We cannot repeat the mistakes that led to the failure of the 2005 Review Conference. The stakes are too high.

As the President of the United States made clear in his speech in Prague: "the existence of thousands of nuclear weapons is the most dangerous legacy of the Cold War". At the 2000 NPT

Review Conference all States Parties agreed to the unambiguous statement that "the total elimination of nuclear weapons is the only absolute guarantee against the use or threat of use of nuclear weapons". This simple truth remains as relevant as ever.

The New Agenda Coalition has never shied away from acknowledging and welcoming progress made on nuclear disarmament. Significant reductions in overall nuclear arsenals have been made, three of the nuclear-weapon States have ratified the CTBT and the other two have recently reaffirmed their commitment to doing so, one nuclear-weapon State has taken all its nuclear weapons off high-alert, another has declared a no-first use policy and yet another has verifiably closed down all of its production facilities for weaponsgrade fissile material. A new nuclear-weapon-free zone has been created in Central Asia.

But we also have to note with concern that a majority of weapons reductions made so far are not irreversible, transparent or verifiable. The role of nuclear weapons in security policies has not yet been diminished and the doctrine of nuclear deterrence is still being advocated. The option of creating new types of and new uses for nuclear weapons has not yet been taken off the table in strategic planning. The CTBT has not yet entered into force. The negotiations for a Treaty ending the production of fissile material for weapons purposes remain to take off.

In addition, we see no real progress in fulfilling the conunitment to create a Middle East free from nuclear weapons as well as other weapons of mass destruction. We therefore urge the Review Conference to address this matter effectively through the adoption of concrete and practical measures leading towards the implementation of the 1995 Resolution on the Middle East.

Within this mixed picture, we see some rays of hope. The New Agenda Coalition was heartened by the increased support given to its resolution in the current General Assembly entitled "Towards a nuclear—weapon—free world: accelerating the implementation of nuclear disarmament commitments". We also welcome the recent joint statement by the Presidents of the two major nuclear-weapon States, reaffirming their commitment to achieve a nuclear-weapon-free world and initiating negotiations for new and verifiable reductions in their nuclear arsenals, beginning with a new legally binding post-START Treaty.... The prospects for further key ratifications of the CTBT were greatly improved by the commitment of the new US administration to "immediately and aggressively" pursue ratification of the Treaty. The consensus for launching negotiations in the CD for a verifiable FMCT is gradually being rebuilt.

The New Agenda Coalition looks forward to concrete and transparent progress on these and other issues before the 2010 Review Conference.

At the 2010 Review Conference we will review the operation of all aspects of the Treaty. This obviously includes assessing the implementation of commitments made by consensus at previous Review Conferences, in particular the Decisions and Resolution of the 1995 Review and Extension Conference and the Final Document of the 2000 Review Conference. But, even more importantly, we must look forward. We must build on previous commitments, take into consideration current challenges and opportunities and forge a renewed commitment to realizing all objectives of the Treaty, and ultimately translate this into concrete and realistic actions to be taken during the following 5 years.

The New Agenda Coalition has submitted working papers on nuclear disarmament to the two previous sessions of this Preparatory Committee. In the first of those working papers we identified seven areas that required urgent attention during the current review cycle: universality, nuclear doctrines, reductions in nuclear forces, security assurances, nuclearweapon-free zones, negotiation of a treaty on fissile material and a prohibition of the testing of nuclear weapons. In our second working paper we focussed on transparency, confidence-building and operational readiness. In this Prepcom session, the New Agenda Coalition will table a further working paper offering some additional reflections and recommendations on ways forward on nuclear disarmament in the current review cycle. We will introduce this third working paper in the session dealing with cluster 1 issues. Let me underline, Mr Chairperson, that all three working papers remain current and could be drawn upon by you when building consensus on substantive recommendations for next year's Review Conference.

34

Statement by Mr. John Sullivan, Assistant Secretary, Arms Control and Counter Proliferation Branch, Department of Foreign Affairs and Trade, Australia, at Third Preparatory Committee for 2010 Nuclear Non-proliferation Treaty Review Conference, New York, U.S.A.

4 May 2009

...

Australia is firmly committed to the goal of a nuclear weapon free world.

In the first instance, we look to those states possessing nuclear weapons to exercise leadership: leadership in reaffirming their shared vision for a world without these terrible weapons; and leadership in taking concrete steps to disarm, consistent both with the obligations they have freely assumed under Article VI of this treaty and with agreed outcomes of past NPT Review Conferences.

In this context we warmly welcome the bold re-statement of US commitment to a world without nuclear weapons and to specific disarmament measures given by President Obama in his speech in Prague. We are also greatly encouraged by the ambitious joint statement delivered by President Obama and Russian President Medvedev in London.... Such commitments by countries which hold some ninety-five per cent of the world's nuclear weapons are deeply significant and demonstrate a momentum towards nuclear disarmament not seen since the immediate post-Cold War period.

A world without nuclear weapons requires an equally strong commitment by non-nuclear-weapon states not to acquire nuclear weapons and to accept stringent international safeguards on their nuclear facilities. The vast majority of the world's nations, including Australia, have made such commitments and honour them scrupulously—because they judge it in their national security interests to do so.

These non-proliferation and disarmament commitments comprise the fundamental collective security bargain which underpinned the NPT when it was negotiated in 1968. Nuclear weapon states and non-nuclear weapon states must join together to reaffirm the vital importance of this Treaty to their security at the Review Conference.

The NPT includes another bargain: states parties accept these commitrnents on the understanding they can participate in exchanges in the peaceful uses of nuclear energy. States' interest in the fullest possible access to nuclear energy and nuclear materials while preventing proliferation risks will be an important issue for the Review Conference.

This Preparatory Committee should pave the way for a successful Review Conference by adopting an agenda quickly and by moving on to identify key issues for consideration in 2010.

Australia has a long history of determined activism in support of non-proliferation and disarmament. In June 2008, the Australian Prime Minister, Mr Rudd, announced the establishment of an International Commission on Nuclear Non-proliferation and Disarmament. The Commission—an independent global panel co-chaired by former Australian Foreign Minister Gareth Evans and former Japanese Foreign Minister Yorilco Kawaguchi—aims to reinvigorate the global effort to curb the proliferation of nuclear weapons and to promote nuclear disarmament. The Commission commenced its work in October 2008 and will present its major report by early 2010 to help forge international consensus in the lead up to the Review Conference and beyond.

The Commission seeks to bring a fresh and imaginative vision to the set of issues that comprise the nuclear non-proliferation and disarmament agenda. The Commission takes a realistic approach to the challenges of nuclear non-proliferation and disarmament, and does not underestimate the magnitude of the tasks it faces.

It is important to recognise the real cuts in nuclear weapons made since the end of the Cold War. The United States and Russia have significantly reduced deployed strategic nuclear warheads in accordance with the Strategic Arms Reduction Treaty (START I) and the Moscow Treaty, Australia welcomes the decision, announced by President Obama and President Medvedev on 1 April 2009, to conclude a legally binding and verifiable successor agreement to the START before its expiration at the end of the year. We have also welcomed significant nuclear reductions by France and the United Kingdom.

We would encourage China to make reductions in a similarly transparent fashion. But more can and must be done. We urge all nuclear weapon states to commit to faster, deeper and irreversible reductions in all categories of nuclear weapons. We urge them to reduce further the role of nuclear weapons in their security policies and to reduce the operational status of such weapons in ways that promote international security and stability. We welcome undertakings on these issues by some nuclear weapon states.

All states should make the entry into force of the Comprehensive Test Ban Treaty (CTBT) a priority, starting with those states possessing a nuclear weapons capability. We welcome the strong commitment by the US Administration to pursue ratification of this treaty. And we encourage all Annex II states which have not yet done so to ratify it.

Australia remains committed to negotiations on a verifiable Fissile Material Cut-off Treaty (FMCT) in the Conference on Disarmament on the basis of the Shannon mandate (CD/1299 of 1995). Negotiation of such a treaty was a recommendation of the 1995 and 2000 Review Conferences. It continues to have very broad support. It's time we made it happen. As one of the

CD Presidents for 2009, Australia is working closely with the other five presidents and CD members to ensure the Conference agrees...to start negotiations in the context of agreement on a balanced program of work. We would like to acknowledge the excellent efforts of the current Algerian CD President, Ambassador Jazairy in producing a document for discussion.

Demonstrated progress on and additional clear commitments by all five nuclear weapon states to take forward nuclear reductions and to support important steps like the entry into force of the CTBT and the commencement of FMCT negotiations will provide necessary momentum and an enabling environment for a successful Review Conference in 2010.

That said, while leadership by the nuclear weapon states is critical, non-nuclear weapon states also have an important role to play in building the climate of stability and trust which allows nuclear disarmament to proceed.

While most NPT parties fully accept the need to comply with the IAEA safeguards arrangements they have freely accepted, the unwillingness by some states fully to cooperate with the Agency raises concerns about the nature of their nuclear programs.

In the case of Iran, we do not question Iran's right, under Article IV, to nuclear energy for peaceful purposes. But that right is not unconditional and must be in conformity with Articles I, II and III—as NPT parties reaffirmed in the Final Document of the 2000 Review Conference.

The international community is gravely concerned about the direction of Iran's nuclear program because Iran has continued to refuse to provide the assurances required by the NPT that its program is purely for peaceful purposes. It has not fully cooperated with the IAEA in response to its repeated requests. Nor is it complying with UN Security Council resolutions. Australia therefore urges Iran to comply with its UN obligations, cooperate fully with the IAEA and engage constructively with the P5+1.

The DPRK's nuclear weapons and missile programs are a serious challenge to international security and to peace and stability on the Korean peninsula. The DPRK's recent announcements to leave the Six-Party Talks, re-start its Yongbyon nuclear facilities and cease cooperation with the IAEA are alarming, as is its 5 April long-range missile launch. We urge the DPRI to reconsider its positions, comply with relevant UN Security Council Resolutions and address international concerns about its missile and nuclear programs.

The case of the DPRK has highlighted the need to increase disincentives to withdraw from the Treaty and strengthen and formalise international responses to any cases of withdrawal, including through automatic referral to the UN Security Council.

That states have developed proliferation sensitive nuclear capabilities in secret while party to this treaty demonstrates a clear need to strengthen the international safeguards system. Australia's firm view is that a comprehensive safeguards agreement combined with an Additional Protocol should be the basic standard of verification for non-nuclear weapons states.

As a major uranium supplier, Australia recognises the important role suppliers play in nuclear non proliferation. We have made adherence to the Additional Protocol a condition of supply for Australian uranium.

Prevention of nuclear terrorism is part of the broader agenda to prevent nuclear proliferation. Terrorists can access information on developing a nuclear weapon on the internet. And we are aware of terrorists' interest in acquiring weapons of mass destruction. So preventing them obtaining relevant material, particularly fissile material, is vital. In this context Australia welcomes President Obama's proposal for a Global Summit on Nuclear Security.

Central to the long-term strength of the NPT is its guarantee of access to peaceful nuclear energy. The recent upsurge of interest in nuclear power to combat climate change and facilitate energy security must be underpinned by strong non-proliferation commitments.

Australia takes seriously its Article IV undertakings to facilitate the exchange of equipment, materials and scientific and technological information for the peaceful uses of nuclear energy.

The IAEA Technical Cooperation Program and Regional Cooperative Agreements are key mechanisms for ensuring that countries are able to benefit from the peaceful uses of nuclear technology. Australia supports a number of Regional Cooperative Agreement programs in the Asia-Pacific.

But the right to peaceful nuclear energy is not unqualified. To access that right NPT parties must fully comply with their NPT non-proliferation obligations.

Australia looks forward to further discussion at this Prepcom on arrangements to ensure that the international nuclear market reinforces non-proliferation without restricting peaceful access to nuclear technology. Australia is interested in hearing more about multilateral approaches to the fuel cycle which might help avoid the unnecessary spread of sensitive nuclear technologies. This discussion is an important one both in supporting the peaceful use of nuclear energy and in upholding the highest nuclear non-proliferation standards.

Australia like other NPT parties continues to call on India, Pakistan and Israel to join the NPT as non-nuclear weapon states. Meantime, we would like to see the extension of non-proliferation disciplines to these states to the maximum extent possible. How to do so will be one key focus of the International Commission's work which, we think, could usefully be discussed at the Review Conference.

Also in this context, we note the importance of outcomes at the Review Conference which assist progress towards the establishment of an effectively verifiable Middle East zone free of nuclear weapons and their means of delivery. Any such progress will need to take account of the legitimate security needs of all regional states.

Finally, we offer some suggestions on outcomes for the Review Conference.

It seems to us the Review Conference could usefully issue some kind of forward looking blue print for action, possibly along the lines of the 2000 Review Conference's 13 steps.

For states parties to have confidence that such a blue print would be implemented, they would need to be reassured that, to the maximum extent possible, all states, particularly the nuclear weapon states, were implementing past Review Conference outcomes. They would also need some assurance that states parties could monitor future implementation more effectively than in the past. In this context, we see merit in exploring ideas, such as those put forward by Canada, for shorter annual meetings of states parties to replace the prepcom process.

NPT parties must seize the opportunity in 2010 to move forward on all the substantive issues covered by this treaty. We should take advantage of the increased interest in nuclear non-proliferation and disarmament generated by former politicians, think tanks and NGOS which play an important role in raising public awareness and building public support. But most significantly, we must take advantage of the new determination of world leaders to tackle these issues by encouraging and supporting them to take crucial decisions vital to the strength of this treaty and to the security of the world.

35

Statement by H.E. Mr. Oh Joon, Deputy Minister for Multilateral and Global Affairs Preparatory Committee for the 2010 NPT Review Conference, Third Session, New York, U.S.A.

4 May 2009

...

For one thing, new visionary initiatives, such as the five-point proposal for nuclear disarmament introduced by Secretary-General Ban Ki-moon, as well as the vision for "a world free of nuclear weapons" offered by US President Obama during his speech in Prague, have intensified the disarmament debate on a global scale.

It is also encouraging to see new policies in nuclear weapon states. We are heartened by the commitments of the US and Russian Presidents, as set out in their Joint Statement..., to fulfil their obligations under the NPT by concluding an agreement to succeed the Strategic Arms Reduction Treaty I (START I). Going one step further, President Obama suggested specific actions during his Prague speech to work towards a global nuclear zero target. We sincerely hope that these initiatives will produce concrete results at an early date.

However, while we hold greater hopes for the future, we must first resolutely confront the grave challenges facing the NPT regime today. The challenges are present in all of three pillars of the NPT. But the most serious ones are found in the area of non-proliferation, such as the nuclear issue of the

Democratic People's Republic of Korea. The DPRK nuclear issue raises a pressing, fundamental question of how the NPT can tackle threats to the foundation of nuclear non-proliferation. Presently, this issue has the risk of constituting the first case where nuclear weapons have been developed within the framework of the NPT.

As such, an early resolution of the DPRK nuclear issue is vital to ensuring the integrity of the global nuclear non-proliferation regime as well as to securing peace on the Korean Peninsula and beyond. Strenuous efforts have been made to achieve the verifiable denuclearization of the DPRK in a peaceful manner through the Six-Party Talks. However, it is extremely regrettable that despite these efforts, the DPRK carried out a rocket launch last month in direct contravention of UN Security Council Resolution 1718, and is further threatening "measures that will include nuclear tests and test-firing of intercontinental ballistic missiles." My Government takes this opportunity to urge the DPRK to fully comply with the obligations under the NPT as well as Resolution 1718, and implement the 2005 Joint Statement and subsequent agreements adopted at the Six-Party Talks.

My delegation continues to hold a firm belief that strengthening the NPT-based regime is the most effective deterrent to the current pressing challenges that threaten it. The Treaty should be buttressed by various creative tools that have been developed so far. In this regard, I would like to highlight the following points to strengthen the NPT regime.

First, the nuclear safeguards regime with the IAEA at its center should be further reinforced. My delegation therefore endorses the necessity to universalize the comprehensive safeguards agreement and the Additional Protocol. We also emphasize the importance of robust international cooperation to prevent nuclear terrorism as shown by the Global Initiative to Counter Nuclear Terrorism (GICNT).

Second, my delegation reiterates its firm conviction in the goal of nuclear disarmament in realizing a world free of nuclear weapons. To effectively pursue both nuclear disarmament and non-proliferation, we share the view that the first order of business should be an early entry into force of the Comprehensive Nuclear Test Ban Treaty (CTBT) and the commencement of negotiations for a Fissile Material Cut-off Treaty (FMCT). In this respect, we welcome President Obama's recent call for CTBT ratification by the US Government. We urge those who have not yet ratified the Treaty, in particular the Annex 2 countries, to do so as soon as possible.

Third, the Republic of Korea attaches great importance to the right to the peaceful uses of nuclear energy. We are of the view that this right is particularly instrumental in sustainable socio-economic development of developing countries. For my country, nuclear energy has been vital to our economic growth during the past decades, currently providing 40% of our electricity needs with the projection of an increase up to 60% by 2030. At the same time, we believe that there should be effective safeguards against the potential misuse of this right.

Fourth, my delegation recognizes the merit of multilateral approaches to the nuclear fuel cycle, as nuclear renaissance may enhance international concerns over nuclear proliferation. A guaranteed and sustainable supply of nuclear fuel through an international mechanism may discourage states in need of peaceful nuclear energy from pursuing their own uranium enrichment technology. In this regard, we believe that such an approach should be based on objective and fair criteria, and should not be implemented in a way that denies or limits the legitimate right for the peaceful use of nuclear energy. It should also serve as a complement to, and back up of, the existing market. The Republic of Korea is willing to constructively participate in the discussions on this subject.

Last but not least, the misuse of Article X (withdrawal) has been the focus of States Parties' attention, following the DPRK's announcement of withdrawal from the Treaty. We believe that it is high time for States. Parties to consider an effective and collective response mechanism to a withdrawal from the Treaty.

In concluding, one important task ahead is mobilizing the political will necessary to strengthen the NPT regime. I believe that we should not waste the opportunity we have today with the positive developments in the nuclear disarmament and non-proliferation field. We need to remind ourselves that we should not repeat the failure of the 2005 Review Conference. The commitments to disarmament should turn into concrete actions promptly. All available mechanisms should be fully utilized both in and outside the UN system. The Republic of Korea will do its part to enable this session to lay solid groundwork for a successful 2010 Review Conference that is essential to furthering international peace and security.

36

Statement of African Group Read by Mr. Lawrence O. Obisakin, Minister, Permanent Mission of Nigeria to the United Nations, New York, U.S.A.

4 May 2009

The African Group, aligning itself with the statement of the Non-Aligned Movement earlier delivered by Cuba, will like to emphasize the following aspects:

Reaffirming the importance of promoting international peace and stability, the group remains strongly committed to the achievement of general and complete disarmament under strict and effective international control premised on the principle of undiminished security for all states.

Informed by this vision, the African group reiterates its firm belief in the achievement of the goals of nuclear disarmament and nuclear non-proliferation, and peaceful uses of nuclear technology for development as enshrined in the NPT.

Nuclear Disarmament

As was clearly articulated by NAM. the African Group wishes to highlight that the total, elimination of all nuclear weapons is the only absolute guarantee against the use and threat of use of nuclear weapons. While recognizing the reported reduction in existing nuclear arsenals, and other positive developments in this regard, especially in recent months. Africa still remains convinced that meaningful nuclear disarmament should be based on the principle of transparency, verifiability and irreversibility in all matters related to nuclear disarmament.

In this regard, Africa believes that within the NPT context there exists a sound consensual basis on how to achieve this goal. While we look forward to a fruitful 2010 Review Conference, Africa believes that it is pertinent that we should not lose sight of the gains of the past. These gains include: the implementation of the 13 practical steps as agreed in the 2000 Review Conference.

Non-proliferation

Africa believes that nuclear weapons still represent the greatest threat to humanity and therefore should be eliminated. Both nuclear disarmament and nuclear non-proliferation in all its aspects should be pursued as our shared goals. It is pertinent to state that Africa has played its part by ensuring the continent's universal membership of the NPT, establishing the ideals of a nuclear weapons-free zone (The Treaty of Pelindaba).

In this connection, we reaffirm and recognize the establishment of nuclear-weapons-free zones (NWFZ) by the treaties of Tlatelolco, Raratonga, Bangkok, Pelindaba and Semipalatinsk. This we believe should serve as a positive step towards the ultimate objective of a world free of nuclear weapons.

In this respect while Africa is working towards the entry into force of the treaty of Pelindaba, we wish to call on NWS to demonstrate their commitment to the nuclear weapon-free zones.

Africa recalls the Resolution on the Middle East adopted in 1995 as well as the final document of the 2000 Review Conference (Part 1) and calls for meaningful progress on this resolution.

Negative Security Assurances

Pending complete and verifiable and irreversible elimination of nuclear weapons, we wish to remind all the nuclear weapons states of their NPT obligations to give non-discriminatory negative security assurances (NSA) to non nuclear weapon states. We call for a finalization of these assurances under a universal and legally-binding instrument as a matter of priority.

While reaffirming the centrality of the NPT, we believe strongly that multilateral forum is the most effective framework for disarmament negotiations for weapons of this magnitude of lethality.

We call on all delegations to demonstrate the necessary political will to enhance progress on the issue of disarmament, non-proliferation and peaceful uses of nuclear technology.

37

Secretary-General Ban Ki-moon's Remarks to the Fourth Biennial Ministerial Meeting in Support of the Comprehensive Nuclear Test Ban Treaty

24 September 2008

...

It is an honour to address you on this vital subject. Since it was opened for signature 12 years ago today, the Comprehensive Nuclear-Test-Ban Treaty has achieved near universal adherence. One hundred and seventy-nine States have signed it, and 144 have ratified it. I am encouraged that in 2008, Barbados, Columbia and Malaysia ratified the Treaty. I also welcome Iraq's recent signature of the Treaty.

However, despite the progress that has been made, the CTBT has still not entered into force. Of the 44 States whose ratifications are required, nine have yet to do so. This is cause for serious concern.

The Treaty's entry into force would be a major step in our effort to build a safer, more peaceful world. It would outlaw all nuclear tests and move us towards the larger goals of ridding the world of nuclear weapons and preventing their proliferation.

It is with profound appreciation that I commend the outreach activities by the Foreign Ministers who are here with us today. Let me say from my heart that your efforts to promote the entry into force of the Treaty are truly appreciated. Some critics are saying it would be unrealistic to expect the entry into force of the

Treaty anytime soon given the overall stalemate in the areas of disarmament and non-proliferation. I flatly reject such a pessimistic view. With the persistence and optimism that you have demonstrated thus far, we can, and we shall, see the day when the Treaty enters into force.

Therefore I very much welcome the launching of the Fourth Joint Ministerial Statement of support for the Treaty. States are not only reaffirming their commitment to its entry into force, but are showing real determination in working towards that important goal.

Having served as chairman of the Preparatory Commission of the CTBTO in 1999, I am personally committed to achieving this objective. Last month in Mexico City, I attended an extraordinary session of OPANAL, the Agency for the Prohibition of Nuclear Weapons in Latin America and the Caribbean. I emphasized the importance of international efforts to prevent proliferation and achieve nuclear disarmament. The global system of nuclear disarmament and non-proliferation faces significant challenges. If not properly handled, these challenges could pose far greater threats to regional and international peace and security.

The prospects for achieving nuclear disarmament and the ultimate objective in the disarmament process—general and complete disarmament under effective international control—hinge on the international security environment. But we cannot wait for the perfect security environment to come along. Rather, I believe that the process of moving forward in disarmament, non-proliferation and against the uses of weapons of mass destruction by terrorists will itself contribute to international peace and security.

It is worthwhile noting that we are already past the mid-point of the preparatory process for the Review Conference of the Nuclear Non-Proliferation Treaty, which will take place in 2010. The CTBT is an integral part of reinforcing the NPT regime. I encourage all States to seize this opportunity.

The United Nations, for its part, will continue to work with the Preparatory Commission for the CTBTO so that it will be ready to fulfil its vital functions upon the Treaty's entry into force. I particularly laud the efforts being made by the Preparatory Commission to establish the Treaty's international monitoring system, and encourage its Member States to continue providing their full support for completion of the global verification regime.

Allow me once again to urge all Governments that have not yet done so to sign and ratify the Treaty without delay. I also call upon States to continue their voluntary adherence to a nuclear-weapon-test moratorium and to refrain from acts contrary to the object and purpose of the Treaty prior to its entry into force. As Depository of the Treaty, I intend to send a letter to the nine countries whose ratifications are required for the Treaty to enter into force, urging them to do so as soon as possible.

The threat to the very survival of humankind posed by the existence of weapons of mass destruction, especially nuclear weapons, is universally recognized. We must redouble our efforts to achieve deeper reductions in nuclear arsenals and to further diminish the role of nuclear weapons in security policies. With persistence and courage, a world free of nuclear weapons—a safer world for present and future generations—can be ours.

38

Statement by Mr. Tibor Toth, Executive Secretary of the CTBTO Preparatory Commission, on the Occasion of the 40th Anniversary of the Treaty for the Prohibition of Nuclear Weapons in Latin America and the Caribbean (Treaty of Tlatelolco), Mexico City, Mexico

14 February 2007

...

1. It is a great honor and pleasure for me to celebrate with you this symbolic anniversary of the Treaty of Tlatelolco, as a historical achievement. It contributed greatly to peace and stability in your region, it fostered confidence and cooperation and it provided a successful example for other initiatives to create Nuclear Weapon Free Zones.

2. While all of us are rightly concerned about the prevailing threat of nuclear proliferation and the continuous lack of progress in nuclear disarmament, the Treaty of Tlatelolco provides us with an example of true success and progress in this area.

3. Big historical achievements are made possible by a combination of visionary leadership and the right circumstances. This leadership to achieve a denuclearization of the Continent was provided in the aftermath of the Cuban Missiles Crisis by several states, among them Bolivia, Brazil, Chile, Ecuador and Mexico. However, I would like to pay special tribute to Alfonso Garcia Robles who was so instrumental in turning this vision into reality.

4. As a young diplomat participating in the work of the Conference on Disarmament in Geneva, in the early 1980s, I

remember the forceful speeches of Alfonso Garcia Robles putting all his moral weight as key architect of the Tlatelolco Treaty into underscoring the urgency for nuclear disarmament and to fight the proliferation of nuclear weapons. One of the issues he spoke of frequently and with deep conviction was the need for a multilateral treaty prohibiting nuclear tests in any environment. Probably only few besides him believed that a decade after he had received the Nobel Peace Prize in 1982, negotiations would start and lead so swiftly to a treaty.

5. This year marks the 25th anniversary of acknowledging with the Nobel Peace Price the dedication and perseverance of Alfonso Garcia Robles. This is the right moment to pay tribute to his visionary statesmanship, even more since we recently celebrated the tenth anniversary of the CTBT, the treaty which was called the "*hardest fought price in the history of arms control negotiations*". As of today, 177 States have signed and 138 have ratified the CTBT. Since 1997, the Preparatory Commission has been working to build up a credible, functional and cost effective verification system to underpin the norm against nuclear testing established by the Treaty. It is a unique feature of the participatory and democratic CTBT verification regime that it empowers each and every State, regardless of its size and wealth, to fully participate in the verification work and to benefit from the wealth of data and data products provided by the monitoring system.

6. In addition to the primary purpose of verification, the CTBT verification technologies have the potential to offer important additional scientific and civilian benefits. Our data can be used in a variety of fields, including studies of the earth's structure as well as for research on earthquakes, volcanic eruption forecasting, underwater explosion location, the monitoring of the sea temperature and climate change. In addition, we are providing our data in real time to tsunami warning systems.

7. The norm against nuclear testing was severely challenged last year, when the Democratic People's Republic of Korea announced that it had conducted a nuclear test on 9 October 2006. This resulted in practically unanimous global expressions of concern and condemnation, in particular also from the

Contracting States of the Treaty of Tlatelolco, with regard to this irresponsible act. This strong reaction of the international community was important and demonstrated impressively how much the international community cares about the nuclear test ban.

8. The explosion was a test for our organization, our technical capabilities, our own procedures and the potential value that our global verification system can bring to States Signatories in a situation of such political importance. I am pleased that we were able to provide States Signatories with reliable data and to prove the value of the significant investment that has been made into the CTBT verification system.

9. While it is primarily for those states listed in Annex 2 of the CTBT whose ratification is necessary for entry into force to consider the value of the Comprehensive Nuclear Test Ban Treaty for their national and for international security, it is also a collective responsibility of all states to do whatever they can contribute to strengthening the norm of the Treaty.

10. I would like to use today's opportunity to appeal to all Contracting States of the Treaty of Tlatelolco to support the CTBT and the upholding of the norm against nuclear testing. In particular, I would like to appeal to those Contracting States that are already committed under Article 1 of the Treaty of Tlatelolco *to prohibit and prevent the testing of any nuclear weapons and* that have not yet signed or ratified the Comprehensive Nuclear-Test–Ban Treaty, to do so at their earliest convenience.

11. Finally, Madam Minister, I would like to use this occasion to express my appreciation for your contribution to the cause of the Treaty and the CTBTO Preparatory Commission, and for the contribution of so many gifted Mexican diplomats, colleagues present here.

39

Statement of the Executive Secretary, Mr. Tibor Toth, on the Occasion of the Scientific Symposium Hofburg, Vienna, Austria

31 August 2006

...

It is a great pleasure to welcome you to this first Scientific Symposium entitled "CTBT: Synergies with Science, 1996-2006 and beyond." Let me start by thanking the Federal Ministry for Foreign Affairs of Austria for providing this wonderful venue for our meeting. Furthermore I would like to thank the Government of Austria and the City of Vienna for being such generous and supportive hosts to the CTBTO Preparatory Commission.

This symposium is the first formal occasion celebrating an ongoing process that started well before the Comprehensive Test Ban Treaty was opened for signature 10 years ago. The Group of Scientific Experts, under the Chairmanship of our Master of Ceremonies, Dr. Ola Dahlman, laid the foundations for a close and fruitful relationship between the scientific community and the CTBT-community. A relationship that was focused very much on the design of a verification regime for the CTBT that would with high accuracy and probability detect nuclear test explosions and any other nuclear explosion.

The challenge of designing, building and operating such a system was very much at the heart of discussions about an international arrangement banning nuclear test explosions since the Indian Prime Minister Nehru first proposed a total ban on nuclear testing in 1954. Doubts about the verifiability of such a ban were strong even among those nations which were most advanced in registering nuclear explosions, mostly to find out what the cold war adversary was up to. This argument became even stronger once nuclear test explosions moved underground as a consequence of the Partial Test Ban Treaty. The PTBT banned tests in the atmosphere after the nuclear powers realized the global environmental impact of their testing programmes.

It is in no small part due to progress in science that by the early 1990s the Members of the United Nations Conference on Disarmament were confident that a legally binding instrument banning all nuclear test explosions could be verified in a credible way.

Today, 10 years after the CTBT was adopted by the United Nations General Assembly, we are proud to state that the scientists and diplomats who predicted that a global verification regime would be feasible and credible were right.

The Provisional Technical Secretariat of the CTBTO Preparatory Commission was mandated to establish an International Monitoring System consisting of 321 monitoring stations in four technologies. Seismic, infrasound and hydroacoustic stations are registering energy propagated through the earth, through the atmosphere and through the oceans. The radionuclide technology allows to filter radioactive particles and the noble gas stations will in addition also register minute quantities of noble gases present in the atmosphere. The geographic distribution of the stations allows for global coverage of the system and, if I may add, to some rather difficult locations to build and operate these stations. It is the combination of these four technologies that should ultimately allow Member States of the CTBT to make an informed judgment about events registered by our system.

As of today 72% of the station-network has been installed and over half of the stations have been certified which means that they meet the stringent specifications of the Preparatory Commission.

The data registered at our stations around the globe is sent to the International Data Centre in Vienna via satellite communication in near real time. Here the data are processed, redistributed to national data centres and archived. According to the CTBT the International Data Centre is supporting member states in the analysis of the data, providing raw and processed data. Our products which are made available to all member states are based on automated as well as human analysis. This should facilitate the task of finding the proverbial needle in the haystack. To give you an idea about the size of the haystack, the quantities of data currently processed by our system you should realize that terabytes of data are transmitted to the IDC and redistributed per year. Roughly 20,000 events are registered annually. After entry into force of the treaty, Member States with the assistance of the CTBTO should be able to identify and locate that one event among the 20,000 mostly natural occurrences which might be a clandestine nuclear explosion.

Once such a suspicious event is identified and located there will be the possibility to dispatch an On-Site Inspection that would have the right to inspect a fairly small area of 1000 square kilometers and look for indications of a nuclear explosion. The on-site inspection regime poses not only a large number of logistical and political challenges but also of technological ones that I hope will be the subject of further discussions with the scientific community.

The verification regime of the CTBT has several unique features which are worth mentioning. Firstly, it is a global regime that allows for no white spots on the map. Every corner of the globe is covered by it and an event even the remotest areas of our planet would be registered by our stations. Sometimes I even get the feeling that the more remote and the more isolated an area, the higher the likelihood that we still need to build a station there.

Secondly, due to the stringent specifications of the stations, we receive consistent data from the stations in near real time and with extraordinarily high reliability. This puts our network apart from other existing networks which operate under less strict rules of reliability.

Thirdly, the CTBT verification regime is a truly democratic and participatory system. The data and products of the CTBTO PrepCom are made available to every Signatory State, regardless of size or wealth or technological prowess, making sure that transparency is not limited to the few states who possess the necessary technical and financial resources. The credibility of our verification system does not only reside in its technical performance but also in the open and equal access of all Signatory States.

Fourthly, to realize the open and democratic nature of the regime the Preparatory Commission is engaged in a wide range of training and capacity building activities that will allow all State Signatories to fully realize the benefits of the Treaty and the manifold potential civil and scientific applications of the verification technologies. In the exhibition you will find a display of our most recent initiative in this field, an e-learning programme, financed through voluntary contributions by the Netherlands, the Czech Republic and the European Union.

The CTBTO PrepCom and the activities of the secretariat are dependent on the assistance and cooperation of many actors. First and foremost the Signatory States whose technical, political and financial support for the organization are vital. With 176 signatures and 135 ratifications the CTBT enjoys near universal support. I would like to use this opportunity to thank all Signatory States for what they are doing in support of the Treaty and its verification system through their delegates, their experts, their political and financial commitment to our common cause.

The second group of actors which I would like to praise and thank here are the staff of the PTS. It is their dedication and talent that have brought us here today.

The third constituency of the CTBT family is the scientific community. Some of you here have worked with the Preparatory Commission on test ban verification, in fact, without your input and constant readiness to advise and share your experience we would not be able to do our work. For many of you, however, this Scientific Symposium is the first direct contact with our organization and I hope that the discussions over the next two days will help us explore new avenues of cooperation.

The science on which our verification regime is based is evolving at a rapid pace, be it in the field of monitoring technologies or in the field of analysis and computing. The success and efficiency of our verification regime relies on a permanent dialogue with scientific institutions about the latest developments in their areas of expertise and their adaptation to our needs.

On the other hand, we hope to explore the vastly untapped scientific and civilian uses of the verification technologies at our disposal. We are having a lively debate about the contribution of the CTBTO Preparatory Commission to Tsunami early warning. Since the Tsunami of December 2004 killed hundreds of thousands and devastated many coasts in the Indian Ocean we have started through the Intergovernmental Oceanographic Commission of UNESCO to cooperate with international and national Tsunami warning centres to explore the potential of our verification regime for this important humanitarian purpose. It was encouraging to hear the almost enthusiastic presentations of the North West Pacific Tsunami warning centre in Japan and the Pacific Tsunami warning Centre in Hawaii who have tested the usefulness of raw data provided by some of our stations to them last year. Meanwhile many more institutions have come to similar conclusions. This is but one of many areas where the data collected by our stations might help not only the advancement of science but also the protection of human lives.

Let me conclude this little introduction by stating the obvious: We are gathered here to celebrate the achievements of the CTBTO Preparatory Commission and explore synergies with science that could be beneficial for our verification work. Ultimately this verification regime will only show its worth once the CTBT has entered into force. It is for those states listed in Annex 2 of the CTBT whose ratification is necessary for entry into force to consider the value of the Comprehensive Test Ban Treaty for their national and for international security. The reliable performance of the verification regime and the example of a growing number of ratifiers should help them with a positive decision.